VICTIMS OF CRIME

SAGE CRIMINAL JUSTICE SYSTEM ANNUALS

Volumes in the **Sage Criminal Justice System Annuals** focus on and develop topics and themes that are important to the study of criminal justice. Each edited volume combines multiple perspectives to provide an interdisciplinary approach that is useful to students, researchers, and policymakers.

Recent Books in This Series:

Volume 25. **Sage** Criminal Justice System Annuals

VICTIMS OF CRIME
Problems, Policies, and Programs

Arthur J. Lurigio
Wesley G. Skogan
Robert C. Davis

Editors

SAGE PUBLICATIONS
The International Professional Publishers
Newbury Park   London   New Delhi

Copyright © 1990 by Sage Publications, Inc.

For information address:

SAGE Publications, Inc.
2111 West Hillcrest Drive
Newbury Park, California 91320

SAGE Publications Ltd.
28 Banner Street
London EC1Y 8QE
England

SAGE Publications India Pvt. Ltd.
M-32 Market
Greater Kailash I
New Delhi 110 048 India

Printed in the United States of America

Library of Congress Cataloging-in-Publication Data

Victims cf crime : problems, policies, and programs / Arthur J.
    Lurigio, Wesley G. Skogan, Robert C. Davis, editors.
        p.   cm. — Sage criminal justice system annuals : v. 25)
    Includes bibliographical references.
    ISBN 0-8039-3369-X. — ISBN 0-8039-3370-3 (pbk.)
    1. Victims of crimes—United States.   I. Lurigio, Arthur J.
II.   Skogan, Wesley G.   III. Davis, Robert C. (Robert Carl)
IV. Series.
HV6250.3.U5V54 1990
362.88'0973—dc20   89-24260
                                                                  CIP

FIRST PRINTING, 1990

Sage Production Editor: Mary Beth DeHainaut

CONTENTS

Chapter 1

CRIMINAL VICTIMIZATION

WESLEY G. SKOGAN
ARTHUR J. LURIGIO
ROBERT C. DAVIS

This book is about victims of crime. There has been a great deal of research on criminal victimization, legislation supporting victims, and victim programs and services, but no book has taken recent stock of these advances. This volume provides a state-of-the-art review of many facets of criminal victimization and many of the efforts that have been made to ameliorate crime victims' pain and loss. It covers a wide range of topics, including chapters on the trends in victimization, the emotional impact of crime, the needs and problems of special classes of victims, the participation of victims in the criminal justice system, the evolution of victim programs and services, policies toward victims in the United States and Europe, and the politics of the crime victim movement.

BACKGROUND

In recent years, one of every four U.S. households has been victimized by personal or property crime. At one time or another, crime will touch most Americans or affect the lives of their relatives, friends, and acquaintances. The consequences of crime can involve financial loss, property damage, physical injury, and death. Less obvious but sometimes more devastating are the psychological wounds left in the wake of victimization, wounds that may never heal.

The threat of crime and fear of victimization alone are enough to diminish the quality of people's lives. For some, the constant specter of violent crime can be overwhelming. In an attempt to prevent or avoid victimization, individuals may move, restrict their daily activities, or purchase expensive security measures. Billions of dollars and man-hours are being extended by governments to apprehend and punish offenders, yet we have started only recently to focus our attention on the victims of crime.

Since the early 1970s, there has been growing concern for crime victims, and some observers have begun to speak of the emergence of a "victims' movement." The discovery of crime victims in the United States represents the confluence of several broad social movements, including the women's movement, the law and order movement, and the civil rights movement (Karmen, 1984). Lying at the heart of the victims movement are desires for the explicit recognition of victims' losses and for more humane treatment for victims by the public and the criminal justice and health systems (Gottfredson, 1989). This new interest in victims of crime has changed general attitudes and policies and spurred federal, state, and local efforts to increase public awareness of victims' rights and needs. At the federal level, for example, President Ronald Reagan proclaimed National Victims of Crime Week in 1981. This has since become an annual event in order to focus attention on victims' problems. Further impetus for improving the plight of crime victims was provided by the President's Task Force on Victims of Crime (1982), which called the neglect of crime victims "a national disgrace" and promoted the expansion of victim assistance efforts (Davis, 1987a; Finn & Lee, 1988). Following on the heels of the Task Force report, legislation was enacted in Congress to secure better treatment for crime victims, and protect crime victims from harassment and threat and to implement crime victims' compensation and assistance programs (see also the American Bar Association, 1979).

The 1982 Omnibus Victim and Witness Protection Act was one of the earliest and most sweeping federal legislative actions concerning victims of crime. Among its numerous provisions, the act mandated the use of victim impact statements at sentences, greater protection of victims from harassment and intimidation, guidelines for the fair treatment of victims and witnesses, and more stringent bail laws. Two years later, the 1984 Federal Victims of Crime Act was passed to establish the Crime Victims Fund, which disburses federal monies to state victim compensation and victim assistance projects throughout the country. The Fund draws its revenues from fines, penalty assessments, and bond forfeitures, and had contributed to nearly 1,400 programs as of early

1987 (Finn & Lee, 1988). This act gives funding priority to programs that cater to victims of sexual assault, domestic violence, and child abuse. To supplement federal efforts, several states also have passed comprehensive legislation to protect the rights of crime victims (e.g., McGuire, 1987), and have legislated victim compensation programs that reimburse victims for medical expenses and lost wages.

Support for victims of crime has also been dramatic at the grass-roots level. There are some 5,000 victim service programs providing a variety of services to crime victims, such as emergency care, crisis intervention, counseling, victim compensation and restitution, witness protection and other court-related services, public education, and victim advocacy (Finn & Lee, 1988; Norquay & Weiler, 1981). Many local programs offer several of these services to clients, and are housed in police departments or prosecutors' offices.

Crime victims could be key actors in the criminal justice process, but more often they are kept at the periphery (Gottfredson, 1989). Studies have shown that victim cooperation may be highly critical in helping the police to make arrests and prosecutors to secure convictions (e.g., Greenwood & Petersilia, 1975; Spelman & Brown, 1981). Despite the value of victims to the system and the location of numerous victim programs in criminal justice and law enforcement settings (Gottfredson), it is widely recognized that in its haste to enhance the efficiency of prosecutions and convictions, the system does not always respond sufficiently to the special demands and challenging problems of crime victims (Villmow, 1984; Young, 1988). Moreover, the response of criminal justice personnel often is regarded as having a negative impact on the emotional problems of victims. So prevalent is the tendency of victims to experience difficulties in their encounters with the criminal justice system, that Symonds (1980) characterized its effect on victims as the "second wound." Crime victims are the "forgotten persons" of the criminal justice system, valued only for their capacity to report crimes and to appear in court as witnesses. Sales, Rich, and Reich (1984) note that victims are expected to support a criminal justice system that has "treated them with less respect that it has treated the offender" (p. 114). Similarly, Siegal (1983) characterized this inequity in the following manner: "Vulnerable, angry, insecure, selfless, the victim who survives observes a criminal who is fed, housed, given legal, medical, psychological, and psychiatric aid—even education and vocational training. The victim . . . suffers alone" (p. 1271).

In a seminal article, Ash (1972) documented the high cost of victim cooperation in the prosecutorial process:

> In the typical situation the witness will several times be ordered to appear at some designated place, usually a courtroom, but sometimes a prosecutor's office or grand jury room. Several times he will be made to wait tedious, unconscionable long intervals of time in dingy courthouse corridors or in other grim surroundings. Several times he will suffer the discomfort of being ignored by busy officials and the bewilderment and painful anxiety of not knowing what is going on around him or what is going to happen to him. . . . In sum, the experience is dreary, time-wasting, depressing, exhausting, confusing, frustrating, numbing, and seemingly endless (p. 390).

Other authors have described the generalized neglect of crime victims by police, prosecutors, and court personnel, citing long waits, loss of wages, poor protection against intimidation, mishandling of property, difficult questioning, unnecessary trips to court, and a variety of other inconveniences (Chelimsky, 1981; Knudten, Meade, Knudten, & Doerner, 1976; Rosenbaum, 1977; Waller, 1982).

Although many of today's most innovative victim programs are built upon research, our knowledge regarding the effects of criminal victimization and victim services programs is limited. For example, research on the psychological consequences of crime has been restricted largely to victims of rape. Much less attention has been paid in the literature to the so-called "forgotten victims" of such other significant crimes as burglary, robbery, and non-sexual assault. In addition, inadequacies in research designs (e.g., failure to include a comparison or control group of nonvictims), measurement procedures (e.g., failure to measure concepts adequately or to include multiple impact variables), and conceptual frameworks (e.g., failure to elaborate or test theoretical models for explaining the reactions to victimization) have sorely limited our understanding of the impact of serious crimes (Lurigio & Davis, 1989; Lurigio & Rosenbaum, in press). According to Chelimsky (1981):

> Given the current inadequate state of knowledge about the problems of victims and the effects of victimization, it will be necessary to build a sound research base from which to structure the development of better victim services. In this effort, evaluation and knowledge diffusion research will necessarily play a major role (p. 95).

Even less is known about the effectiveness of victim services programs. Although there have been some studies regarding the needs of
victims (Friedman, Bischoff, Davis, & Person, 1982; Maguire &
Corbett, 1987; Roberts, 1987), there have been few experiments examining the impact of victim assistance programs (Skogan & Wycoff,
1987). According to a national assessment of victim/witness programs,
evaluation designs typically have not been powerful enough to detect
program impacts or to answer such fundamental questions as (1) are
victims and witnesses better off emotionally or "healthier" in the long
run for having received assistance? and (2) are victims and witnesses
now receiving better treatment at the hands of local criminal justice and
social service agencies as a consequence of project efforts? (Cronin &
Bourque, 1981, p. 41).

The American Psychological Association's Task Force on the Victims of Crime and Violence (Kahn, 1984) also lamented the lack of solid
data on crime victim programs. The Task Force stated emphatically:
"Both those who seek help and those who pay for services deserve
interventions for which the efficacy is known or is under systematic
study. Little is known about the effectiveness of services currently
being offered to victims" (Kahn, p. 100). Davis (1987b) compares the
paucity of knowledge in the area of crime victim services to that of other
fields where crisis intervention techniques are utilized, e.g., suicide
prevention, psychiatric treatment, and acute medical care (see Auerback
& Kilman, 1978). A series of unresolved issues for investigators to
explore in future studies includes (Davis, 1987a):

- Which counseling techniques are most effective for victims?
- How do victims who cope effectively in the aftermath of the crime differ
  from victims who do not cope effectively?
- Are victim compensation programs assisting victims with the greatest
  needs?
- Do most victims want the opportunity to submit victim impact statements?
- Do the elderly and child victims have special needs that are not being
  addressed?

There are several new directions for practitioners to pursue in the
areas of victim services and rights. A number of states, for example,
have acted to tip the balance away from offenders' rights in favor of
victims. Efforts in this regard include increasing the penalties for victim

intimidation, involving victims in the plea bargaining process, and denying bail to suspects who would be a threat to victims if released. Other proposals are being considered to create new and more ambitious victims' rights. They are aimed at institutionalizing a more definitive role for victim advocates in the criminal justice system and at bringing together victims and offenders in dispute resolution and reconciliation programs (Karmen, 1984).

CONTENTS

Victims of Crime begins with Chapter 2, by John H. Laub, who describes patterns of criminal victimization in the United States. He traces recent trends in crime, describes who is victimized and how, and discusses some of the consequences of crime, including physical injury and financial loss. Laub's chapter underscores the importance of understanding how we *know* about crime, i.e., how we access and document details regarding criminal victimization and its effects. Crime is a furtive event, and most offenders do their best to keep victims and the police from discovering what happened. Also, many crimes are not reported to the police, while others are not recorded officially. The police generally focus their efforts on criminals, and typically there is little in their files concerning information about victims. As a result, official crime statistics need to be supplemented by extensive interviews with victims and offenders to fill fundamental gaps in our knowledge and understanding of crime. Chapter 2 is a synthesis of all these sources of information.

While crime is fairly prevalent overall in the United States, more serious crimes occur less frequently than less serious crimes. Property crime is more common than violent crime, and less serious personal crimes (those involving no injuries and in which no weapons are used) are more likely to occur than more violent personal crimes. Crime victims are disproportionately young; in most offense categories, they are more likely to be male, and blacks and the poor are more likely to be victimized than whites and persons in higher income brackets. National victimization surveys indicate that the crime rate has been stable or even declining (depending upon the crime category) through most of the 1970s and 1980s. Quite the opposite impression is given by police statistics, which have gone up considerably over the same period. Most crimes have relatively trivial consequences for their victims. The value of stolen goods often is not very high, the biggest losses are more likely to be insured, and in most categories relatively few victims are harmed physically.

Despite the minor physical and financial repercussions of crime for most victims, the adverse emotional effects can be quite devastating. However, there is great variation in the duration and seriousness of psychological impacts (Gottfredson, 1989). Chapter 3, by Arthur J. Lurigio and Patricia A. Resick, examines the antecedents of psychological distress. In their comprehensive review of research, they describe how victim characteristics and prior experiences, features of the crime incident, and post-victimization events influence victim adjustment and recovery.

In their presentation of the findings of research on victim adjustment, Lurigio and Resick report, for example, that men tend to cope better with crime than women and that victims without a history of prior victimization or preexisting emotional problems tend to exhibit fewer symptoms following the event. The authors conclude their chapter by pointing to the usefulness of this research for victim service providers. Knowing which victims are likely to be affected adversely by crime can help practitioners to organize their outreach efforts, to develop special interventions, and to formulate more effective client assessment strategies.

Sexual assault is the first of the special classes of crimes to be discussed in this volume. In Chapter 4, Patricia A. Resick discusses the impact of sexual assault and some of the implications of this research for redressing victims' needs. Estimates of the extent of sexual assault vary widely; Resick reports that a woman's chance of being victimized in her lifetime might be anywhere from between 14 and 44%. The impact of sexual assault can be painful and persistent. Research indicates that rape victims are likely to be depressed, anxious, and fearful, and to feel helpless. They report lower levels of self-esteem, drug and alcohol problems, and difficulties in their relationships with others. These reactions spill over and affect the entire population; it appears that concern about rape accounts for much of the fear and avoidance behavior reported by women in surveys.

Psychological theories that explain reactions to rape provide some guidance for helping victims. Crisis theory, for example, points to the importance of early intervention; getting victims assistance quickly makes a difference. Learning theory helps us understand why the impact of victimization can persist for years; victims can have flashbacks during which they relive their experience and feel its effects all over again. Finally, cognitive theory helps us understand why some victims blame themselves for their fate and are plagued by recrimination and self-doubt as a consequence.

In Chapter 5, Lucy Friedman and Minna Shulman examine the criminal justice system's response to domestic violence. This is an area in which policy and practice is in tremendous flux. Before the 1970s, police generally were reluctant to treat domestic violence as a crime. They rarely made arrests in those cases, and few abusers ever came to trial. Now there is increased pressure to take domestic violence more seriously, but Friedman and Shulman argue that treating it like any other crime is not likely to protect victims and their families adequately, and that victims of domestic violence actually need special treatment.

Domestic violence cases involve conflict among intimates. The relationship between the parties may be complex (they may, for example, share children) and worth trying salvage. These cases may involve continuous abuse of varying levels of severity, and victims may fear reprisal if they try to summon help. Domestic violence often is not reported to police, who are frequently in a quandary about what to do when they arrive at the scene. Beginning in the 1970s, police were urged to deal with these cases as "crises," and to intervene and mediate between the parties. Critics charged that this only legitimated the continued battering of women, and that it blamed victims for their condition. They advocated arrests and pushed for greater police authority to make arrests even when they did not witness the alleged abuse. This criticism was buttressed by a number of significant legal challenges that encouraged changes in how police treated domestic violence. By the 1980s, police were much more likely to view domestic violence as a serious offense, officers were empowered legally to intervene in more effective ways, and many departments had adopted mandatory arrest policies. The courts also were more likely to take domestic violence seriously, and prosecutors were less likely to dismiss domestic violence cases out of hand when faced with a victim's ambivalence about whether to proceed.

Child sexual abuse is another problem that has come to the fore in recent years, and it, too, presents special challenges to the criminal justice system; in Chapter 6, Barbara E. Smith details how police and the courts have responded. Child abuse cases question some time-honored criminal procedures. The victims are young—sometimes very young—and they can find elements of the adversary process like cross-examination to be confusing and frightening. Offenders are rarely predatory strangers; usually they are family members, relatives, or friends of the family, and it is not clear that they respond in the traditional way to the threat of criminal sanctions. There also are frequently no witnesses to what they have done and little physical evidence of any kind. The media may become acutely interested in these cases, especially if the abuse has ritualistic or sadistic overtones. This puts tremendous pressure on public officials who are responsible for the victims. Charges of abuse fall under the jurisdiction of multiple agencies, including those entrusted with mental health and child protection. Child sexual abuse raises complex medical issues and commands the careful attention of several branches of the criminal justice system. The resulting jurisdictional squabbles can lead to disagreements about how to proceed and may contaminate cases from a legal standpoint. All this can be traumatic for victims, and it is not clear that handling those cases as crimes will do much to help the victimized children.

There is a great deal of interest in devising more appropriate legal procedures for processing child abuse cases. One tack is to assemble interdisciplinary teams of police, prosecutors, and social workers to investigate them. Special techniques have been developed for interviewing children (including using anatomical dolls) and for presenting their testimony (videotape, closed-circuit television, excluding outsiders from courtrooms). However, these may impinge on the constitutional rights of the accused, and courts have approached them with a great deal of caution. The general pattern still seems to be one of nonprosecution, and research reveals that in cases that are pursued, offenders usually are put on probation and typically are directed to counseling or therapy.

Recent research provides suggestive evidence that persons close to crime victims (who can be thought of as "indirect victims") often suffer emotionally during the aftermath of the incident. In Chapter 7, David S. Riggs and Dean Kilpatrick review a number of studies that show that the relatives or intimate partners of crime victims may manifest many of the same symptoms reported by the victims themselves, such as anxiety, depression, intrusive thoughts and memories, and diminished self-esteem. A case in point involves the surviving family members of homicide victims, who not only experience the stress resulting from the loss of a loved one but also have problems with anxiety and other clinical symptoms. It appears that the family's level of dissatisfaction with the criminal justice system is related to the intensity of these symptoms.

As the authors note, it is not easy to explain the reactions of indirect victims of crime. However, there are some theoretical frameworks that help to shed light on the phenomenon. For example, "attribution" theory suggests that indirect victims may change their basic perception of the world as a predictable and safe place and may believe that they have also become more vulnerable to criminal victimization. "Learned helplessness" theory predicts that indirect victims experience problems because they feel that the crime incident was out of their control, and they feel further out of control in their contacts with the criminal justice system. According to "learning theory," victims may become anxious and depressed by sharing the experience of the crime vicariously with direct victims. Riggs and Kilpatrick have advice for practitioners in the field of victim services. First and foremost, they should be aware of the difficulties encountered by indirect victims and offer them diagnostic and treatment services. For practitioners in the criminal justice system, the authors recommend providing indirect victims with information about the progress of the case.

When crime occurs, the police are usually the first on the scene. In Chapter 8, Irvin Waller highlights the importance of the police for victims. In addition to their traditional duty to apprehend criminals, police are in a strategic position to assist victims in a number of ways. They can offer practical assistance to victims, including helping them deal with insurance forms and smashed-in doors, advising them on how to prevent future victimization, and protecting them from reprisal if they cooperate with the prosecutor. It is crucial that police remain in continued contact with victims, keep them informed about their case, and help them get into contact with service agencies and compensation programs. The police—who Waller describes as being "first in aid"—need to be trained to help victims deal with the emotional trauma that many of them experience in the hours and days immediately following the crime.

Chapter 8 illustrates these general points by describing victim service programs in several Canadian cities. Police there have organized volunteers to staff crisis intervention units and routinely refer victims to needed social services, and have instituted a number of simple procedures designed to make the lives of victims run more smoothly. The chapter concludes with a call for police in the United States to follow Canada's lead in providing police help for crime victims.

In Chapter 9, Robert C. Davis and Madeline Henley survey the range of services available to victims in the United States. They trace the growth of service programs over time. Twenty years ago, there were practically none; now there are at least 5,000 programs, and there is good reason to believe they have become a permanent part of the criminal justice system. Many publicly run programs are administered by prosecutors' officers, while others operate within police departments or are independent city or county agencies. There also are some privately run services for victims. Grass-roots groups were early supporters and advocates for rape victims and battered women; they were run without government funding, and some even took an adversarial stance toward the police and courts. More recently, they have been joined by service and advocacy groups, such as Parents of Murdered Children and Mothers Against Drunk Driving. As the criminal justice system has become more responsive to victims and as federal and state funding has become available to support their efforts, private groups have come to work more closely with public agencies.

Davis and Henley also summarize what is known concerning the effectiveness of these programs. Evaluations reveal that they frequently miss their mark. Although the most common needs reported by victims are for improved household security and financial assistance, relatively few programs provide either kind of support. Furthermore, they reach only a small percentage of those in need. A basic reason for this is that victims commonly do not know about the availability of program services; this finding recommends that victim programs be more aggressive in their outreach efforts. Another problem is the dearth of research to speak conclusively about the effect of support services, especially on the emotional trauma that affects many victims. It is not clear whether programs can substitute for the vital role played by family and friends in alleviating the impact of crime.

In Chapter 10, Deborah Kelly examines a series of reforms designed to increase victim participation in the criminal process. They were made in response to massive victim dissatisfaction with their role in the criminal justice process. During the early 1970s, a number of studies documented how frequently cases had to be dropped due to problems in securing the continued cooperation of victims and witnesses. In light of considerable evidence that victims and witnesses felt victimized by the system as well as by offenders, there have been new efforts to institute reforms that make their lives easier and their cooperation more meaningful. Some of the changes were simple efforts to attend to their practical needs; for example, in many jurisdictions, victims are notified routinely of the various proceedings and events that affect their cases, and attempts are made to see that they do not have to show up and wait unnecessarily in court and that they have a separate and secure place to sit during hearings and trials. Efforts to promote their participation in the prosecutorial process have been more controversial. These have included rules (1) involving victims in plea negotiations between prosecutors and defense attorneys, (2) allowing victim participation in sentencing, and (3) assuring the right of victims to be present in court when their cases are being heard. (It may surprise most readers to learn that in a majority of jurisdictions, they were *excluded* specifically from the courtroom.)

Research to date indicates that these reforms have not had a substantial impact on how the system actually works. Prosecutors often were opposed to them because they threatened to break up cozy coalitions of courtroom lawyers and erode their control of the process. However, most victims do not claim their new rights, and few have even heard of them. Research suggests that those who participate more heavily in the process are more satisfied with it and are more likely to cooperate fully, but thus far only a small number of victims has been very involved.

Most of the state legislatures and the federal government have inaugurated compensation programs that reimburse victims for some of the costs of crime. These programs are discussed in Chapter 13, and their European equivalents are described in Chapter 12. Chapter 11, by Susan Hillenbrand, explores another approach to compensating victims—making offenders pay. Almost every state has passed legislation enabling judges to issue orders calling for offenders to pay or somehow make up the losses that victims have suffered. There is ample historical precedent for this policy of restitution; early American courts frequently awarded damages to victims. Interest in restitution has revived for two reasons. One is the new attention being focused on victims' concerns; the other is that jails in the United States are overcrowded, and the nation is casting about for alternative forms of punishment. Making the offender pay seems to respond to both needs.

Restitution programs take several forms. Court-ordered victim-offender reconciliation programs are designed to heal the breech between the parties to certain kinds of conflicts. Sometimes restitution is seen as a form of victim assistance, and is conducted as part of such service programs. Restitution employment programs match offenders with jobs, using the "stick" of mandatory repayment to keep them there.

However, restitution is usually a condition of probation or parole, or is ordered along with a suspended sentence. Sometimes offenders agree to make restitution in lieu of a sentence; in this case, payment is the penalty. As these examples suggest, restitution programs can have mixed goals. Hillenbrand argues that they are not really victim oriented, but rather, employ rhetoric about victims to legitimize what is in fact an alternative to incarceration.

Chapter 12 describes the development of the victim movement and trends in victim policy in Europe. Mike Maguire and Joanna Shapland observe that, as in the United States, European interest in victims mushroomed during the early 1970s in response to rising crime rates, the apparent ineffectiveness and uncaring attitude of their criminal justice systems, and growing awareness of the complex and enduring impact of crime on victims. However, the victim movement took a somewhat different course in Europe. It focused on victim services rather than on victims' "rights." Advocates did not press for legislation to empower victims, as they have done in the United States by pushing for participation in sentences, impact statements, and other special roles for victims. European movements were less overtly political than in the United States and instead worked with government ministries to deliver and improve specialized services for their constituents. European programs also are not part of the criminal justice system. Whereas in the United States they are frequently adjuncts of prosecutors' officers or the police, in Europe they are independently organized social agencies. In Great Britain, for example, most services are coordinated and delivered by volunteer networks, while victims' programs in Holland are staffed by professionals. They are all funded directly by central governments, except in West Germany, where they are the responsibility of the states.

Chapter 13 presents a thorough review of recent innovations in victim policy, examining some of the assumptions and political forces that underlie these changes. Legislative policy with regard to victims was born in California in the mid-1960s; there were steady gains during the 1970s, but the real outpouring of initiatives did not begin until the 1980s. In Chapter 13, Robert Elias summarizes policy activity in the following areas: services for victims, changes in the criminal justice process, expanding rights for victims, special protection for particular groups of victims, and measures to deal more harshly with offenders. His legislative review documents the extent of the "policy boom" during the 1980s. There are more victim programs and more money to support them than ever before. States have enacted victims' bills of rights, and some have put them into their constitutions. Groups like children, the elderly, and the mentally impaired have been granted special status as crime victims. Sentences have gotten longer.

Not everyone is satisfied with the consequences. Critics charge that victim services remain understaffed and underfunded, that the rules determining who is qualified for benefits are drawn too narrowly and are bureaucratically enforced, and that programs for victims are among the first to be cut when hard budget decisions must be made. Only a small percentage of victims is being served, and they remain mostly irrelevant to the routine prosecution of criminal cases. Politicians have seized upon the cause of victims to justify narrowing the constitutional rights of criminal defendants, increasing the length of prison sentences, and diverting popular attention from other injustices and abuses of power. This chapter raises disturbing questions about the character of the alliances that shape criminal justice policy in the United States.

In the final chapter of this book, Gilbert Geis presents his assessment of recent trends in victim policy. He traces the origins of the victim movement in the United States to national politics. Seeking to protect himself from charges that he was soft on crime, President Johnson appointed a commission to investigate the entire problem. The commission's research focused new attention on victims and sponsored surveys that documented the extent of crime, widespread fear of crime, and dissatisfaction with the criminal justice system. Geis points out how insistence on victims' concerns since that time has shaken up parts of the criminal justice system, which raises questions concerning whose interests the system should serve. Rhetoric about victims cuts across some unlikely coalitions. For example, elements of the women's movement pressing for the suppression of pornography, mandatory arrests, and stern treatment of sex offenders have come into conflict with some of their otherwise natural political allies. Larger ideological conflicts are played out in the politics of the victim movement because it provides an advantageous field both for liberals and conservatives. It seems that no one can be *against* doing something for victims; as Geis notes, "The plight of crime victims is traumatic and determinable. Their relief is feasible. It has strong social, political, and personal appeal. Any of us, at any time, could become a crime victim." However, views on *what to do* about crime and victims vary widely.

REFERENCES

American Bar Association (1979). *Reducing victim/witness intimidation: A package.* Washington, DC: American Bar Association.

Ash, M. (1972). On witnesses: A radical critique of criminal court procedures. *Notre Dame Lawyer, 48,* 386-425.

Auerback, S. M. & Kilman, P. R. (1978). Crisis intervention: A review of outcome research. *Psychological Bulletin, 84,* 1189-1217.

Chelimsky, E. (1981). Serving victims: Agency incentives and individual needs. In S. Salasen (Ed.), *Evaluating victim services* (pp. 73-98). Beverly Hills, CA: Sage.

Cronin, R., & Bourque, B. (1981). *Assessment of victim/witness projects.* Washington DC: U.S. Government Printing Office.

Davis, R. C. (1987a). *Crime victims: Learning how to help them—NIJ Reports.* Washington, DC: National Institute of Justice.

Davis, R. C. (1987b). *Providing help to victims: A study of psychological and material outcomes.* Final report of the Victim Services Agency (New York) to the National Institute of Justice.

Finn, P., & Lee, B. N. W. (1988). *Establishing and expanding victim-witness assistance programs.* Washington, DC: National Institute of Justice.

Friedman, K., Bischoff, H., Davis, R., & Person, A. (1982). *Victims and helpers: Reactions to crime.* Washington, DC: U.S. Government Printing Office.

Gottfredson, G. D. (1989). The experiences of violent and serious victimization. In N.A. Weiner and M. E. Wolfgang (Eds.), *Pathways to criminal violence* (pp. 202-234). Newbury Park, Sage.

Kahn, A. S. (Ed.). (1984). *Victims of crime and violence.* Washington, DC: American Psychological Association.

Karmen, A. (1984). *Crime victims: An introduction to victimology.* Monterey: Brooks/Cole.

Knudten, R. D., Meade, A., Knudten, M., & Doerner, W. (1976). *Victims and witnesses: The impact of crime and their experience with the criminal justice system.* Washington, DC: U.S. Government Printing Office.

Lurigio, A. J., & Davis, R. C. (1989). *Adjusting to criminal victimization: The correlates of post-crime distress.* Manuscript submitted for publication.

Lurigio, A. J., & Rosenbaum, D. P. (in press). The psychological effects of criminal victimization: Past and future research. *Victimology.*

Maguire, M., & Corbett, C. (1987). *The effects of crime and the work of victims' support schemes.* Hampshire, England: Gower House.

McGuire, S. (1987). Victims' rights laws in Illinois: Two decades of progress. *Crime and Delinquency, 33,* 532-540.

Norquay, G., & Weiler, R. (1981). *Services to victims and witnesses of crime in Canada.* Ottawa: Solicitor General of Canada, Research Division.

President's Task Force on Victims of Crime. (1982). *Report of the President's Task Force on Victims of Crime.* Washington, DC: U.S. Government Printing Office.

Roberts, A. (1987). National survey of victim services completed. *NOVA Newsletter, 11,* 1-2.

Rosenbaum, D. P. (1977). *Reactions to criminal victimization: A summary report of victim, community, and police reactions.* Unpublished doctoral dissertation, Loyola University, Chicago.

Sales, B., Rich, R. F., & Reich, J. (1984). Victims of crime and violence: Legal and policy issues. In A. S. Kahn (Ed.), *Victims of crime and violence* (pp. 113-154). Washington, DC: American Psychological Association.

Siegal, M. (1983). Crime and violence in America: The victims. *American Psychologist, 38,* 1267-1273.

Skogan, W. G., & Wycoff, M. (1987). Some unexpected effects of a police service for victims. *Crime and Delinquency, 33,* 490-501.

Spelman, W., & Brown, D. K. (1981). *Calling the police: Citizen reporting of serious crime.* Washington, DC: Police Executive Research Forum.

Villmow, B. (1984). *Implications of research on victimization for criminal and social policy.* Paper presented at the Council of Europe, Sixteenth Criminological Research Conference, Strasbourg, France.

Waller, I. (1982). *Crime victims: Needs, services and reforms—orphans of social policy.* Paper presented at the Fourth International Symposium on Victimology, Tokyo, Japan.

Young, M. (1988). The crime victims' movement. In F. Ochberg (Ed.), *Post-traumatic therapy and victims of violence* (pp. 13-57). New York: Brunner-Mazel.

Chapter 2

PATTERNS OF CRIMINAL VICTIMIZATION IN THE UNITED STATES

JOHN H. LAUB

Despite daily attention to crime in the newspaper, television reports, and radio talk shows, it is surprising that we know so little about crime and its impact on society. For instance, estimates as to the system size and shape of the crime problem vary considerably even among so-called crime experts. Policy decisions are often made in a seemingly ad hoc fashion. And, until recently, information on the experiences of crime victims themselves was virtually nonexistent. Nonetheless, concerns about personal and community safety are among the most important in the United States today.

In this chapter, I seek to bring together the best available empirical information on criminal victimization in order to provide a comprehensive, systematic review of the current state of our knowledge. More precisely, I address four important dimensions of criminal victimization in the United States. The first concerns the *level* of victimization. For example, how many victimizations occur each year? What is the rate of criminal victimization? Is the rate of criminal victimization increasing or decreasing over time? The second issue regards *correlates* of victimization. For instance, who are the typical victims of crime? Do victim characteristics vary by crime type? How is victimization distributed across time and space? The third area addresses the *dynamics* of victimization. What is the nature of the relationship between victims and their

AUTHOR'S NOTE: *I thank Wes Skogan, Art Lurigio, and Rob Sampson for their helpful comments on an earlier version of this chapter. I also thank Jamie Fox for his technical assistance in producing the figures for this chapter.*

offenders? Do victims in any way contribute to their victimizations? Conversely, do victims typically resist during the victimization occurrences and, if so, what are the results of that resistance? Finally, I examine the *consequences* of criminal victimization. How often to victims report their victimization to the police? What is the extent of injury suffered by victims of crime? Similarly, what is the extent of economic loss? Answers to these questions can provide a solid foundation upon which to build theories of victimization, as well as effective policies relating to victims of crime. But before presenting the empirical findings. I turn to a brief discussion of the available sources of data.

DATA SOURCES

Most criminologists distinguish between official and unofficial sources of data. Official sources of data generally consist of records generated by criminal justice agencies (e.g., police, courts, and corrections). In contrast, unofficial sources of data primarily include social surveys conducted independently of criminal justice agencies (e.g., victimization surveys and self-reported delinquency surveys). Unfortunately, efforts to obtain useful information on victims and victimizations from official data sources like the *Uniform Crime Reports* face two interrelated problems. First, information regarding victim characteristics are not routinely collected by criminal justice agencies. On the contrary, criminal justice records tend to be *offender focused*. Second, and perhaps more important, information that is collected by criminal justice agencies only relates to those criminal events that have come to the attention of the criminal justice system. More precisely, crimes that are not reported (or recorded) to the police are not included in these official measures.

If the reporting or non-reporting of crimes to the police were random, there would be little problem in using crimes known to the police as an indicator of crime. Although we would not know about the total *number* of crimes occurring, the data could be used with confidence to analyze the *correlates* and *characteristics* of crime. However, reporting crimes to the police is not a random process. There are certain factors, such as weapon use and victim injury, that are systematically related to the likelihood that a crime will come to the attention of the police, that the police will record it, that an arrest will be made, and the case will be followed up on (see, for example, Block & Block, 1980).

To overcome problems with official data, I will focus on the National Crime Survey (NCS) victimization data. This survey was designed to collect information on crime victims from a large sample of the U.S. population. Conducted by the Bureau of the Census and the Bureau of Justice Statistics, the NCS is a household-based survey that is national in scope and has been ongoing since its inception in 1972.[1] The NCS is the only data source on the national level that allows individual-level analyses of victims and their victimizations across a variety of crime categories. It is also the only national indicator of the level of crime that attempts to record crimes that do not come to the attention of the police. These two characteristics make the NCS a rich source of information on the nature and extent of criminal victimization and victims in the United States.

The offenses covered in the NCS are rape, robbery, assault, and personal larceny (theft), with and without contact. In addition, such household crimes as burglary, household larceny, and motor vehicle theft are included. Information is available regarding the basic demographic characteristics of the victim, the alleged offender, the victimization event itself, and the consequences of the crime. Information on personal victimizations is collected directly from victims themselves.[2]

INCIDENCE AND PREVALENCE

This next section focuses on the substantive findings generated from the NCS data. Attention is given only to the major questions regarding the nature and extent of criminal victimization and the characteristics of victims. More detailed information is available in the Bureau of Justice Statistics (BJS) annual reports, *Criminal Victimization in the United States*.

Rates of Victimization

In 1986, the NCS estimated that 34.1 million victimizations (including both attempts and completed crimes) were committed throughout the United States. In general, the more serious the victimization, the less frequently it occurred. Also, property crimes were far more frequent than crimes of violence. In fact, the most frequently committed crime was a theft against a household or individual. Violent crimes accounted for 16% of all the victimizations reported to the NCS in 1986;

the most common violent crime reported to survey interviewers was simple assault. Of all household crimes reported, the most common was household larceny (theft).

A better way of assessing victimization patterns is by constructing a *victimization rate* (the number of victimizations divided by the number of persons/households in a specific category of interest, that category being the United States). Rates of victimization standardize the population for a given time and place and provide a measure of the *incidence* of victimization. In 1986, the victimization rate for violent crimes (rape, robbery, and assault) was 28 per 1,000 population age 12 and over.[3] The overall victimization rate for personal crimes of theft (purse snatching and pocket-picking along with thefts away from home) was 68 per 1,000. The victimization rate for household crimes (burglary, larceny-theft, and motor vehicle theft) was 170 per 1,000 households. The victimization rate for burglary alone was 62 per 1,000 households in 1986 (BJS, 1988a).

Another way of assessing the extent of victimization is by constructing a *prevalence* rate of victimization. The numerator of the prevalence rate is the number of persons/households victimized one or more times in a given time period divided by the population of interest. Recently, the Bureau of the Census and the Bureau of Justice Statistics developed a new crime indicator, "Households Touched by Crime," which measures the annual prevalence of victimization among households. In 1987, about 24% of the more than 91 million households in the United States were victimized by some type of crime, with crimes of violence occurring less frequently, (4.6%), compared with crimes of theft, 17.1% (BJS, 1988b).

In order to provide a context in which to better understand victimization risk, one can compare the risks for other life events (e.g., traffic accidents, house fires, serious illness) to the risk of victimization. As revealed in Table 1, all else equal, the risk of criminal victimization is less than the risk of accidental injuries. Although the risk of violent crime is higher than that of death by cancer or death in a house fire, a person is more likely to die from natural causes than from a criminal victimization. At the same time, the risk of personal theft is quite high relative to other life events (BJS, 1988c).

Trends in Victimization

In 1986, the overall level of crimes reported to the NCS decreased to their lowest level in the 14-year history of the survey. This pattern of

TABLE 2.1

A Comparison of Adult Crime Rates with the
Rates of Other Life Events, 1982-1984 Data

Events	Rate per 1,000 Adults
Accidental injury, all circumstances	242
Accidental injury at home	79
Personal theft	72
Accidental injury at work	58
Violent victimization	31
Assault (aggravated and simple)	24
Injury in motor vehicle accident	17
Death, all causes	11
Victimization with injury	10
Serious (aggravated) assault	9
Robbery	6
Heart disease death	4
Cancer death	2
Rape (women only)	2
Accidental death, all circumstances	.5
Pneumonia/influenza death	.3
Motor vehicle accident death	.2
Suicide	.2
Injury from fire	.1
Homicide/legal intervention death	.1
Death from fire	.03

SOURCE: BJS (1988c). *Report to the Nation on Crime and Justice, Second Edition*, p. 24.

declining victimization rates generally held true for personal crimes, as well as household ones, over the 1973-1986 period. What is particularly noteworthy is the robbery rate for 1986 — a crime of high concern — is the lowest it has been in the NCS history. At the same time, it is important to note that the rate of reporting crimes to the police by victims did not change dramatically during the time period in question. Accords to NCS data, about half of all violent crimes, two fifths of all household crimes, and one fourth of all personal theft crimes are reported to the police each year (see Figure 2.1). Not surprisingly, the number of households touched by crime also declined over the same period. In 1975, nearly one of three households were touched by crime, compared with one of four in 1987, the lowest figure in the 11 years for which the indicator has been kept (BJS, 1988b).

A major concern among criminologists has been the comparison of NCS and UCR data over time (see O'Brien, 1985; Gove, Hughes, & Geerken, 1985). In fact, examining the UCR and NCS trend data from

28

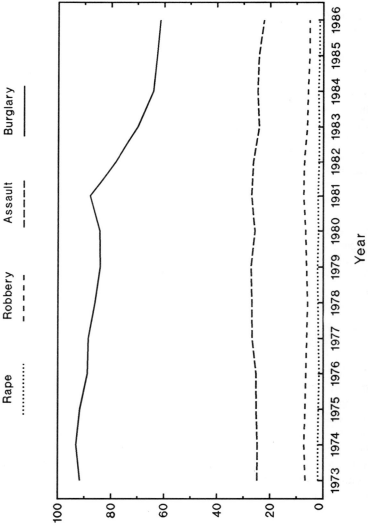

Figure 2.1. Victimization Rates (per 1000 persons/households) for Selected Personal and Household Crimes, 1973-1986 National Crime Survey Data

SOURCE: BJS (1987). "Criminal Victimization, 1986" p. 3.

1973 through 1986 for the crimes of rape, robbery, aggravated assault, burglary, and motor vehicle theft reveal radically different portraits. While the UCR show percentage increases for the five crimes under discussion over the 1973-1986 time frame, the NCS data reveals stability or a declining trend for the same crime types. Whether or not the differences are artifacts of the different methodologies used to gather these data or reflect the fact that the UCR and the NCS measure different phenomenon is unknown.[4]

Correlates of Victimization

Risk of criminal victimization is linked to lifestyle and routine activities (Garofalo, 1987; Maxfield, 1987). What people do, where they go, and who they associate with all affect their likelihood of victimization. In part, lifestyle and routine activities are a reflection of a person's individual characteristics. For example, teenagers typically go to school five days a week for nine months of the year and associate primarily with other teenagers. Similarly, elderly persons spend considerable time at home, often do not work, and associate with friends of the same age or family members. This section will explore how victimization is distributed across key demographic dimensions. There is considerable evidence that criminal victimization is not evenly distributed across demographic subgroups in the population, but instead follows the patterns suggested by the ideas of lifestyle and routine activities.

Age

Age is one of the strongest correlates of victimization. The NCS data show an inverse relationship between the age of victim and the risk of both personal and household victimization. In other words, elderly persons (age 65 and older) are victimized at a rate far less than that of younger persons. In fact, rates of victimization seem to peak in the 16- to 24-age group and decline as age increases. The relationship between age and victimization is especially strong with regard to the crimes of aggravated assault and robbery. The exception to this pattern is personal theft, which displayed much more stability across age categories than any other crime type.

Sex

The NCS data show that the rate of victimization of personal crimes for males is twice the rate for females. The relationship between sex and victimization is especially strong for aggravated assault. Of course, one exception to this pattern is the crime of rape. But, in addition to rape, the rate of victimization for males and females is virtually identical for the crime of personal theft (see Figure 2), a category that includes purse snatching.

The relationship between the sex of victim and victimization is also influenced by victim's age. As displayed in Figure 2.2 rates of violent victimization for those 35 and older reveal far less difference by sex of victim compared with other younger age groups. Moreover, for crimes of personal theft, rates for females aged 20 and older surpass comparable rates for males in similar age groupings.

Race

Rates of victimization also vary across racial subgroups in the population. The NCS data tell us that the rate of violent victimizations—especially aggravated assaults and robberies—is greater for blacks than whites. However, for crimes of personal theft, whites have a slightly higher rate compared with blacks. The NCS indicates that black males have the highest rate of violent crime victimization and white females the lowest. Blacks also have the highest rate of overall household victimization. This is particularly striking for the crime of burglary. The burglary rate for blacks is 92 per 1,000 households compared with 58 per 1,000 households for whites.

Family Income

Income is also related to the risk of personal victimization. As income goes up, the risk of personal victimization goes down. This is particularly true for crimes of robbery and aggravated assault. However, the pattern changes for personal theft crimes. While poor people are more often victimized by purse snatching and pocket picking, individuals with family incomes of $30,000 and over face higher risks for personal thefts that involve no victim/offender contact compared to other income groups (see Figure 2.3).

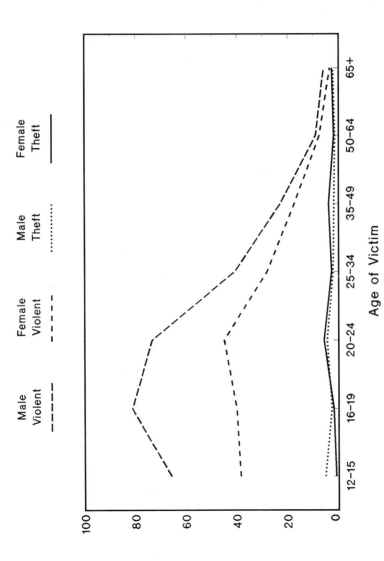

Figure 2.2. Victimization Rates (per 1000 persons) by Type of Crime and Age and Sex of Victim, 1986 National Crime Survey Data

SOURCE: BJS (1988a). Criminal Victimization in the United States, 1986, pp. 18-19.

Although total household victimization rates are highest for families making less than $9,999, the rates are virtually identical for the remaining income groups. The crime of household burglary, however, displays an interesting pattern. The data in Figure 2.3 reveal that burglary rates are highest for those households with less than $7,500 income. At the same time, burglary rates for those households with $50,000 and over are among the highest. Burglary rates are the lowest for those households with moderate incomes, in the range of $15,000 to $50,000. It should also be noted that renters experience the greatest rates of household victimization, especially for burglary.

Urbanization

Those who live in urban areas suffer more victimizations than residents of suburban or rural areas. This pattern holds for all person and household crimes, and is particularly noteworthy for the crime of robbery. Robbery is a big city phenomenon. Overall, even though there is considerable city-to-city variation, people who live in cities face higher crime rates regardless of their personal characteristics.

Of course, other correlates of victimization can be found in the NCS. For instance, marital status is related to victimization; singles or divorced/separated persons face higher rates of victimization than those married or widowed. Since most single people are also young, some of the risk may be accounted for by age. However, those that are married, regardless of age group, have the lowest rates of personal victimization. Furthermore, rates of victimization are related to a person's position in the labor force. The NCS shows that persons who are employed, housewives, or retirees have rates of personal victimization that are lower than for those who are unemployed.

It is important to point out that these relationships vary somewhat when one or more of the other demographic variables are taken into account and when specific sub-categories of crime are examined. Nonetheless, the five correlates of victimization discussed above are quite robust and hold up quite well when controlling for other variables.[5]

Time and Space Dimensions

In addition to examining the distribution of victimization across demographic subgroups in the population, lifestyle and routine activities theories hold that victimization patterns will vary across space and

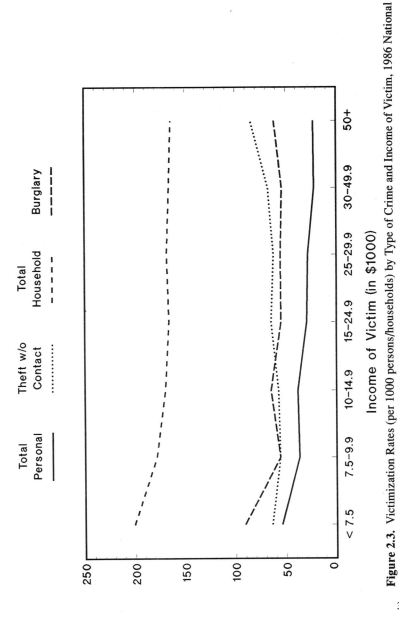

Figure 2.3. Victimization Rates (per 1000 persons/households) by Type of Crime and Income of Victim, 1986 National Crime Survey Data

SOURCE: BJS (1987). Criminal Victimization in the United States, 1986 pp. 26-27 and 34-35

time. To the extent that lifestyle and routine activities increase an individual's chances of being in public places at night, for example, victimization risk is heightened. Victimizations are not randomly distributed across time or space dimensions.

Unfortunately, the NCS data set contains only crude indicators of the time and place where victimizations occur. For instance, the NCS indicates that about half of all violent crimes take place during the nighttime hours (6:00 p.m. to 6:00 a.m.), with the largest proportion occurring between 6:00 p.m. and midnight. Household crimes occur more frequently at night, but overall are much more variable. In fact, 28% of household crime victims do not even know the time their victimization occurred. As for place, the most common site of personal victimizations was on the street. This was true for all personal crime categories. Overall, the NCS data are in agreement with patterns found in official records regarding the time and space dimensions of crime (BJS, 1988a).

In summary, the NCS strongly supports the notion that criminal victimization is linked to lifestyle and routine activities as reflected in basic demographic characteristics. Those individuals whose lifestyle and routine activities lead them away from home to public places, especially at night and in association with young people, are at greater risk of victimization. This is not to say that lifestyle and routine activities explain all victimization risk. What is argued is that certain lifestyles and routine activities increase on a probabilistic basis the opportunities one faces for victimization. This general model of victimization fits quite well with the existing data on crime patterns (see Gottfredson, 1981; Cohen, Cantor, & Kluegel, 1981; Maxfield, 1987).

Homicide

There are numerous questions about the crime of homicide. For example, are the correlates of homicide different from other violent crimes? Is homicide linked to lifestyle and routine activities? Is the rate of homicide in the United States increasing? What do we know about the circumstances of homicide? What can be done to prevent homicide?

In 1987, there were 20,096 murder and nonnegligent manslaughter offenses reported to the UCR; the rate per 100,000 inhabitants was 8.3. The murder rate is higher in urban areas than in suburban and rural areas, although there is a great deal of variation from city to city. Trend data show fairly large increases in the homicide rate since 1960.

However, since 1980 the rate of homicide declined each year until 1986. There were 3% fewer murders in 1987 than in 1986 (Federal Bureau of Investigation, 1988).

Based on UCR reports, three out of four victims were males, almost half were between the ages of 20 and 34, and two out of every five homicide victims were black. An examination of single offender and single victim incidents reveals that homicide is disproportionately an intraracial event with blacks killing blacks and whites killing whites. In a similar vein, males were most often killed by other males; however, females were far more likely to be slain by males as opposed to females (FBI, 1988).

In 1987, firearms were the weapon of choice in three of every five homicides, with handguns accounting for 44% of all murders. Moreover, three of every five murders in 1987 involved relatives of persons acquainted with the victim. Almost two out of every five murders were the result of arguments, 20% were felony murders, and the motives were unknown in 25% of the incidents (FBI, 1988).[6]

Maxfield (1988) has recently begun to sort out the various types of incidents that fall under the general rubric of homicide. Specifically, he distinguishes between *conflict* homicides (generally resulting from arguments), *instrumental* homicides (resulting from other felonies, such as robbery or sexual assault), *other felony* homicides (resulting from burglaries and other such crimes), *drug traffic* homicides, and *youth gang* homicides. These types of homicide clearly display age-related patterns that reflect differences in lifestyle and routine activities. However, in contrast to other forms of personal victimization, a significant proportion of homicide victims are killed in their own homes (Maxfield, 1988; also see Warr, 1988, for a discussion of rape in the home).

DYNAMICS OF VICTIMIZATION

This section examines the nature of the victim/offender relationship in criminal events. One concern is whether the risk of victimization is greater from strangers or from loved ones. Another is whether the threat of victimization from strangers is greater for particular types of crime. Answers to these questions are crucial from both a theoretical and public policy standpoint in light of the widespread belief that at the core of fear of crime is a fear of victimization by a stranger (see Garofalo & Laub, 1978; Reidel, 1987).

In addition, this section analyzes interactions between the victim and the offender during the victimization event, specifically with regard to victim resistance and victim precipitation. A major policy concern is what concrete advice can be offered potential victims of crime so that they may protect their property as well as themselves during a victimization encounter. Although relatively understudied, understanding the dynamics of victimization is critically important in order to develop reasonable victim-oriented policies.

Victim-Offender Relationships

Typically, three victim-offender categories have been used in victimization research—crimes committed by relatives, including spouses, ex-spouses, parents, and children: crimes committed by acquaintances, including casual acquaintances as well as close friends; and crimes committed by strangers, including those known by "sight only." Unfortunately, it is difficult to adequately assess the extent of crime committed by strangers for a variety of reasons. Most important is that victim-offender relationships can only be determined in crimes that typically involve some face-to-face contact, like robbery and assault. In contrast, victims of burglary, auto theft, and household larceny do not typically see who their assailants were. However, even in crimes involving a confrontation, the victim-offender relationship may not be known or be reported inaccurately. Indeed, the nature of the victim-offender relationship is unknown in approximately 30% of the homicides reported to the police each year (Reidel, 1987: p. 225). Secondly, research has consistently shown that a large number of crimes committed by relatives, friends, and lovers are not reported to the police *or* to NCS interviews (see Skogan, 1981). Therefore, both official and unofficial data sources limit what is known about victim-offender relationships.

According to 1982-1984 NCS data for the violent crimes of rape, robbery, and assault, 57% of the victimizations were committed by strangers, 31% were committed by acquaintances and friends, and 8% were committed by relatives (Timrots & Rand, 1987). This pattern has remained generally stable since 1973, when the NCS was launched. The nature of the victim-offender relationship varies by type of crime. Generally, crimes of theft are more commonly committed by strangers than are crimes of violence. For instance, 77% of the robberies reported to crime survey interviewers were attributed to strangers. In sharp contrast, available UCR data on homicide from 1985 reveal that three of every five murders involved relatives or persons acquainted with the victim. However, there is some reason to believe that over the last 20 years, stranger homicides have been on the rise (Reidel, 1987: p. 240).

At the micro-level, males, younger people, and single/divorced individuals are more likely to be victimized by strangers, compared to their demographic counterparts. At the macro-level, persons living in areas characterized by high levels of family disruption and residential mobility, and with a large proportion of single individuals, experience above average risks of stranger violence independently of their personal characteristics (Sampson, 1987).

Finally, crimes committed by strangers differ from crimes committed by nonstrangers in that stranger-to-stranger crimes are more likely to occur on the street, are more likely to involve two or more offenders, and are more likely to involve the presence of a weapon. However, those victimized by nonstrangers are more likely to be injured compared with stranger-to-stranger crimes (Timrots & Rand, 1987; Hindelang, 1976).

Victim Resistance and Precipitation

A small amount of contemporary research has been done on victim resistance and precipitation. Victim precipitation is defined here as actions by the victim that encourage a behavioral response or arouse emotions in the offender that increase the chance of victimization (Sparks, 1982: p. 26-27). Unfortunately, this research suffers from a number of problems, ranging from inadequate or unavailable data to faulty conceptualization and measurement. Undoubtedly, the two topics are fraught with conceptual ambiguities, including the lack of a clear distinction between victim precipitation and victim resistance. There is also a tendency to interpret victim behavior during the victimization event solely in the context of the outcome of the event (Fattah, 1984). Although early victimology focused quite heavily on the role of the victim in crime causation (see von Hentig, 1948), this perspective was not informed by sound empirical research. Moreover, this focus often led to what has come to be viewed as "victim-blaming" (Bard & Sangrey, 1979: p. 65). At the same time, issues surrounding victim resistance were virtually ignored until very recently.

In his seminal work on criminal homicide, Wolfgang (1958; p. 252) defined victim-precipitated homicides as those in which

. . . the victim is a direct, positive precipitator in the crime. The role of the victim is characterized by his having been the first in the homicide drama to use physical force directed against his subsequent slayer. The victim precipitated cases are those in which the victim was the first to show and use a deadly weapon, to strike a blow in an altercation—in short, the first to commence the interplay of resort to physical force.

Using this definition, Wolfgang found 26% of the homicides in Philadelphia during the period 1948 to 1952 were victim precipitated. Generally speaking, similar results were found in more recent studies of homicide, although problems with missing data make such findings very tentative (see Sparks, 1982: p. 22-25, for a review).

Victim precipitation has been examined for the crimes of aggravated assault, rape, and robbery. For instance, Mulvihill & Tumin (1969) found in their study of offense patterns in 14 large cities that 14% of the aggravated assaults, 4% of the rapes, and 8% of the robberies can be classified as victim precipitated. Again, it is important to stress the definitional problems of victim precipitation and the heavy reliance on police data in these studies. In fact, one researcher has suggested that

with the exception of homicide there is no adequate operational definition of VP; that the measures used in the past have been highly unreliable from a methodological point of view because they are highly dependent on a researcher's interpretation rather than on a fixed criteria (Silverman, 1974: p. 104).

Recently, Sparks (1982) attempted to distinguish a range of behaviors among victims that in some way may contribute to their victimization. His list includes precipitation, facilitation, vulnerability, opportunity, attractiveness, and impunity. To the extent that these concepts are useful in explaining the variation in victimization risk and understanding the dynamics of victimization awaits further research. It is interesting to note that, unlike some criminologists, Sparks does not want to abandon the topic of victim precipitation, despite its serious conceptual and ideological difficulties.

Unlike research on victim precipitation, research on victim resistance has been more recent and often uses victimization data as well as police records. At Block and Skogan (1986: p. 242) observe, "police reports generally distort the apparent effects of victim resistance because they greatly underrepresent instances of *successful* resistance." Victims can and do resist their assailants in a variety of ways. According to available NCS data, approximately three of every four victims of violent crime took some form of self-protective measures, ranging from trying to reason with the offender to using a weapon. The most common form of self-protection among victims who reported using such measures was nonviolent resistance and evasion. Victims of rape and assault were more likely to use self-protective measures than were victims of robbery. Also, victims were more likely to employ such measures when the offender was known to them (BJS, 1988a: p. 63-65).

In a recent study of resistance in stranger-to-stranger crime using NCS data from 1973 to 1979, Block and Skogan (1986) distinguished two types of resistance: *nonforceful* resistance, which includes talking with the offender, yelling for help, and trying to flee, and *forceful* resistance, which includes physically fighting with the offender, with or without a weapon. Using a multivariate analysis they found that forceful victim resistance may have reduced the likelihood of robbery completion, though such resistance may have increased the risk of physical attack to the victim. Forceful resistance in rape victimizations was related to a higher risk of attack and injury to victims with no apparent effect on the likelihood of rape and completion. In contrast, victims using nonforceful methods of resistance in robbery reduced the risk of robbery completion *and* suffered less attack and injury. Nonforceful resistance in rape victimizations was linked to a lower rate of completed rapes, but was not related to attack or other nonrape injuries (Block & Skogan, 1986).

It is important to note that a major weakness of this study and any study using NCS data (or most data from the police) is the lack of information on the sequencing of events *during* crimes. We generally do not know whether the resistance on the part of the victim is in response to some offender action, or vice versa (see Cook, 1986). Such information is crucial for criminologists seeking to give advice to victims regarding resisting potential offenders.

CONSEQUENCES OF VICTIMIZATION

This section examines what happens after a victimization occurs. For instance, what is the nature and extent of victim reporting to the police? This issue is important because reports by victims formally trigger action by the criminal justice system. Citizens have been said to act as "gatekeepers" to the formal system of social control (Gottfredson &

Gottfredson, 1980). Therefore, the extent of victim reporting, as well as the correlates of nonreporting, can reveal critical information relating to victims, the police, and the criminal justice system at large.

This section also reviews what is known regarding the consequences of victimization, including the extent of physical injury and property loss. For example, how often are victims physically injured as a result of their victimizations? What is the severity of their injuries? Similarly, how often do victims suffer economic loss from their victimizations, and what is the extent of economic loss? What are the costs of crime for society at large? Answers to such questions are crucial for the development of adequate compensation programs, among other police considerations.

Victim Reporting to the Police

Until the development of victimization surveys, there was no empirical data on the nature and extent of victim reporting to the police. Speculation about the "dark figure" of unreported crime suggested that a considerable number of crimes did not come to the attention of the police. Once available, the NCS confirmed this speculation. Indeed, according to 1986 NCS, a little more then a third of all crimes reported to survey interviewers are also reported to the police. Reporting rates also vary by crime type. In 1986, for instance, violent crimes were more often reported to the police than crimes of theft (50% vs. 28%), although the reporting rates for motor vehicle theft (93%) are among the highest (BJS, 1987). Importantly, rates of reporting to the police reveal no substantial variation over the 1973-1986 period. This is illustrated in Figure 2.4.

Research has consistently established that an important determinant of victim reporting to the police is the seriousness of the incident (Skogan, 1984). That is, completed thefts resulting in large losses and completed violent crimes involving injury and/or weapons are most likely reported to the police. In contrast, reporting to the police seems to be independent of the victim's personal characteristics (Skogan, 1984). Small differences are noted in reporting rates by sex and age: older victims are more likely to report than younger ones, and female victims are more likely to report than males. No differences are found by race and income. Surprisingly, the NCS data reveal no differences in the extent of victim reporting to the police in crimes committed by strangers as compared with nonstrangers. Given the concerns about the

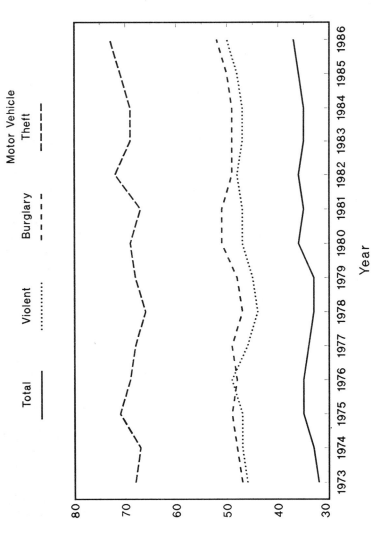

Figure 2.4. Percent Reporting Victimizations to the Police for Selected Personal and Household Crimes, 1973-1986 National Crime Survey Data

SOURCE: BJS (1987). "Criminal Victimization, 1986" p. 4

NCS measuring nonstranger victimizations, this finding is in all likelihood a methodological artifact and should be viewed cautiously.

In the NCS, victims are also asked to state their *reasons* for reporting or not reporting their victimization experiences to the police. A large number of crimes are not reported because victims believe they were "not important enough" or "nothing could be done/lack of proof," perhaps reflecting the nonserious nature of a number of crimes reported in the survey. However, a number of violent crimes were not reported to the police because victims felt they were *private matters.*" As to reasons for reporting, victims of violent crimes most often reported crimes out of a sense of duty or obligation, or as a way of preventing reoccurrences of the victimization in the future. On the other hand, victims of theft reported in order to recover their losses, primarily through insurance claims (BJS, 1988c: p. 35).

Physical Injury

Over 18,000 people are murdered each year in the United States, and more than two million are injured in rapes, robberies, and assaults. In fact, about one of every three victims of violent crime suffers some form of physical injury. However, serious injury is less common. About one in seven victims requires some medical care, and one in ten victims spent at least one night in the hospital (BJS, 1988c).

Not surprisingly, the likelihood of injury varied by crime type and victim characteristics. For example, the NCS shows that 24% of the victims of rape suffered injuries serious enough to require medical attention, compared with 15% of robbery victims, 18% of the victims of aggravated assault, and 7% of the victims of simple assault. Furthermore, rape victims were more likely than other victims of violent crime to receive treatment in a hospital emergency room. Such hospital treatment is often required for evidentiary reasons in rape cases, and this may vastly inflate this figure. It should be noted, though, that the average length of hospitalization does not vary by crime type (BJS, 1988c: p. 25). With regard to victim characteristics, the risk of physical injuries is greater for females than males and for persons from lower income families compared to higher income families. Also, blacks are more likely than whites to receive injuries that require some medical attention (BJS, 1988c: p. 25).

It should be recognized that using hospitalization as a measure of injury severity has been criticized by some researchers (see Allen,

1986). Allen (1986: p. 141) argues that hospitalization is dependent upon a number of factors (e.g., delay in time between injury and medical intervention) in addition to the severity of the injury itself. Therefore, data on physical injury derived from the NCS must be viewed with these considerations in mind.

Economic Loss

Individuals may suffer a wide range of economic penalties if they become victims of crime. These may include direct cash and property losses, property damage, medical expenses, work time loss, and security costs, as well as more intangible costs, such as fear of crime, a potentially trying involvement with the criminal justice system, and a general deterioration of the quality of their life.

The NCS contains some information regarding direct economic costs of victimization to individual victims of crime. For instance, the 1985 NCS reveals that the direct cash and property losses for victims of personal robbery, personal and household larceny, household burglary, and motor vehicle theft totaled 13 billion dollars. The bulk of these costs resulted from losses suffered as a result of the household crimes of burglary, larceny, and motor vehicle theft. Among the violent crimes of rape, robbery, and assault, the crime of robbery accounts for a disproportionate share of the total economic loss in violent crimes (BJS, 1988c: p. 25). It is believed that these estimates are low and that they exclude such important categories as mental health costs (Cohen, 1988). At the same time, only 3.9 billion dollars (36% of all losses) are recovered or reimbursed by insurance within six months of the victimization incident (BJS, 1988c: p. 114).

The 1986 NCS data show 42% of all losses from personal crimes and 30% of all losses from household crimes involved less than $50 per victimization. In contrast, only 16% of the personal crimes and 24% of the household crimes resulting in losses greater than $250 or more (BJS, 1988a: p. 72). Using NCS data from 1981, Shenk and Klaus (1984) found that the median loss was $45 in personal crimes, compared with $65 in household crimes. Not surprisingly, the highest median loss was for completed motor vehicle thefts.

Examining medical expenses for injured victims of violent crime, the 1986 NCS revealed that 12% incurred costs of less than $50, 25% were between $50 and $249, and 29% suffered costs greater than $250. Note, though, that 34% of the victims did not know the amount of their

medical costs at the time of interview (BJS, 1988a: p. 67). Shenk and
Klaus (1984) reported that the median loss due to medical expenses in
violent crimes was $120. However, about 1 in 4 victims spent $375 or
more on their medical bills.[7]

In addition to the costs for individual victims, there are costs of
crime to society at large. The Bureau of Justice Statistics (1988c:
p. 114) has estimated that the cost of criminal justice at the local, state,
and federal level is 45.6 billion dollars a year. Moreover, private security costs have been estimated to be more than 20 billion dollars (BJS,
1988c: p. 114). Finally, Skogan (1986) has noted the indirect effects of
crime and fear of crime on neighborhood disinvestment, deindustrial-
ization, demolition and construction activities, and declining commercial activity. Assessing the monetary cost of community decay is nearly
impossible.

CONCLUDING REMARKS

Our knowledge regarding the nature and extent of victimization and
the characteristics of victims in crimes other than homicide is almost
wholly dependent upon the NCS. Of course, the NCS is not without
its problems, and a variety of questions have been raised regarding the
validity and reliability of the NCS procedures. The importance of these
methodological concerns depend on part upon the substantive question
being asked; namely, whether one is interested in addressing the level
of victimization (or changes in that level) compared with examining the
correlates of victimization (Gottfredson, 1986). More important, perhaps, are the general problems inherent in victimization surveys. Victimization surveys attempt to capture in a uniform and systematic
manner very complex interactions between people under stressful circumstances. Research has indicated that memory problems are significant in victim surveys (Skogan, 1981: p. 15-22). In addition, affective
factors like shame and embarrassment make the reporting of certain
events to survey interviewers more difficult. Finally, the setting of the
home interview may also inhibit the reporting of certain crimes (such
as domestic violence) to survey interviewers. These problems can affect
both estimates of the level of victimization in the United States and
descriptions of the correlates of victimization.[8]

Some evidence of systematic response bias has been discovered
within the NCS. For example, it is generally recognized that victimizations committed by offenders known to the victim, especially relatives,

are less likely to be reported to survey interviewers, even though the incident was reported to the police (see Skogan, 1981). This is particularly problematic for the crimes of rape and assault, especially date rape, spouse abuse, and elder abuse.

In sharp contrast to the NCS data, official data on crimes from the police and other agencies reveal that a much higher proportion of incidents of assaultive violence involves friends and family members (Skogan, 1981: p. 30-31). Skogan argues that this makes the NCS even more suspect

> because we also believe that violence between friends and relatives is less likely than stranger violence to be reported to the police. That police files contain approximately 3½ times more acquaintance violence than revealed in interviews does not add to our confidence in the validity of the survey findings. (p. 30)

In addition, Cook (1985) has found that compared with police data, the NCS undercounts (by a factor of about 3.0) serious assaults that involve gunshot woundings. In light of this concern, it is unfortunate that the NCS does not collect more information on the dynamics of victimization or the situational context of victimization. More specifically, no information is collected on the time ordering of events—Who said what to whom? Who spoke first? Who acted first? What happened then? Little information on the victimization *process* is collected, which has hampered the development of comprehensive theory and policy for crime victims.

Nevertheless, we can draw some broad conclusions on the basis of the available data:

1. Serious crimes, especially violent offenses, are relatively rare events. The comparative risk of various life events reveals that accidental injuries at home and work are more likely to occur than a victimization of a violent crime. Similarly, persons are more likely to die from natural causes (e.g., heart disease) than homicide. Overall, the risk of personal theft is greater than the risk of violent victimization.

2. The risk of victimization varies across population groups, time, and space. It is largely consistent with the exposure to victimization that is linked to lifestyle and routine activities. Although there are exceptions, young persons, males, blacks, and low income groups are at greater risk of both personal and household victimization, perhaps due to their typical day-to-day behavior.

3. The NCS shows an overall decline in crime over the 1973-1986 period. For the same time period, the NCS indicates stability in the rates of victim reporting to the police. In contrast, the UCR reveals large percentage increases in many crime categories for the same time period. This suggests that the NCS and UCR are measuring different phenomena, and one should exercise caution in making trend comparisons.

4. While the direct economic costs of crime for individual victims are not generally large, the indirect costs for the criminal justice system and communities as a whole are enormous. Although difficult to quantify, the indirect costs of fear of crime are believed to be quite large. At the same time, it should be recognized that while fear of crime is largely a fear of victimization by strangers, a large proportion of crimes, especially violent crimes, are committed by friends, lovers, and relatives.

Overall, these findings reveal the striking importance of the effect of crime on the quality of life in families and neighborhoods across the United States.

NOTES

1. Detailed reviews of the methodology of the National Crime Survey are available elsewhere (see Garofalo & Hindelang, 1977; Skogan, 1981; Sparks, 1982).

2. To date, the NCS has focused on a relatively narrow, albeit important, set of crime types. For instance, no information on homicide is available in the NCS data set. Since children under 12 are not interviewed, the NCS data do not provide any information on child abuse or child pornography. Commercial crimes, such as robbery, are not covered in the survey, nor is vandalism of public structures and facilities. Moreover, since respondent knowledge is necessary for certain crimes, it is extremely difficult to collect information on organizational crimes, such as consumer fraud. So called "victimless" crimes are also not studied in this survey. Respondent knowledge also limits the types of information that can be collected on the crimes contained in the survey. For instance, victims are asked only a few questions regarding offender characteristics.

3. The population base is 12 and older because the NCS does not interview persons under the age of 12; thus, they are excluded from the denominator of the rate. Sparks (1980) has argued that incidence rates of victimization can be misleading indicators because the distribution of victimization events is skewed; namely, a large proportion of persons experiences *no* victimizations in a given time period, while at the same time, a small proportion of the population experiences a great many victimizations.

4. As will be seen below, the basic correlates of personal and household victimization have not changed over the time period for which data are available (see Gottfredson, 1986).

5. One puzzling finding has been the relationship between educational attainment and victimization. Sparks (1981: p. 32-36) has found that social-class-linked variables, like

educational attainment, positively affect the reporting of victimizations to survey interviewers. This suggests that highly educated members of the sample are more productive respondents than victims at greater risk. Skogan (1981) and Gottfredson (1984) have shown that once the educational effect is controlled, major patterns in the data (e.g., age, income, major activity) general hold. In addition, the correlates of victimization found in the NCS generally parallel those found in foreign victimization surveys, such as the British Crime Survey (see Gottfredson, 1984, and, more generally, Block, 1984, for a review).

6. The UCR has also calculated the lifetime probability murder victimization (Federal Bureau of Investigation, 1982: Appendix V). Overall, the lifetime chance of U.S. citizens becoming a murder victim in the United States is 1 out of 153. For non-white males, the probability is 1 out of 47, compared with 1 out of 450 for white females. One key difference in calculating lifetime probabilities of murder is that multiple victimizations cannot occur as with other crime types.

7. A recent study examined all firearm victims who were hospitalized in San Francisco's regional trauma center in 1984, and estimated the annual hospital costs to be $905,809, or $6,915 per patient. Extrapolating to the United States as a whole, the researchers estimated the total costs of firearm injuries to be $429 million per year (Martin, Hunt, & Hulley, 1988).

8. Victimization surveys are best for capturing discrete crimes that have a clear-cut beginning and end. More difficult to measure are crimes that are of a continuous nature. For instance, a dispute between neighbors evolving over a period of time; a series of domestic assaults occurring sporadically over a long period of time; or daily "shakedowns" of lunch money at school. These kinds of victimizations present unique measurement concerns; to date, no adequate mechanism has been found to record these victimizations.

REFERENCES

Allen, R. B. (1986). Measuring the severity of physical injury among assault and homicide victims. *Journal of Quantitative Criminology*, 2, 193-156.

Bard, M., & Sangrey, D. (1979). *The crime victim's book*. New York: Basic Books.

Block, R. editor. (1984). *Victimization and fear of crime: World perspectives*. Washington, DC: U.S. Government Printing Office.

Block, R., & Block, C. (1980). Decisions and data: The transformation of robbery incidents into official robbery statistics. *Journal of Criminal Law and Criminology*, 71, 622-636.

Block, R., & Skogan, W. G. (1986). Resistance and nonfatal outcomes in stranger-to-stranger predatory crime. *Violence and Victims*, 1 (Winter), 241-253.

Bureau of Justice Statistics (1987). *Criminal victimization, 1986*. Washington, DC: U.S. Department of Justice.

Bureau of Justice Statistics (1988a). *Criminal victimization in the United States, 1986*. Washington, DC: U.S. Department of Justice.

Bureau of Justice Statistics (1988b). *Households touched by crime, 1987*. Washington, DC: U.S. Department of Justice.

Bureau of Justice Statistics (1988c). *Report to the nation on crime and justice* (2nd ed.). Washington, DC: U.S. Department of Justice.

Cohen, L. E., Cantor, D. Kluegel, J. R. (1981). Robbery victimization in the U.S.: An analysis of a nonrandom event. *Social Science Quarterly, 62*, 644-657.

Cohen, M. A. (1988). Some new evidence on the seriousness of crime. *Criminology, 26*, 343-353.

Cook, P. J. (1985). The case of the missing victims: Gunshot woundings in the national crime survey. *Journal of Quantitative Criminology, 1*, 91-102.

Cook, P. J. (1986). The relationship between victim resistance and injury in noncommercial robbery. *The Journal of Legal Studies, 15*, 405-416.

Fattah, E. A. (1984). Victims' response to confrontational victimization: A neglected aspect of victim research. *Crime and Delinquency, 30*, 75-90.

Federal Bureau of Investigation (1982). *Crime in the United States, 1981*. Washington, DC: U.S. Government Printing Office.

Federal Bureau of Investigation (1988). *Crime in the United States, 1987*. Washington, DC: U.S. Government Printing Office.

Garofalo, J. (1987). Reassessing the lifestyle model of criminal victimization. In M. Gottfredson and T. Hirschi (Eds.), *Positive criminology*. Newbury Park, CA: Sage Publications.

Garofalo, J., & Hindelang, M. J. (1977). *An introduction to the national crime survey*. Washington, DC: U.S. Government Printing Office.

Garofalo, J., & Laub, J. H. (1978). The fear of crime: Broadening our perspectives. *Victimology, 3*, 242-253.

Gottfredson, M. R. (1981). On the etiology of criminal victimization. *Journal of Criminal Law and Criminology, 72*, 714-726.

Gottfredson, M. R. (1984). *Victims of crime: The dimensions of risk*. London: H. M. Stationery Office.

Gottfredson, M. R. (1986). Substantive contributions of victimization surveys. In M. Tonry and N. Morris (Eds.), *Crime and justice: An annual review of research*. Chicago: University of Chicago Press.

Gottfredson, M. R., & Gottfredson, D. M. (1980). *Decisionmaking in criminal justice*. Cambridge, MA: Ballinger.

Gove, W. R., Hughes, M., & Geerken, M. (1985). Are uniform crime reports a valid indicator of the index crimes? An affirmative answer with minor qualifications. *Criminology, 23* (August): 451-503.

Hindelang, M. J. (1976). *Criminal victimization in eight American cities*. Cambridge, MA: Ballinger.

Martin, M. J., Hunt, T. K., & Hulley, S. B. (1988). The cost of hospitalization for firearm injuries. *Journal of American Medical Association, 60*: 3048-3050.

Maxfield, M. G. (1987). Lifestyle and routine activity theories of crime: Empirical studies of victimization, delinquency, and offender decision-making. *Journal of Quantitative Criminology, 3*: 275-282.

Maxfield, M. G. (1988, September). *The comparative development of routine activity theories of victimization*. Paper presented at the 10th International Congress on Criminology, Hamburg, Federal Republic of Germany.

Mulvihill, D., & Tumin, M. (1969). *Crimes of violence*. A staff report submitted to the U.S. Commission on the Causes and Prevention of Violence (Vol. 11). Washington, DC: U.S. Government Printing Office.

O'Brien, R. M. (1985). *Crime and victimization data*. Beverly Hills, CA: Sage.

Reidel, M. (1987). Stranger violence: Perspectives, issues, and problems. *The Journal of Criminal Law and Criminology*, 78: 223-258.

Sampson, R. J. (1987). Personal violence by strangers: An extension and test of predatory victimization. *The Journal of Criminal Law and Criminology*, 78: 327-356.

Shenk, J. F. & Klaus, P. A. (1984). *The economic cost of crime to victims*. Washington, DC: U.S. Department of Justice.

Silverman, R. (1974). Victim precipitation: An examination of the concept. In I. Drapkin and E. Viano (Eds.), *Victimology: A new focus*. Lexington, MA: Lexington Books.

Skogan, W. G. (1981). *Issues in the measurement of victimization*. Washington, DC: Bureau of Justice Statistics.

Skogan, W. G. (1984). Reporting crimes to the police: The status of world research. *Journal of Research in Crime and Delinquency*, 21: 113-138.

Skogan, W. G. (1986). Fear of crime and neighborhood change. In A. J. Reiss and M. Tonry, (Eds.), *Communities and crime*. Chicago: University of Chicago Press.

Sparks, R. F. (1980). Criminal opportunities and crime rates. In S. Fienberg and A. Reiss, (Eds.), *Indicators of crime and justice: Quantitative studies*. Washington, DC: U.S. Government Printing Office.

Sparks, R. F. (1981). Surveys of victimization—An optimistic assessment. In M. Tonry and N. Morris (Eds.), *Crime and justice: An annual review of research*. Chicago: University of Chicago Press.

Sparks, R. F. (1982). *Research on victims of crime*. Washington, DC: U.S. Government Printing Office.

Timrots, A. D., & Rand, M. R. (1987). *Violent crime by strangers and nonstrangers*. Washington, DC: U.S. Department of Justice.

von Hentig, H. (1948). *The criminal and his victim*. New Haven, CT: Yale University Press.

Warr, M. (1988). Rape, burglary, and opportunity. *Journal of Quantitative Criminology*, 4: 475-488.

Wolfgang, M. E. (1958). *Patterns in criminal homicide*. Philadelphia: University of Pennsylvania Press.

Chapter 3

HEALING THE PSYCHOLOGICAL
WOUNDS OF CRIMINAL VICTIMIZATION
Predicting Postcrime Distress and Recovery

ARTHUR J. LURIGIO
PATRICIA A. RESICK

INTRODUCTION

Each year, approximately one in four households is victimized by at least one crime of violence or theft, which amounts to more than 35 million victimizations at an estimated cost of nearly 13 billion dollars (Bureau of Justice Statistics, 1988a; Laub, this volume). Recent statistics suggest that the average American is more likely to become a victim of violent crime during his or her lifetime than to become involved in an automobile accident (Bureau of Justice Statistics, 1988b). Being a crime victim may have profound psychological repercussions. Studies show that the emotional concomitants of serious crime can be more disruptive than the loss of property or physical injury, which are commonly regarded as the most unsettling aspects of criminal victimization. The crime of rape is particularly traumatic (see Resick, this volume).

Several investigations have documented the devastating and often lifelong effects of rape (e.g., Atkeson, Calhoun, Resick, & Ellis, 1982; Katz & Mazur, 1979; Norris & Feldman-Summers, 1981; Symonds, 1980). Some of the most prominent and debilitating reactions to sexual assault are fear and anxiety, suicidal ideation, sexual dysfunction, diminished self-esteem, depression, persistent somatic complaints, and drug abuse. Data indicate that reactions to rape can persist for months and even years following the incident (Kilpatrick & Veronen, 1983).

Evidence is mounting that victims of other serious crimes also may suffer adverse psychological consequences. For example, in a study of burglary, robbery, and non-sexual assault victims, Lurigio (1987) found that these crime victims expressed higher levels of vulnerability, fear, and disturbing symptoms (e.g., anxiety, unpleasant thoughts, upset stomach) than a comparable sample of non-victims. In a more recent investigation, Lurigio and Davis (1989) revealed that burglary, robbery, and non-sexual assault victims reported greater levels of distress and symptoms on several outcome measures when compared to standardized norms.

Similarly, a study of the prevalence of criminal victimization and its effects indicated that substantial numbers of non-sexual assault, burglary, and robbery victims developed a psychiatric disorder known as post-traumatic stress syndrome (Kilpatrick, Saunders, Veronen, Best, & Von, 1987), which is defined by a persistent reexperiencing of a traumatic event through intrusive memories and dreams and by a variety of anxiety-related symptoms (American Psychiatric Association, 1987). An investigation by Hough (1985) showed that, overall, more than half of a sample of burglary victims suffered fear, loss of confidence, sleep difficulties, and depression. In addition, the works of Cohn (1974), Horowitz (1976), and Krupnick (1980) support the notion that victims of serious crime other than rape also experience disabling psychological responses to the episode (see also Leymann, 1985).

Reactions to crime and other deleterious experiences are often quite varied. Hence, it is important to study individual differences in response to criminal victimization (Lurigio, 1987). According to Kilpatrick, Veronen, and Best (1985), researchers should eschew the "client uniformity myth" when examining crime victim distress and adjustment. Indeed, findings suggest that victims of crime and other traumatic episodes manifest varying levels of distress and symptoms (Janoff-Bulman & Frieze, 1983). Variability in victim recovery can be a function of victim characteristics and predispositions, the nature of the incident, victims' perceptions and interpretations of the occurrence, and events that transpire in the aftermath of the crime (Janoff-Bulman & Frieze; Kilpatrick, Veronen et al., 1985; Sales, Baum, & Shore, 1984).

This chapter provides a comprehensive review of the correlates of recovery from criminal victimization. While Resick's work in this volume focuses on the adverse consequences of victimization, our contribution is concerned with the antecedents, or correlates, of postcrime distress and recovery. We describe previctimization, victimization, and postvictimization factors that predict adjustment. To date, the bulk of studies on the psychological sequelae of crime have dealt with rape (Lurigio & Rosenbaum, in press), so much of the data we report here are based on investigations of rape victims.

THE CORRELATES OF
POSTCRIME DISTRESS AND RECOVERY

Previctimization Factors

Demographic characteristics

Age. A series of studies has found that younger victims cope more effectively than older victims of crime. For example, Sales et al. (1984) reported that whereas older rape victims evidenced more serious and protracted symptoms, younger rape victims evidenced more acute symptoms of relatively short duration. Atkeson et al. (1982) found that older victims of rape displayed a greater tendency to become depressed 12 months following the incident when compared to younger victims of rape. McCahill, Meyer, and Fischman (1979) and Ruch and Chandler (1980) showed that adult victims of rape suffered from more serious trauma than child and adolescent victims of rape (non-incest). Burnham, Stein, Golding, Siegel, Sorenson, Forsythe, and Telles (1988) reported that younger rape victims were more likely to display drug abuse problems, whereas older rape victims were more likely to display symptoms of obsessive-compulsive disorder following assault.

In contrast to most of the previous investigations that have examined the effects of age, Lurigio and Davis (1989) revealed that younger victims of robbery, burglary, and non-sexual assault were more likely to report physical symptoms (e.g., headaches, nausea, trembling) and depression in the immediate aftermath of the incident and at three months postcrime. Age was shown to have little or no effect on recovery by Kilpatrick, Best, Veronen, Amick, Villeponteaux, and Ruff (1985a).

Marital status and race. Research on the relationship between recovery and the marital status and race of the victim has yielded conflicting results. In some studies, married rape victims had a more difficult time adjusting than unmarried rape victims (McCahill et al., 1985a). Burnam et al. (1988), Kilpatrick, Veronen et al. (1985), and Morelli (1981) found no relationship between race and crime victim recovery, whereas Ruch and Chandler (1980) reported that race was a significant predictor of victim trauma.

Sex. Women have been shown generally to be more distressed by crime than men (Friedman, Bischoff, Davis, & Person, 1982; Harrell, Smith and Cook, 1985). For example, in the investigation by Lurigio and Davis (1989), female crime victims were more fearful and symptomatic than male crime victims during the immediate aftermath of the episode. However, in studies by Goyer and Eddleman (1984) and Johnson and Shrier (1985), male sexual assault victims evidenced symptoms that were highly comparable to female sexual assault victims. In addition, Burnam et al. (1988) found that sexually assaulted men were more likely than sexually assaulted women to develop alcohol abuse or dependence problems in the aftermath of the incident.

Resick's (1987) study of male and female victims of robbery revealed a complex pattern of findings. She reported that there were no differences between men and women on many of her measures of symptoms: self-esteem, work adjustment, and sexual functioning. Although female robbery victims in her study were more distressed than male robbery victims immediately following the incident, they were no more distressed than men three months postcrime. Both genders reported a variety of symptoms throughout an 18-month period following the victimization.

Education and income. Research suggests that victims with little formal education and low incomes are more traumatized than victims from higher socioeconomic and educational groups (Calhoun & Atkeson, 1982; Friedman et al., 1982; Harrell et al., 1985). For example, a longitudinal study of rape victims, which traced their recovery at 4 to 6 years postcrime, demonstrated that economically impoverished rape victims evidenced a greater number of psychiatric symptoms (Burgess & Holmstrom, (1978). Lurigio and Davis (1989) revealed that immediately following the crime, victims reporting less income were more fearful, while unemployed victims displayed more negative emotions. Lower income also was related to recovery three months postcrime. Further, the relative importance of SES as a predictor of adjustment has been found to be greater several months succeeding the incident than shortly after the crime, i.e., victims who occupy higher income brackets recover relatively quickly whereas those who are less affluent continue to experience distress months after the episode (Friedman et al., 1982). For exceptions, see Burnam et al. (1988); Kilpatrick, Veronen et al. (1985); and McCahill et al. (1989).

Previctimization adjustment and stress

   Previctimization adjustment. A number of investigations relying on retrospective reports have demonstrated that crime victims' previctimization adjustment is strongly predictive of their postcrime functioning (Resick, 1987). For example, Calhoun and Atkeson (1982) found that one year after the crime, the best predictor of depression, fear, and anxiety among rape victims was whether they had been experiencing psychological difficulties prior to the rape. Additional studies have shown that rape victims with pre-existing emotional or physical health problems were more likely to express difficulties in coping with the incident (Burgess & Holmstrom, 1979; McCahill et al., 1979; Sales et al., 1984). Atkeson et al. (1982) reported that pre-existing psychiatric symptoms, such as anxiety attacks and obsessive-compulsive behaviors, were significant predictors of depression in rape victims at 4, 8 and 12 months after the incident.

   Frank, Turner, Stewart, Jacobs, and West (1981) found that victims who had been treated for psychiatric disturbances prior to being raped or who had a history of alcohol abuse or suicide attempts experienced more difficulty adjusting to the incident when compared to victims who had not been treated for psychiatric disturbances. A more recent investigation by Frank and Anderson (1987) showed that rape victims who had received a previous psychiatric diagnosis were more likely to be classified with a psychiatric disorder one month after the crime than victims with no prior history of psychiatric disorders. In similar studies, Krupnick and Horowitz (1980) and Symonds (1980) both reported that pre-existing emotional distress aggravated the emotional impact of violent assaults. (See Kilpatrick, Veronen et al., 1985 and Lurigio & Davis, 1989, for exceptions to these findings.)

   Life stress. Research also has examined the relationship between life stress and victim recovery. Some studies have demonstrated that prior life stress has an untoward impact on postcrime adjustment (e.g., Harrell et al., 1985; Kilpatrick, Best et al., 1985). Burgess and Holmstrom (1978) reported that rape victims who had persistent economic difficulties, such as limited income and unemployment, displayed lengthier and more serious reactions to the crime. Moreover, their results showed that acute or transient life stress had no impact on recovery, whereas chronic life stress was extremely disruptive to the coping process. Kilpatrick and Veronen (1984) and Kilpatrick, Veronen et al. (1985) found that the most distressed rape victims had lost their spouse in the year preceding the victimization, and that the least distressed rape victims had higher self-esteem (as measured early in the recovery process) and more stable relationships with their male companions one year preceding the attack.

Other investigations suggest a curvilinear or qualified relationship between life stress and psychological reactions to crime. For example, Ruch, Chandler, and Harter (1980) found that women who experienced a moderate number of recent life changes showed fewer effects of rape when compared to women who experienced many or no recent life changes. Similarly, Bard and Sangrey (1980) reported that victims experiencing a major crisis preceding the crime incident were better able to cope with the victimization. Taken together, these findings suggest that transient life stress may equip victims with more effective coping skills, while major life stress may have a *numbing* effect that can facilitate recovery (Sales et al., 1984).

Being a previous victim of crime is an important life stressor that can affect current recovery. A history of prior victimizations is associated generally with poorer adjustment. Resick (1987) found that rape victims' reactions were exacerbated if they had undergone a prior episode of criminal victimization or domestic violence (cf. Miller & Porter, 1983). Burnam et al. (1988) reported that rape victims initially assaulted in childhood were more likely to suffer from a mental disorder than those initially assaulted in adulthood. Similarly, Glenn and Resick (1986) revealed that a history of domestic or parental violence, child abuse, or incest was associated with more severe reactions to rape and complications in the adjustment process. Several additional studies present comparable findings (e.g., Frank & Anderson, 1987; McCahill et al., 1979; Resick, 1988).

Victimization Factors

Features of the crime incident

Seriousness of crime. Some studies that have examined episode variables show that the severity of victim symptoms is related directly to the degree of violence or injury occurring in the incident (Bard and Sangrey, 1980; Ellis, Atkeson, & Calhoun, 1981; McCahill et al., 1979; Peters, 1977). For example, Lurigio and Davis (1989) revealed that victims who reported injury were more likely to be symptomatic both immediately and three months following the incident. Sales et al. (1984) found that physical injury and the perceived threat of violence or death during the crime episode were significant predictors of victim symptoms. They reported further that incident violence was most predictive of coping. Harrell et al. (1985) also demonstrated a significant relationship between crime severity and the emotional trauma of victims. Resick's (1988) study, however, showed that the amount of injury sustained by female victims of robbery and rape did not predict the extent of their reactions.

Other investigations have explored the effect of brutality on rape victims' reactions by developing brutality scores or indices based on several assault variables. Results of these efforts have been mixed. Atkeson et al. (1982) reported that the amount of rape "trauma" did not predict later reactions, but Cluss, Boughton, Frank, Steward, and West (1983), Ellis et al. (1981), Norris and Feldman-Summers (1981), and Resick (1986) all found a combination of assault variables to be predictive of greater distress.

Sales et al. (1984) have suggested that "it is possible that the actual violence of an attack is less crucial to victim reaction than the felt threat" (p. 125). A few investigations have tested this hypothesis. Girelli, Resick, Marhoefer-Dvorak, and Hutter (1986) reported that subjective distress was predictive of later fear reactions, whereas other assault variables, such as threats, weapons, and injuries, were not significant predictors. Kilpatrick et al. (1987) also found that victims' subjective interpretations of the event predicted later distress. Another study reported greater distress among victims who perceived their life as being threatened during the episode (Lurigio & Davis, 1989). Resick (1988) explored the effect of the perception of imminent death or injury during the episode on subsequent reactions and recovery. She found that rape victims had significantly more perceptions of death or injury than robbery victims but found no differences in perceptions between male and female robbery victims. These within-assault perceptions were found to be predictive of greater fear and postcrime distress in robbery victims overall but were not good predictors of recovery in rape victims, probably because they were uniformly high.

Relationship between victim and offender. Studies examining the impact of the victim-offender relationship on victim recovery have found few differences between victims of stranger and non-stranger sexual assault. For example, Kilpatrick et al. (1987) reported no differences in adjustment between victims who were raped by their husband, a date, or a stranger. Similarly, Hassell (1981) revealed that the levels of recovery and distress manifested by stranger and non-stranger victims of rape were highly comparable. Investigations by Girelli, Resick, Marhoefer-Dvorak, and Hutter (1986) and by Resick (1986) also failed to uncover any differences between stranger and non-stranger victims of rape on symptoms and recovery. Koss, Dinero, and Seibel (1988) compared the experiences and reactions of 52 stranger-rape victims with those of 416 acquaintance-rape victims. They found that acquaintance-rape victims were more likely to involve a single offender and multiple episodes. Rapes perpetrated by acquaintances were reported to be less violent than those perpetrated by strangers. The victims of acquaintance rape were less likely to label the event as rape or report the victimization. However, there were no differences in resistance and no differences in psychological reactions.

In contrast to the aforementioned studies, Ellis et al. (1981) found that women sexually assaulted by strangers were more anxious and depressed than women sexually assaulted by acquaintances. In addition, Steward, Hughes, Frank, Anderson, Kendall, and West (1987) reported that women raped by an acquaintance were less likely to fend off their attackers and more likely to delay treatment in the aftermath of the episode.

Type of crime. A few comparative studies have tested whether type of criminal victimization has an effect on psychological recovery. For example, Friedman et al. (1982) revealed that robbery and assault victims fared less well than burglary victims on several indices of recovery from the incident. Lurigio (1987) reported that there was no pattern of clear or consistent differences between victims of burglary, robbery, or non-sexual assault on numerous measures of psychological impact. But he did find that burglary victims were more unfavorably affected, which was reflected in a greater tendency to report vulnerability, fear, and sleep disturbances. Lurigio and Davis (1989) found that burglary and robbery victims were more bothered by disturbing and repetitive thoughts about the episode than non-sexual assault victims at three months postcrime.

Resick (1988) conducted a longitudinal study comparing the reactions of rape and robbery victims. She assessed the recovery of both groups at 1, 3, 6, 12, and 18 months postcrime. As with other longitudinal studies, she found that the greatest improvement of both groups occurred between 1 and 3 months postcrime. After controlling for differences between rape and robbery victims, she also found that rape reactions are, for the most part, similar to robbery reactions. Rape reactions are usually more severe because of the longer duration of the crime and other within-crime variables, such as greater threats and injury. The one exception was sexual functioning, which would be expected to differ in kind as well as degree. Initial analyses of data emerging from the first three measurement sections indicated that while both rape and robbery victims experienced some disruptions in sexual activity for the first few months after the crime, rape victims reported greater sexual dysfunction and sexual fears (Resick, 1986). Sexual dysfunctions represent a specific type of anxiety disorder that is conditioned in rape victims because of the pairing of terror with sexual contact.

Postvictimization Factors

Victims' perceptions

Postcrime perceptions of the incident and its causes may be viewed as reactions to the crime and as attempts to cope with the victimization and its consequences. Perceptions include self-blame and cognitive restructuring.

Self-blame. Victims' self-blame can influence psychological well-being. Self-blame or the tendency of victims to make personal attributions about the causes of their victimization has been the focus of several studies. According to Janoff-Bulman (1979, 1982), behavioral self-blame, i.e., imputing the causes of victimization to alterable behaviors, fosters a belief that future events can be readily controlled or avoided. Behavioral self-blame diminishes victims' sense of vulnerability and is therefore functional. Friedman et al. (1982) found that crime victims who blamed themselves for not preventing the incident reported fewer psychological disturbances at both two weeks and four months after the crime when compared to victims who did not blame themselves. In a similar study, Rosenbaum (1980) reported that crime victims who engaged in behavioral self-blame were more likely to contend that their victimization was avoidable. Lurigio and Davis (1989) demonstrated that victims who engaged in behavioral self-blame were less likely to suffer from distressing thoughts and dreams.

In contrast, characterological self-blame, i.e., imputing the causes of victimization to enduring or stable personality traits and inadequacies, leaves victims with little confidence that future victimization is avoidable. Characterological self-blame is associated with depression (Janoff-Bulman, 1979; Peterson, Schwartz, & Seligman, 1981) and helplessness (Peterson & Seligman, 1983), and is basically maladaptive. Janoff-Bulman (1979), for example, indicated that rape victims who engaged in characterological self-blame were more likely to view themselves as "deserving" to be raped. Studies utilizing global measures of self-blame reveal no association or a negative association between self-blame and adjustment (Meyer & Taylor, 1986; Taylor, Lichtman, & Wood, 1984).

Cognitive restructuring. Cognitive restructuring is a coping mechanism in which victims reinterpret their experience to ameliorate the adverse effects of the incident. It can take several forms, such as finding meaning in the episode, engaging in downward comparisons (i.e., thinking about themselves as being better off than other real or imagined victims), comparing themselves to a hypothetical "worst world scenario" in which they are harmed to a much greater extent than in reality, and evaluating the event as occasioning personal growth or some other benefit (Taylor, Wood, & Lichtman, 1983).

There is a growing literature that indicates that people have a strong need to search for the meaning of negative events (Silver & Wortman, 1980). According to an early study on the effects of crime, victimization destroys the illusion that we live in a predictable, controllable, and comprehensible world (Lejeune & Alex, 1973). As noted by Bard and Sangrey (1979), crime victims undergo a "loss of equilibrium. The world is suddenly out of whack. Things no longer work the way they used to" (p. 14). In an investigation of incest victims, Silver, Boon, and Stones (1983) found that women who were still actively searching for the meaning of the experience were more likely to report recurrent, intrusive, and disruptive ruminations than those who were not searching for meaning. Women who reported that they were able to make some sense out of their experience also reported less psychological distress, better social adjustment, greater self-esteem, and greater resolution of the experience than women who were not able to find any meaning but were still searching.

Researchers have found that rape victims strive to enhance self-esteem by either comparing themselves to less fortunate victims or redefining their situation as not being a genuine rape (Bart & Scheppele, 1980; Burgess & Holmstrom, 1979; Scheppele & Bart, 1983). Lurigio and Davis (1989) studied several aspects of cognitive restructuring, including downward comparisons. Their results showed that victims who believed that they were coping well with the event, that they had gained something favorable from the experience (e.g., to believe that "since their experience as a crime victim, they were better able to handle themselves well in a crisis"), or that other crime victims were "worse off than they are" reported more positive affect and fewer event-related intrusive thoughts.

Participation in the Criminal Justice System

The participation of victims in the prosecution of cases has been regarded commonly as stressful and disruptive to their recovery, especially among victims of sexual assault (e.g., Brownmiller, 1975; President's Task Force on Victims of Crime, 1983; Kelly, this volume). Symonds (1980) characterized the impact of the criminal justice system on victims as "the second wound." Others have referred to crime victims as the "forgotten persons" of the criminal justice system (Schneider & Schneider, 1977). A number of documented cases reflect a generalized neglect of crime victims by police, prosecutors, and court systems. Insensitivity toward crime victims includes long waits, loss of wages, poor protection against intimidation, mishandling of property, difficult questioning by police and attorneys, unnecessary trips to court, and a variety of other inconveniences (Chelimsky, 1981; Knudten, Meade, Knudten, & Doernev, 1977; Rosenbaum, 1977; Stein, 1977).

Few studies, thus far, have systematically examined the effect of participation in the criminal justice system on victim disturbances. Cluss et al. (1983) found that at 12 months post-rape, there were no differences in the levels of depression or social adjustment between victims who wished to prosecute the crime and those who did not. However, women who wished to prosecute reported greater self-esteem. Further, women who wished to prosecute but were not able to (no arrest or insufficient evidence), showed better work adjustment at six months postcrime and more rapid improvement in self-esteem than women who were proceeding with prosecution.

Sales et al. (1984) reported that female victims of sexual assault who began the process by reporting the case and whose charges held, showed fewer symptoms at an initial interview and a six-month follow-up. However, there were indications that additional progress toward trial left victims with more symptoms. The authors concluded that extended court proceedings may inflict continual demands on these women and keep them in a victim role. Although they were not studying the influence of the criminal justice system on victims directly, two studies (Calhoun & Atkeson, 1982; Kilpatrick, Veronen, & Resick, 1979) have found that participating in court may be quite stressful. Using a standard fear scale in both investigations, the item "testifying in court" emerged as one of the most fear-provoking stimuli reported by victims when compared to nonvictims.

As part of her longitudinal study, Resick (1988) compared the reactions of crime victims who completed the criminal justice process through trial or guilty plea with 24 matched subjects who did not enter the system because no suspect was ever apprehended. She first compared them on a battery of self-report symptom measures and other variables at 18 months postcrime and found that the two groups did not differ with respect to symptoms, the quality of social support they received, their work adjustment, or whether they received therapy. In examining earlier time periods, the only difference she found was that criminal justice participants reported greater self-esteem at 6 months postcrime (Cf. Cluss et al., 1983). This result may have been spurious due to the number of analyses conducted; however, Cluss et al. reported a similar finding.

Social Support

A considerable body of research has demonstrated a link between social support and adaptation to adverse life events, such as illness, depression, victimization, and bereavement (see Brownell & Shumaker, 1984; Wortman & Conway, 1985). For example, some studies have shown that positive social support following life stressors can maintain and enhance self-esteem (Cobb, 1976; Kutash, 1978; Silver & Wortman, 1980). Evidence also suggests that the support of family and friends is vital to the adjustment of crime victims (Krupnick & Horowitz, 1980; Symonds, 1980). Bard and Sangrey (1980) underscore the importance of providing crime victims with tolerance, sensitivity, and reassurance during the initial stages following the victimization. Friedman et al. (1982) reported that crime victims were more likely to recover from the trauma of the episode with the support of family and friends.

In other investigations, Ruch and Hennessey (1982) revealed that 72% of their sample of rape victims reported that their families were supportive and 87% reported having supportive friends. The authors did not report whether this perception of support continued over time or whether the support influenced recovery. Sales et al. (1984) found that neither the initial reactions of significant others nor the quality of rape victims' central relationships to men at the time of the crime was related to their reactions. They did, however, find that victims reporting greater closeness to family members had fewer symptoms. Ruch and Chandler (1980) also reported that victims with supportive families experienced lower levels of trauma fairly soon after the assault. Atkeson et al. (1982) demonstrated that social support predicted victim depression at four and eight months post-rape. Norris and Feldman-Summers (1981) studied long-term reactions and found that the presence of understanding persons in the victim's life was related to less reclusiveness.

Popiel and Susskind (1985) studied 25 rape victims at three months post-assault and did not find an overall relationship between social support and adjustment. They did report a relationship between the perceived supportiveness of physicians and adjustment. Generally, physicians were viewed as the least supportive and female friends as the most supportive people following rape. West, Frank, Anderson, and Steward (1987) asked 52 women to rate the supportive or unsupportive reactions they received from their family, friends, and acquaintances in the first two to four weeks following the rape. They found that women who had one or more unsupportive persons in their lives had more symptoms than the women with only neutral or supportive persons. Moss, Frank, and Anderson (1987) showed that poor spousal support was associated with more symptoms postcrime, particularly when the absence of support was unexpected. Cluss et al. (1983) examined positive and negative responses from others and found them to be unrelated to whether the victim wished to prosecute the assailant.

Gerrol & Resick (1988) compared the social support received by male and female robbery victims following victimization. They examined three variables: perceived social support, the range and frequency of people the victim talked to about the crime, and the number of people available to provide support (i.e., social network size). They found that, at one month postcrime, female robbery victims talked to more people and talked to them more frequently about the crime than male robbery victims. There were no other sex differences on that variable or the other two variables. Analyses to examine the effect of social support on reactions indicated that perceived social support was predictive of fewer symptoms and greater self-esteem following the crime. Network size was only predictive of better recovery in female victims and was not as predictive as perceived social support. On the other hand, talking about the crime with more people was associated with greater symptoms for both sexes.

SUMMARY AND CONCLUSIONS

Our survey of the literature indicates that there are several reliable predictors of recovery that may be drawn together to create a composite portrait of crime victims who are more likely to adjust successfully in the aftermath of the incident. According to prior research, it appears that, on balance, victims suffering from lower levels of postcrime distress are: (1) younger, male, better educated, and employed; (2) freer of pre-existing psychiatric disturbances and a history of previous criminal victimization; (3) experiencing moderate recent life stressors; (4) less severely victimized, threatened, or injured during the episode; (5) inclined to blame themselves behaviorally rather than characterologically for the crime, to find meaning in the incident, and to perceive themselves as coping well when compared with other crime victims; and (6) willing to participate in the prosecution of the case and to be surrounded by supportive relatives and friends.

The findings reviewed in this chapter have relevance for victim service providers. The most apparent practical implications stem from the wide range of individual differences affecting victim adjustment. Variation in victim characteristics, episode features, and postcrime experiences may be seen as prodromal factors heralding emotional disturbances and helping to identify victims who may be in greater need of therapy or other types of *psychological* interventions.

Davis (1987, this volume) notes that intensive services (e.g., long-term counseling sessions) are probably not warranted for the vast majority of crime victims apart from victims of rape and domestic violence. Nonetheless, as we discussed in our introduction, several studies have shown that victims of other serious crimes also may manifest significant levels of symptoms and distress. Hence, routine screening techniques are necessary to determine which categories of victims are more likely to exhibit difficulties coping in the aftermath of the incident. Empirically derived correlates of distress can be incorporated into such guidelines for assessment, triage, and outreach. In short, victim service providers will become more effective and efficient if they aim their efforts selectively at victims who are most in need of attention. Finally, research also can suggest ways for service providers, criminal justice personnel, and members of victims' social networks to help facilitate the recovery of crime victims.

References

American Psychiatric Association (1987). *Diagnostic and statistical manual of mental disorders* (3rd ed., revised). Washington, DC: American Psychiatric Association.

Atkeson, B., Calhoun, K., Resick, P., & Ellis, E. (1982). Victims of rape: Repeated assessment of depressive symptoms. *Journal of Consulting and Clinical Psychology, 50,* 96-102.

Bard, M., & Sangrey, D. (1979). *The crime victim's book.* New York: Basic Books.

Bard, M., & Sangrey, D. (1980). Things fall apart: Victims in crisis. In L. Kivens (Ed.), *Evaluation and change: Services for survivors* (pp. 28-35). Minneapolis, MN: Minneapolis Research Foundation.

Bart, P. B., & Scheppele, K. L. (1980 August). *There ought to be a law: Women's definitions and legal definitions of sexual assault. Paper presented at the annual meeting of the American Sociological Association, New York, NY.*

Brownell, A., & Shumaker, S. A. (1984). Social support: An introduction to a complex phenomenon. *Journal of social issues, 40,* 1-9.

Brownmiller, S. (1975). *Against our will: Men, women, and rape.* New York: Simon and Schuster.

Bureau of Justice Statistics (1988a). *Criminal victimization in the United States, 1986.* Washington, DC: Department of Justice.

Bureau of Justice Statistics (1988b). *Reported update on criminal victimization in the United States* (May, 1988). Washington, DC: Department of Justice.

Burgess, A., & Holmstrom, L. (1979). Rape: Sexual disruption and recovery. *American Journal of Orthopsychiatry, 49,* 658-669.

Burgess, A., & Holmstrom, L. (1978). Recovery from rape and prior life stress. *Research in Nursing and Health, 1,* 165-174.

Burnam, M. A., Stein, J. A., Golding, J. M., Siegel, J. M., Sorenson, S. B., Forsythe, A. B., & Telles, C. A. (1988). Sexual assault and mental disorders in community populations. *Journal of Consulting and Clinical Psychology, 56,* 843-850.

Calhoun, K., & Atkeson, B. (1982). *Rape-induced depression: Normative data.* Report submitted to the National Institute of Mental Health (Grant No. MH29750).

Chelimsky, E. (1981). Serving victims: Agency incentives and individual needs. In S. Salasen (Ed.), *Evaluating victim services* (pp. 73-98). Beverly Hills, CA: Sage.

Cluss, P. A., Boughton, J., Frank, L. E., Stewart, B. D., & West (1983). The rape victims: Psychological correlates of participation in the legal process. *Criminal Justice and Behavior, 10,* 342-357.

Cobb, C. (1976). Social support as moderator of life stress. *Psychosomatic Medicine, 38,* 300-314.

Cohn, Y. (1974). Crisis intervention and the victim of robbery. In I. Drapkin and E. Viano (Eds.), *Victimology: A new focus* (pp. 11-16). Lexington, MA: Lexington Books.

Ellis, E. M., Atkeson, B. M., & Calhoun, K. S. (1981). An assessment of long-term reaction to rape. *Journal of Abnormal Psychology, 90,* 263-266.

Frank, E., & Anderson, B. P. (1987). Psychiatric disorders in rape victims: Past history and current symptomatology. *Comprehensive Psychiatry, 28,* 77-82.

Frank, E., Turner, S. M., Stewart, B. D., Jacobs, J., & West, D. (1981). Past psychiatric symptoms and the response to sexual assault. *Comprehensive Psychiatry, 22,* 479-487.

Friedman, K., Bischoff, H., Davis, R., & Person, A. (1982). *Victims and helpers: Reactions to crime.* Summary of Grant Report, National Institute of Justice (Grant No. 79-N1AX0059).

Gerrol, R., & Resick, P. A. (1988, November). *Sex differences in social support and recovery from victimization.* Paper presented at the 22nd Annual Meeting of the Association for the Advancement of Behavior Therapy, New York, NY.

Girelli, S. A., Resick, P. A., Marhoefer-Dvorak, S., & Hutter, C. K. (1986). Subjective distress and violence during rape: Their effects on long-term fear. *Victims and Violence, 1,* 35-45.

Glenn, F., & Resick, P. (1986). *The effects of family violence on coping ability to a later victimization.* Unpublished manuscript, University of Missouri—St. Louis.

Goyer, P. F., & Eddleman, H. C. (1984). Same-sex rape of nonincarcerated men. *American Journal of Psychiatry, 141,* 576-579.

Harrell, A. V., Smith, B. E., & Cook, R. F. (1985). *The social psychological effects of victimization.* Final Grant Report, National Institute of Justice.

Hassell, R. A. (1981, March). *The impact of stranger vs. nonstranger rape: A longitudinal study.* Paper presented at the Eighth Annual Conference of the Association for Women in Psychology, Boston, MA.

Horowitz, M. (1976). *Stress response syndromes.* New York: Jason Aronson.

Hough, M. (1985). The impact of victimization: Findings from the British Crime Survey. *Victimology, 10,* 498-511.

Janoff-Bulman, R. (1979). Characterological versus behavioral self-blame: Inquiries into depression and rape. *Journal of Personality and Social Psychology, 37,* 1798-1809.

Janoff-Bulman, R. (1982). Esteem and control bases of blame: Adaptive strategies for victims versus observers. *Journal of Personality, 50,* 180-192.

Janoff-Bulman, R., & Frieze, I. (1983). A theoretical perspective for understanding reactions to victimization. *Journal of Social Issues, 39,* 1-18.

Johnson, R. L., & Shrier, D. K. (1985). Sexual victimization of boys. *Journal of Adolescent Health Care, 6,* 372-376.

Kahn, A. S. (Ed.). (1984). *Victims of crime and violence.* Washington, DC: American Psychological Association.

Katz, S., & Mazur, M. (1979). *Understanding the rape victim: A synthesis of research findings.* New York: Wiley.

Kilpatrick, D., Best, L., Veronen, A., Amick, E., Villeponteaux, L., & Ruff, G. (1985). Mental health correlates of criminal victimization: A random community survey. *Journal of Consulting and Clinical Psychology, 53,* 873-886.

Kilpatrick, D., Saunders, B., Veronen, L., Best, C., & Von, J. (1987). Criminal victimization: Lifetime prevalence, reporting to police, and psychological impact. *Crime and Delinquency, 33,* 479-489.

Kilpatrick, D. G., & Veronen, L. J. (1983, December). *The aftermath of rape: A three-year follow-up.* Paper presented at the World Congress of Behavior Therapy, 17th Annual Convention, Association for the Advancement of Behavior Therapy, Washington, DC.

Kilpatrick, D. G., & Veronen, L. J. (1984, February). *Treatment of fear and anxiety in victims of rape.* Final report of NIMH Grant no. MH29602.

Kilpatrick, D. G., & Veronen, L. J. (1984a). *The psychological impact of crime*. Washington, DC: National Institute of Justice.

Kilpatrick, D. G., Veronen, L. J., & Best, C. L. (1985). Factors predicting psychological distress among rape victims. In C. R. Figley (Ed.), *Trauma and its wake* (pp. 114-141). New York: Charles R. Figley.

Kilpatrick, D. G., Veronen, L. J., & Resick, P. A. (1979). Assessment of the aftermath of rape: Changing patterns of fear. *Journal of Behavioral Assessment, 1*, 133-148.

Knudten, R. D., Meade, A. C., Knudten, M. S., & Doernev, W. G. (1977). *Victims and witnesses: Their experience with crime and the criminal justice system*. Washington, DC: U.S. Government Printing Office.

Koss, M. P., Dinero, T. E., & Seibel, C. A. (1988). Stranger and acquaintance rape: Are there differences in the victim's experience? *Psychology of Women Quarterly, 12*, 1-12.

Krupnick, J. (1980). Brief psychotherapy with victims of violent crime. *Victimology, 5*, 347-354.

Krupnick, J., & Horowitz, M. (1980). Victims of violence: Psychological responses, treatment implications. In L. Kivens (Ed.), *Evaluation and change: Services for survivors* (pp. 42-46). Minneapolis, MN: Minneapolis Research Foundation.

Kutash, I. (1978). Treating the victim of aggression. In I. Kutash & L. Schlesinger (Eds.), *Violence: Perspective on murder and aggression*. San Francisco: Jossey-Bass.

Lejeune, R., & Alex, N. (1973). On being mugged: The event and its aftermath. *Urban Life and Culture, 2*, 259-287.

Leymann, H. (1985). Somatic and psychological symptoms after the experience of life threatening events: A profile analysis. *Victimology, 10*, 512-538.

Lurigio, A. J. (1987). Are victims all alike? The adverse, generalized, and differential impact of crime. *Crime and Delinquency, 33*, 452-467.

Lurigio, A. J., & Davis, R. C. (1989). *Adjusting to criminal victimization: The correlates of post-crime distress*. Unpublished manuscript, Northwestern University, Center for Urban Affairs and Policy Research, Evanston, IL.

Lurigio, A. J., & Rosenbaum, D. P. (in press). The psychological effects of criminal victimization: Past and future research. *Victimology*.

McCahill, T., Meyer, L., & Fischman, A. (1979). *The aftermath of rape*. Lexington, MA: Heath.

Meyer, C. B., & Taylor, S. E. (1986). Adjustment to rape. *Journal of Personality and Social Psychology, 50*, 1226-1234.

Miller, D., & Porter, C. (1983). Self-blame in victims of violence. *Journal of Social Issues, 39*, 139-152.

Morelli, P. H. (1981, March). *Comparison of the psychological recovery of black and white victims of rape*. Paper presented at the annual meeting of the Association of Women in Psychology, Boston.

Moss, M., Frank, E., & Anderson, B. (1987). *The effects of marital status and partner support on emotional response to acute trauma: The example of rape*. Unpublished manuscript, University of Pittsburgh.

Norris, J., & Feldman-Summers, S. (1981). Factors related to the psychological impact of rape on the victim. *Journal of Abnormal Psychology, 90*, 562-567.

Peters, J. (1977). The Philadelphia victim project. In D. Chappell, R. Geis, & G. Geis (Eds.), *Forcible rape: The crime, the victim and the offender* (pp. 339-355). New York: Columbia University Press.

Peterson, C., Schwartz, S. M., & Seligman, M. E. P. (1981). Self-blame and depressive symptoms. *Journal of Personality and Social Psychology, 41*, 253-259.

Peterson, C., & Seligman, M. E. P. (1983). Learned helplessness and victimization. *Journal of Social Issues, 39*, 103-116.

Popiel, D. A., & Susskind, E. C. (1985). The impact of rape: Social support as a moderator of stress. *American Journal of Community Psychology, 13*, 645-676.

President's Task Force on Victims of Crime (1983). *Report of the President's Task Force on Victims of Crime*. Washington, DC.

Resick, P. (1987). Psychological effects of victimization: Implications for the criminal justice system. *Crime and Delinquency, 33*, 468-478.

Resick, P. A. (1986). *Reactions of female and male victims of rape or robbery*. Final report of NIMH Grant No. MH 37296.

Resick, P. A. (1988). *Reactions of female and male victims of rape or robbery*. Final report of NIJ Grant No. 85-IJ-CX-0042.

Rosenbaum, D. P. (1977). *Reactions to criminal victimization: A summary of victim, community, and police responses*. Evanston, IL: Evanston Police Department.

Rosenbaum, D. P. (1980). *Victim blame as a strategy for coping with criminal victimization; An analysis of victim, community, and police reactions*. Unpublished doctoral dissertation, Loyola University, Chicago.

Ruch, L. O., & Chandler, S. M. (1980, September). *The impact of sexual assault on three victim groups receiving crisis intervention services at a rape treatment center; Adult rape victims, child rape victims and incest victims*. Paper presented at the Annual American Sociological Meetings, New York, NY.

Ruch, L. O., & Chandler, S. M. (1983). Sexual assault trauma during the acute phase: An exploratory model and multivariate analysis. *Journal of Health and Social Behavior, 24*, 174-185.

Ruch, L., Chandler, S., & Harter, R. (1980). Life change and rape impact. *Journal of Health and Social Behavior, 21*, 248-260.

Ruch, L. O., & Hennessey, M. (1982). Sexual assault: Victim and attack dimensions. *Victimology, 7*, 94-105.

Ruch, L. O., & Leon, J. J. (1983). Sexual assault trauma and trauma change. *Women and Health, 8*, 5-21.

Sales, E., Baum, M., & Shore, B. (1984). Victim readjustment following assault. *Journal of Social Issues, .40*, 117-136.

Scheppele, K. L., & Bart, P. B. (1983). Through women's eyes: Defining danger in the wake of sexual assault. *Journal of Social Issues, 39*, 63-80.

Schneider, A. L., & Schneider, P. R. (1977). *Issues in victim-witness assistance programming*. Eugene, OR: Institute for Policy Analysis.

Silver, R. L., Boon, C., & Stones, M. H. (1983). Searching for meaning in misfortune: Making sense of incest. *Journal of Social Issues, 39*, 81-103.

Silver, R. L., & Wortman, C. B. (1980). Coping with undesirable life events. In J. Garber & M. E. P. Seligman (Eds.), *Human helplessness: Theory and applications* (pp. 279-375). New York: Academic Press.

Stein, J. H. (1977). *Better services for crime victims: A prescriptive package*. Washington, DC: Blackstone Institute.

Stewart, B. D., Hughes, C., Frank, E., Anderson, B., Kendall, K., & West, D. (1987). Profiles of immediate and delayed treatment seekers. *The Journal of Nervous and Mental Disease, 175*, 90-94.

Symonds, M. (1976). The rape victim: Psychological patterns of response. *American Journal of Psychoanalysis, 36,* 27-34.

Symonds, M. (1980). The "second injury" to victims. In L. Kivens (Ed.), *Evaluation and change: Services for survivors.* (pp. 36-38). Minneapolis, MN: Minneapolis Research Foundation.

Taylor, S. E., Lichtman, R. R., & Wood, J. V. (1984). Attributions, beliefs in control, and adjustment to breast cancer. *Journal of Personality and Social psychology, 46,* 489-502.

Taylor, S. E., Wood, J. V., & Lichtman, R. R. (1983). It could be worse: Selective evaluation as a response to victimization. *Journal of Social Issues, 39,* 19-40.

West, D. G., Frank, D., Anderson, B., & Stewart, B. D. (1987). *Social support and post-rape symptomatology.* Unpublished manuscript, Western Psychiatric Institute, Pittsburgh, PA.

Wortman, C. B., & Conway, T. L. (1985). The role of social support in adaptation and recovery from physical illness. In S. Cohen & L. Syme (Eds.), *Social support and health* (pp. 281-302). New York: Academic Press.

Chapter 4

VICTIMS OF SEXUAL ASSAULT

PATRICIA A. RESICK

Sexual assault is a problem of great personal and societal significance. In recent random surveys of the population, the lifetime prevalence of sexual assault has been estimated between 13.5% and 44% of woman (Kilpatrick, Best, Veronen, Amick, Villeponteaux, & Ruff, 1985; Koss, Gidycz, & Wisniewski, 1987; Russell, 1982). It is a problem that impacts on both the physical and psychological functioning of victims as measured by chronic medical and mental health service usage (Golding, Stein, & Siegel, 1988; Koss, 1988). Furthermore, nearly 20% of rape victims attempt suicide, and 44% contemplate suicide in its aftermath (Kilpatrick, Veronen, Saunders, Best, Amick-McMullen, & Paduhovich, 1987; Resick, Jordan, Girelli, Hutter, & Marhoefer-Dvorak, 1988). Rape is also a problem that is reflected in our non-victimized population through fear of crime and restriction of lifestyles (Riger & Gordon, 1981).

Rape is probably the most thoroughly studied single-incident crime with regard to victim reactions. It has also been considered the most traumatic adult crime, short of murder, and has, therefore, been the subject of greater scrutiny and intervention. Whether rape does, in fact, produce greater trauma is, of course, an empirical question. Also in question is whether the rape reaction is different qualitatively or whether it is different only in degree. If the latter is the case, then research that has been compiled on reactions and treatment of rape victims should be directly applicable to other types of crime victims. The purpose of this chapter is to examine research on reactions to rape, to describe current theories explaining these reactions, and to discuss implications of these findings and theories for intervention with adult victims of rape.

THE PSYCHOLOGICAL AFTERMATH OF SEXUAL ASSAULT

Research on Victim Reactions

Generally, there are three types of studies that have examined the psychological reactions of rape victims. Each type has advantages and disadvantages in methodology, but together they provide a very good picture of the reactions and recovery of rape victims. The first type of research is the longitudinal study (e.g., Atkeson, Calhoun, Resick, & Ellis, 1982; Kilpatrick, Resick, & Veronen, 1981; Resick, 1988). In such a study, rape victims are compared to either nonvictims or other crime victims over a specified period of time in order to determine the pattern of reactions and recovery unique to rape victims. The advantage of these studies is that they are prospective; that is, they examine the victims shortly after the crime and are sensitive to changes in the victims' responses over time. It was this type of research that clearly demonstrated that rape victims were indeed suffering from distinct symptoms beyond those that are found among the general population. This research also brought into question the validity of the crisis theory model of victim reactions.

The disadvantage of this type of research is that findings are limited to those women who report the crime to some agency fairly soon after it occurs. It is known that many women do not report rape in the immediate aftermath and that some women do not define themselves as rape victims, even though they suffer from its effects. This is particularly true of acquaintance rape victims, who may have only defined rape as an attack by a stranger. Therefore, by definition, this type of research carries some potential bias. Another possible source of bias is the attrition in longitudinal studies, an element that researchers cannot control completely. Attrition has been examined by the comparison of victims who completed longitudinal studies versus those who withdrew. Although no differences have emerged, it is possible that these groups differ on some variable(s) that have not been examined (Kilpatrick, 1984, Resick, Calhoun, Atkeson, & Ellis, 1981).

The second type of research is the random population survey. Because of the problem of nonreporting, this type of research was conducted to assess reactions of rape victims in the general population, as well as to determine more accurately the prevalence of sexual assault. Random population surveys have been conducted by means of telephone survey, written questionnaire, and house-to-house survey. The purpose of random population surveys is to provide information regarding the long-term reactions of victims who may not have reported their crimes or perhaps not even identified themselves as rape victims using everyday definitions.

The greatest disadvantage of this type of research is that it is retrospective and is therefore subject to memory bias. Many of the women surveyed in these studies were victimized many years earlier and may misremember events or their reactions to them. These studies also cannot control for intervening events that could account for some of the symptoms that are reported. However, they do provide interesting information regarding current functioning in women who were sexually assaulted in the past.

The third type of research is designed to identify factors that may influence the reaction and recovery of rape victims. A range of studies has examined precrime, within-crime, and postcrime events and variables that may exacerbate or ameliorate the traumatic impact of rape. Although they provide important supplementary information regarding the effects of sexual assault, these studies are, at times, difficult to evaluate because they use idiosyncratic rather than standard questionnaires and interviews. It is difficult to generalize from one study to the next when every study uses a different methodology and different means to assess the variables of interest. While the results from the longitudinal and random population surveys have been rather consistent, the third type of research has produced a variety of findings that are frequently contradictory. Furthermore, these studies have rarely included comparison groups of other types of crime victims. Nevertheless, they have indicated some potentially important intervening variables for reactions and recovery of which practitioners should be aware.

Symptoms and Patterns of Recovery

Although most recent studies have focused on specific diagnoses of disorders, most of the research begun in the 1970s regarding reactions to rape did not use diagnostic categories or labels and examined the range and occurrence of individual symptoms (Atkeson et al., 1982; Kilpatrick et al., 1981; Kilpatrick, Veronen, & Resick, 1979a). Some of the early resistance to diagnosis stemmed from a reluctance to label victims as pathological when so little was known about what constituted a "normal" reaction to such an event. There was also concern with the classification models that existed prior to 1980 because they were so theory-laden, subjective, and unreliable. Furthermore, there was no clear diagnostic category that captured the essential features of rape reactions. With the advent of the third edition of the *Diagnostic and Statistical Manual* (DSM-III) in 1980, diagnosis became much more empirically based. The new classification, post-traumatic stress disorder, did appear to apply to the trauma reactions that had been observed in rape victims. By this time as well, enough evidence had been compiled to specify typical reactions to sexual assault.

Symptomatology and distress. Rather than determine whether and how many rape victims met the criteria for major depression or post-traumatic stress disorder, most of the early studies merely compared whether rape victims suffered from more depressive symptoms or greater fear and anxiety than nonvictims or victims of other crimes. Generally, the longitudinal studies found that victims suffered from a wide range of symptoms for several months after the crime. While much of the distress diminished by three months postcrime, there were often enduring problems with fear, anxiety, and sexual dysfunctions for a substantial minority of victims, according to these studies (Atkeson et al., 1982; Calhoun, Atkeson, & Resick, 1982; Kilpatrick et al., 1981; Kilpatrick & Veronen, 1983a; Resick, 1988).

Calhoun and her colleagues (Atkeson et al., 1982; Calhoun et al., 1982; Resick et al., 1981; Ellis, Calhoun, & Atkeson, 1980) compared the reactions of 93 rape victims and 87 nonvictims at six postcrime intervals: 2 weeks and 1, 2, 4, 8, and 12 months. They found that rape victims scored significantly higher than nonvictims on depression measures at 2 weeks, 1 month, and 2 months postcrime, but not at later sessions. At the 2 week session, 75% of rape victims reported at least mild depressive symptoms. The pattern of recovery with regard to fear was somewhat different. Rape victims exhibited improvement between the 2-week and 2-month session, but they continued to report more fear and anxiety than nonraped women through the 12-month assessment.

With regard to sexual functioning, these researchers found that sexual activity was curtailed for the first month after the assault in 43% of the sample, but by 12 months postcrime, activity level had returned to normal for those women who had frequent or somewhat frequent sexual activity prior to the crime. Those women who had infrequent sexual activity prior to the crime did not return to precrime levels by 12 months. They continued to avoid sexual contact. Social functioning was also disrupted until the 4-month assessment session. Of particular types of social adjustment, they found that work adjustment was affected the longest, for 8 months after the crime.

Kilpatrick and his colleagues also conducted a longitudinal study comparing rape victims with a sample of nonraped women (Kilpatrick et al., 1981; Kilpatrick & Veronen, 1983a, Kilpatrick, 1984; Kilpatrick, Veronen & Resick, 1979a, 1979b). For the most part, their findings are similar to those of Calhoun et al. (1982). Kilpatrick's project compared the two groups at the following postcrime intervals: 6 to 21 days, 1 month, 3 months, 6 months, 1 year, 2 years, and 3 years. In an early report with a smaller sample size, Kilpatrick and his colleagues reported that raped women scored significantly higher than nonraped women on 25 of 28 measures of distress at 1-month postcrime but scored higher on only 7 of the 28 measures at 3 and 6 months postcrime. All 7 measures were indicators of fear and anxiety. Depressive symptoms had dropped out by 3 months postcrime. Greater fear reactions continued through the 3-year assessment.

However, in the final report for the project, analyses were conducted with a much larger sample (Kilpatrick, 1984). In this larger sample, raped women continued to report significantly greater distress than non-raped women on 26 of 28 measures at 3, 6, and 12 months postcrime, including measures of depression. Through the three-year assessment, there were differences reported on fear and anxiety scales. Self-esteem was examined separately (Murphy, Amick-McMullan, Kilpatrick, Haskett, Veronen, Best, & Saunders, 1988). An examination of 9 self-esteem subscales indicated that rape victims experienced significantly poorer self-esteem than nonvictims during the two years that were examined. Particularly affected were relationships with self, parents, and others.

Resick (1988) has recently completed a study that compares the reactions of rape victims with those of robbery victims. She assessed these two groups at 1, 3, 6, 12, and 18 months postcrime in order to determine whether the reactions observed are unique to the crime of rape or whether they are similar to another life-threatening crime. She found that both rape and robbery victims experienced considerable distress following their victimization. For example, at one month postcrime, on a measure of global distress, 48% of rape victims scored one standard deviation above the normative mean for the scale, and another 35% scored at least two standard deviations above the mean. In the sample of robbery victims, 37% scored one standard deviation above the mean, while another 31% were elevated at least two standard deviations. At 18 months postcrime, 55% of the rape victims and 36% of the robbery victims reported scores that were still elevated at least one full standard deviation.

Sexual dysfunction. Other retrospective studies of rape victims have reported chronic problems with sexual functioning (Becker, Abel, & Skinner, 1979; Becker, Skinner, Abel, & Cichon, 1986; Becker, Skinner, Abel, & Treacy, 1982; Burgess & Holmstrom, 1979a; Ellis et al., 1980; Feldman-Summers, Gordon, & Meagher, 1979; Miller, Williams, & Bernstein, 1982). The most typical reaction in the immediate aftermath is avoidance of sex. Ellis et al. (1980) reported that, of rape victims who had been sexually active prior to the crime, 29% completely stopped having sex with their partner, and 32% had sex less often at a two-week postcrime assessment. At the four-week assessment, 43% of the sample had not been sexually active. By one-year postcrime, those women who had sex frequently or somewhat frequently before the crime had returned to normal levels. Women who had sex infrequently before the crime had not returned to pre-rape levels at the end of a year. Continued avoidance is apparently easier for those women who do not have a regular partner in their lives.

In the largest study of sexual functioning in sexual assault survivors, Becker et al. (1986) found that 59% of 372 sexual assault victims had at least one sexual dysfunction compared to 17% of the 99 comparison sample. Of the sexually dysfunctional victims, 88% reported early-response-cycle-inhibiting problems, which include fear of sex, arousal dysfunction, and desire dysfunction. In a more global assessment of sexual dysfunctions in a retrospective study conducted as a follow-up to a random population survey, Kilpatrick et al. (1987) found that while only 15% of nonvictims reported sexual disorders at the time of the survey, 30% of one-incident rape victims and 40% of two-incident rape victims were experiencing significant sexual disorders. Over their lifetime, 65% of the one-incident and 90% of the two-incident rape victims report sexual dysfunctions compared to 45% of the nonvictims.

Diagnosis of Psychological Disorders in Rape Victims

The two major psychological disorders examined most frequently in rape victims are post-traumatic stress disorder (PTSD) and major depression. Other disorders that have also been associated with rape are phobias (including simple phobias, social phobia), obsessive-compulsive disorder, and chemical dependency. Several studies have determined the frequency of these disorders. In their clinical follow-up of a random population survey, Kilpatrick et al. (1987) found that 16% of 81 victims of one completed rape and 20% of two completed rapes currently met the diagnostic criteria for PTSD. These figures compared to 3.4% of female victims of crimes other than rape. Almost 60% of the rape victims met the criteria for having had PTSD at some time in their lives, compared to less than 15% of nonrape victims.

Kilpatrick et al. (1987) also found that 8.6% of victims of one rape and 20% of victims of two rapes currently met the diagnosis for major depressive disorder, while 46% of victims of one rape and 80% of the victims of two rapes met the lifetime diagnosis of major depressive disorder, compared to 28% of woman who had not been raped. It should be noted that all of the comparisons between victims and nonvictims reported above were statistically significant. Frank and Stewart (1984) found a similar percentage to the lifetime depression figure found by Kilpatrick et al. In a sample of 90 recent rape victims, Frank and Stewart found 43% met the criteria for major depression.

Examination of social phobia and obsessive-compulsive disorder were similar. At the time of the interview, 3% of the nonvictims reported social phobia, while 12% of one-incident and 10% of two-incident rape victims reported meeting the diagnostic criteria for social phobia (Kilpatrick et al., 1987). Only 2 percent of the nonvictims reported obsessive-compulsive disorder, while 12% of the rape victims were currently experiencing the disorder.

As part of a larger epidemiology study, Stein, Golding, Siegel, Sorenson, Forsythe, & Telles (1988) compared the lifetime diagnoses of nine major mental disorders of those who had been sexually assaulted at some time in their lives and those who reported no sexual assault. Their sample included men as well as women. They found that sexual assault predicted later onset of major depression, substance abuse disorders, and anxiety disorders (including phobia, panic disorder, and obsessive-compulsive disorder), but did not predict later onset of mania, schizophrenic disorders, or antisocial personality. Unfortunately, they did not assess post-traumatic stress disorder.

They found that 13% of those who had been sexually assaulted developed major depression after the assault, while only 6% of the nonvictims reported major depression during the same time period. Ten percent of the victims developed phobias compared to 3% of the nonvictims. Three percent of the victims developed panic disorder compared to 1% of the nonvictims, and 4% of the victims developed obsessive-compulsive disorder compared to 1% of the nonvictims. The victims of sexual assault were also more likely than the nonvictims to develop alcohol abuse or dependence (16%) or drug abuse or dependence (18%) than the nonvictims (7% each). Those who were assaulted in childhood were more likely to develop those disorders than those who were assaulted first in adulthood. Sexually assaulted men were more likely to develop alcohol abuse or dependence than women, but there were no other sex differences in reactions.

Overall, the preceding studies indicate that with the exception of PTSD, which was reported by 80% of rape victims postcrime, the major psychological disorders do not develop in a majority of rape victims. However, there is a significant minority of rape victims who do develop serious psychological disorders as a result of the assault. And while many victims do not meet the criteria to be diagnosed as suffering from a major disorder, the majority of rape victims do report some psychological disruption in the months or years that follow the assault.

THEORIES OF PSYCHOLOGICAL REACTIONS TO SEXUAL ASSAULT

Crisis Theory

The first theory of victim reactions was crisis theory (Burgess & Holmstrom, 1974, 1979b; Sales, Baum, & Shore, 1984), which proposes that following an event that is beyond a person's normal resources and abilities to cope, she/he experiences psychological distress. If new attempts to cope are ineffective, the agitation and symptomatology will increase. However, it has always been proposed that such distress is time limited: within 4 to 6 weeks, the person will resolve the crisis either adaptively or maladaptively (through such inappropriate coping strategies as denial or alcohol use). Either way, overt distress should be alleviated within approximately six weeks. The purpose of crisis therapy is to help the person resolve the crisis as quickly as possible and to avoid developing maladaptive coping strategies.

There are several major problems with crisis theory with regard to victims of rape. Although no one would argue that many rape victims experience a "crisis" after the assault, crisis theory does nothing to explain why certain symptoms are developed; it does not predict who is likely to have more problems with recovery or what variables may affect reactions and recovery. Furthermore, the longitudinal studies have all disconfirmed the time schedule proposed by the crisis theorists. All of the studies have found that the bulk of improvement occurs within the first three months after the crime, but that many rape victims continue reporting problems with fear, anxiety, self-esteem, depression, sexual dysfunction, intrusion and avoidance for years after the event. Rape victims report experiencing distress in these studies, so clearly they have not become symptom-free in six weeks.

Learning Theory

Two-factor learning theory was next proposed as the best explanation for the reactions of rape victims (Becker, Skinner, Abel, Axelrod, & Cichon, 1984; Holmes & St. Lawrence, 1983; Kilpatrick, Veronen, & Resick, 1982). Learning theory hypothesizes that at the time of the assault, the victim's fear reactions are great enough to classically condition fear reactions to previously neutral cues that happen to be present during the crime. These cues, or stimuli, are then capable of triggering flashbacks and fear reactions in other nondangerous situations. The victim then develops escape and avoidance behavior to cope with what she subsequently perceives as a dangerous situation (dangerous because she feels terror just as she did during the crime) or merely to avoid the unpleasant experience of fear even if she recognizes that she is not really in danger in some other cue situation. Avoidance learning is the most powerful form of learning and is quite resistant to extinction or unlearning. Two-factor theory explains sexual dysfunctions and avoidance, as well as other fear reactions and anxiety.

Depressive reactions also are explained by learning theory as being secondary to the anxiety reactions. Because of the helplessness experienced during the crime, the victim may perceive she is helpless in other situations in which she could have some control (Peterson & Seligman, 1983). This and the loss of the usual reinforcers of the victim's life that occur as a result of avoidance (refusing to go out in the evening or to date) can lead to a state of depression. The treatments that have been developed based on learning theory all emphasize anxiety management and/or exposure to nondangerous, but fear-inducing cues that were conditioned during the assault and avoided in the aftermath of the rape.

While two-factor theory does much to explain many of the symptoms that develop and why they may persist indefinitely, it does not completely explain the intrusion symptoms of PTSD; that is, why the recurrent recollections, flashbacks, and nightmares occur. Although it could be argued that some, possibly unrecognized, cues in the environment trigger these memories, it is more likely that there is some important cognitive function for the intrusive memories. Some of the experimental psychologists in the 1960s and 1970s recognized that a cognitive component needed to be added to the two-factor theory and learned helplessness theory. For the most part, the variables that were studied concerned attributions regarding events or expectancies regarding future events.

Cognitive Theories

Although there is a very large body of research on attribution theory in psychology, very little of it has been applied to the experience of rape. There is increasing evidence, however, that people have a strong need to search for the meaning of negative events (Silver & Wortman, 1980). Criminal victimization destroys the illusion that we live in a safe, predictable, controllable world. In order to regain that sense of safety and controllability, many women blame themselves for being raped rather than blaming the rapist, who is uncontrollable (Janoff-Bulman, 1979). Usually, self-recrimination is in the form of behavioral self-blame; in such an instance, the victim says to herself/himself, "If only I had not accepted that date (gone to that party, been more careful, etc.), the rape would not have happened. If I just avoid such behavior in the future, it will not happen again."

Another less common form of self-blame has been identified by Janoff-Bulman (1979) as characterological self-blame. In this case, victims blame themselves for the victimization because they are bad or victim-types. Although Janoff-Bulman predicted that behavioral self-blame would lead to more effective post-rape adjustment than characterological self-blame, Meyer and Taylor (1985) found that both types of self-blame lead to poorer adjustment post-rape.

In addition to the postcrime attributions of blame made by victims, it may be the case that precrime appraisals affect postcrime adjustment. Schepple and Bart (1983) found that women who believed the rape situation was safe prior to the crime were more likely to have severe reactions than those who suspected they might be in danger. Perloff (1983), after reviewing a wide range of studies, has proposed that nonvictims may perceive themselves as uniquely invulnerable, being less vulnerable to victimization. Those individuals who hold this view and who are subsequently victimized appear to have more severe reactions than those who do not believe they are uniquely invulnerable. After being victimized, illusions of invulnerability are shattered and the situation must be reappraised. Perloff proposed that those victims who now feel uniquely vulnerable (more vulnerable than others) will have more problems than those who adopt a perception of universal vulnerability (equally vulnerable to others).

The most recent cognitive theory being applied to the reactions of rape victims is the emotional processing theory (Foa & Kozak, 1986; Foa, Steketee & Olasov, in press). The emotional processing model treats attributions and expectations as specific content but also focuses much of its attention on the structure and process by which information and events are encoded, integrated, and retrieved in memory. They propose that when a rape victim's concepts of safety are shattered, the victim develops an internal fear structure that is a program for escape and avoidance behavior and elicits the symptoms of PTSD.

CONCLUSIONS AND IMPLICATIONS
FOR PRACTITIONERS

With very little effort on their parts, practitioners in the criminal justice system are in the position to help rape victims recover. They are also in a position to assess which victims may have more difficulty with recovery and to refer them for treatment. While obtaining statements about the crime, investigating officers are likely to hear from victims about whether they were terrified or fairly calm during the crime. They may also hear from victims as to whether they believed the assailant was going to kill them. And they, of course, will learn about the extent of threats, restraint, violence, and the duration of the crime. Although the police who investigate cases may disagree with the victims' appraisal of the imminent danger posed by the situation based on their experience, they should not disregard the victims' perceptions. It is those perceptions that will, in all likelihood, determine whether they will suffer from a severe trauma reaction and whether they will recover from the crime. Investigators and other criminal justice system personnel should make a special effort to refer victims to counseling who describe the crime as an imminent death situation or who describe themselves as being terrified during the crime.

Over the months that follow the crime, the extent of avoidance can be assessed simply. Victim assistance counselors and attorneys are usually in good position to do so. Rape victims sometimes profess to be recovered; that is, they are not depressed and are no longer having intrusive memories or anxiety reactions. However, they may be avoiding any reminders of the incident and have restructured their lives rather than recover. Specifically, they may deny having problems but will admit upon further questioning, that they are asymptomatic only because they refuse to go out after dark, date, be home alone, and so forth. Were they to attempt these activities, they would experience great distress.

It may still be painful for them to discuss the crime, and they may make great efforts not to think about it or encounter any reminders. A few simple questions about whether the victim is doing everything she did before the crime (going out, being home alone) should give a fairly good indication as to whether she has recovered or is avoiding. If any of the facts regarding the case are known to the practitioner, then specific questions can be asked about situations that are likely to be causing the victim problems. For instance, if the victim was raped while home alone, the practitioner could ask if the victim is able to stay at home alone comfortably. If she was raped while out on a date, has she resumed dating, or at least going out in the evening with friends? Resick (1988) found that among lifestyle questions, the best single predictor of the continuing problems with recovery was whether the victim avoided being alone. That question accounted for 73% of the variance in a measure of PTSD at 18 months postcrime in rape victims. Again, those who are exhibiting difficulties in recovery should be referred for therapy.

How a victim is treated by criminal justice practitioners may affect how the rape victim psychologically processes the event. Investigations can and should be conducted without implying that the victim brought on the crime (should be blamed for the incident, did not resist sufficiently) even when the investigator feels that the victim put herself at risk by her own behavior. Most people occasionally have less than optimal judgment as they move through the world, particularly if they believe that their corner of the world is safer than it actually is (e.g., locks aren't always locked, they open their doors when someone knocks). Usually a lapse in judgment does not have catastrophic consequences. Teenagers are particularly naive and cannot always discriminate safe from potentially unsafe situations. Poor judgment is not an offense punishable by rape. Furthermore, it is impossible to know, after the fact, which and/or whether prevention or resistance techniques may have been effective with that particular assailant in that particular situation.

Police, counselors, and attorneys need to be careful in their phrasing of questions. For example, "What happened next?" or "What did you do then?" are neutral questions, whereas, "Why did you . . . ?" implies blame and puts the victim on the defensive. It is important that victims understand that, regardless of what they did, the offender had no right to rape them and that no one can second-guess how they behaved during the crime. They resisted and coped during the crime as best they could being given that particular set of circumstances.

A few judicious statements by the criminal justice practitioner may help greatly in a victim's recovery. Statements about the normal course of recovery (months, not days or weeks) and normal symptoms, such as flashbacks, nightmares, intrusive memories, the desire to avoid reminders, sleeping problems, and roller-coaster emotions, may help victims know that their reactions are normal and that they are not crazy. Rape victims should be advised to take things one step at a time but to return to normal activities as soon as they are able rather than avoid nondangerous "danger" cues that were conditioned during the crime. They should be encouraged to mobilize their social support network and tell loved ones what they need. In this author's experience, most often, families and friends want to be supportive but do not know what to do or say.

Finally, because the goal for victims is to accept what happened and recover rather than to develop amnesia, they should be warned that they may be given bad advice from well-meaning but uninformed people. Our society appears to subscribe to the "stiff-upper-lip school of psychology" in which people are supposed to disregard their emotions, forget the fact that someone almost killed them, put the event behind them, and get on with their lives in a few days or weeks. This advice, if followed, will give the appearance that victims have recovered. The advice serves to remove uncomfortable emotions and reactions from view of family, friends, and acquaintances. However, as everyone who works with crime victims knows, such behavior is just another form of avoidance that postpones recovery. In a recent treatment study, Resick et al. (1988) reported that the average length of time it took rape victims to seek therapy was five years.

It is fairly common for mothers to have trauma reactions about their own unresolved rape years earlier when one of their children is assaulted. It is also not uncommon for victims to have their rape trauma suddenly reemerge after many years and after some other trauma, such as the death of a loved one, another crime, or when they finally attempt to develop intimacy with someone. The intense reactions of the second event probably reactivate memories and emotions that were encoded years earlier. Postponing recovery from the rape trauma complicates recovery from later traumas because it appears that when the first event was not resolved and processed to the point where the emotions had dissipated, it is left encoded with all of the intense emotions intact. Furthermore, it is possibly more difficult to enlist social support years after an event than immediately after it occurs. Family and friends are likely to be confused as to why the victim is so upset years after an event occurred.

Although there has not been extensive research thus far, several types of therapy techniques have been developed and appear promising in treating symptoms that rape victims experience. *Systematic desensitization* (Becker & Abel, 1981; Frank & Stewart, 1983, 1984; Frank, Anderson, Stewart, Dancu, Hughes, & West, 1988; Turner, 1979; Wolff, 1977), *cognitive therapy* (Forman, 1980; Frank & Stewart, 1984, Frank et al., 1988), *flooding* (Haynes & Mooney, 1975; Rothbaum & Foa, 1988), *sexual dysfunction therapy* (Becker & Skinner, 1983, 1984), and *stress inoculation training* (Rothbaum & Foa, 1988; Kilpatrick, Veronen, & Resick, 1982; Veronen & Kilpatrick, 1983; Resick, Jordan, Girelli, Hutter, & Marhoefer-Dvorak, 1988) have all been used successfully with rape victims. Most of these therapy procedures serve to reduce anxiety and break up avoidance patterns, to treat sexual dysfunctions, or to treat the symptoms of depression. These single case reports and the few treatment outcome studies that have been conducted indicate that cognitive and behavioral therapies are effective, with no one technique being demonstrated superior thus far. More comparison studies are needed to determine which procedures are most beneficial for which rape victims.

Sexual assault is a shockingly common crime. It would be easy to conclude that rape is not very serious because it is a common occurrence in our society and is infrequently accompanied by other serious physical injuries. This is not the case. Although the incidence of murder during rape is actually rather infrequent, rape is a life-shattering event because the victim perceives that she is about to die due to threats, the presence of weapons, being choked, and other factors (Resick, 1988). The majority of victims experience severe psychological reactions in its wake, which in many cases last for years. A substantial minority of victims are so distressed that they contemplate and/or attempt suicide. We have no statistics on how many successful suicides were precipitated by rape. Because of prevailing attitudes of victim-blame, victims frequently do not receive the support they need to recover successfully.

We do know, however, that many victims *do* recover successfully. When they receive nonjudgmental support from their loved ones and the professionals they encounter, they are many steps closer to recovery. There are now available effective therapies for the treatment of rape victims. Victims may need help in finding therapists who can supply appropriate treatment. Practitioners in the criminal justice system and victim assistance agencies are often in a good position to make appropriate referrals. Most of all, they are in the best position to lead the way in changing attitudes toward rape victims by their humane treatment of victims, by the example they set, and by the dissemination of accurate information and training to other professionals and the general public.

REFERENCES

Atkeson, B. M., Calhoun, K. S., Resick, P. A., & Ellis, E. m. (1982). Victims of rape: Repeated assessment of depressive symptoms. *Journal of Consulting and Clinical Psychology, 50*, 96-102.

Becker, J. V., & Abel, G. G. (1981). Behavioral treatment of victims of sexual assault. In S. M. Turner, K. S. Calhoun, & H. E. Adams (Eds.), *Handbook of clinical behavior therapy* (pp. 347-379). New York, John Wiley.

Becker, J. V., Abel, G. G., & Skinner, L. J. (1979). The impact of a sexual assault on the victim's sexual life. *Victimology: An International Journal, 4*, 229-235.

Becker, J. V., & Skinner, L. J. (1983). Assessment and treatment of rape-related sexual dysfunctions. *The Clinical Psychologist, 36*, 102-105.

Becker, J. V., & Skinner, L. J. (1984). Behavioral treatment of sexual dysfunctions in sexual assault survivors. In I. Stuart & J. Greer (Eds.), *Victims of sexual aggression* (pp. 211-234). New York: Van Nostrand Reinhold Co.

Becker, J. V., Skinner, L. J., Abel, G. G., Axelrod, R., & Cichon, J. (1984). Sexual problems of sexual assault survivors. *Women & Health, 9*, 5-20.

Becker, J. V., Skinner, L. J., Abel, G. G., & Cichon, J. (1986). Level of postassault sexual functioning in rape and incest victims. *Archives of Sexual Behavior, 15*, 37-49.

Becker, J. V., Skinner, L. J., Abel, G. G., & Treacy, E. C. (1982). Incidence and types of sexual dysfunctions in rape and incest victims. *Journal of Sex and Marital Therapy, 8*, 65-74.

Burgess, A. W., & Holmstrom, L. L. (1974). Rape trauma syndrome. *American Journal of Psychiatry, 131*, 981-986.

Burgess, A. W., & Holmstrom, L. L. (1979a). Rape: Sexual disruption and recovery. *American Journal of Orthopsychiatry, 49*, 648-657.

Burgess, A. W., & Holmstrom, L. L. (1979b). *Rape: Crisis and Recovery*. Bowie, MD: Robert J. Brady Co.

Burnam, M. A., Stein, J. A., Golding, J. M., Siegel, J. M., Sorenson, S. B., Forsythe, A. B., & Telles, C. A. (1988). Sexual assault and mental disorders in a community population. *Journal of Consulting and Clinical Psychology, 56*, 843-850.

Calhoun, K. S., Atkeson, B. M., & Resick, P. A. (1982). A longitudinal examination of fear reactions in victims of rape. *Journal of Counseling Psychology, 29*, 655-661.

Ellis, E. M., Calhoun, K. S., & Atkeson, B. M. (1980). Sexual dysfunctions in victims of rape: Victims may experience a loss of sexual arousal and frightening flashbacks even one year after the assault. *Women and Health, 5*, 39-47.

Feldman-Summers, S., Gordon, P. E., & Meagher, J. R. (1979). The impact of rape on sexual satisfaction. *Journal of Abnormal Psychology, 88*, 101-105.

Foa, E. B., & Kozak, M. J. (1986). Emotional processing of fear: Exposure to corrective information. *Psychological Bulletin, 99*, 20-35.

Foa, E. B., Steketee, G., & Olasov, B. (in press). Behavioral/cognitive conceptualizations of post-traumatic stress disorder. *Behavior Therapy*.

Forman, B. D. (1980). Cognitive modification of obsessive-thinking in a rape victim: A preliminary study. *Psychological Reports, 47*, 819-822.

Frank, E., Anderson, B., Stewart, B. D., Dancu, C., Hughes, C., & West, D. (1988). Efficacy of cognitive behavior therapy and systematic desensitization in the treatment of rape trauma. *Behavior Therapy, 19*, 403-420.

Frank E., & Stewart, B. D. (1983). Physical aggression: Treating the victims. In E. A. Bleckman (Ed.) *Behavior modification with women* (pp. 245-272). New York: Guilford Press.

Frank, E., & Stewart, B. D. (1984). Depressive symptoms in rape victims: A revisit. *Journal of Affective Disorders, 7*, 77-85.

Golding, J. M., Stein, J. A., & Siegel, J. M. (1988). Sexual assault history and use of health and mental health services. *American Journal of Community Psychology, 16*, 625-644.

Haynes, S. N., & Mooney, D. K. (1975). Nightmares: Etiological, theoretical, and behavioral treatment consideration. *Psychological Record, 25*, 225-236.

Holmes, M. R., & St. Lawrence, J. S. (1983). Treatment of rape-induced trauma: Proposed behavioral conceptualization and review of the literature. *Clinical Psychology Review, 3*, 417-433.

Janoff & Bulman, R. (1979). Characterological versus behavioral self-blame: Inquiries into depression and rape. *Journal of Personality and Social Psychology, 37*, 1798-1809.

Kilpatrick, D. G. (1984, February). *Treatment of fear and anxiety in victims of rape*. Final report, NIMH Grant No. MH29602.

Kilpatrick, D. G., Best, L., Veronen, A., Amick, E., Villeponteaux, L., & Ruff, G. (1985). Mental health correlates of criminal victimization: A random community survey. *Journal of Consulting and Clinical Psychology, 53*, 873-886.

Kilpatrick, D. G., Resick, P. A., & Veronen, L. J. (1981). Effects of a rape experience. *Journal of Social Issues, 37*, 105-122.

Kilpatrick, D. G., & Veronen, L. J. (1983a, December). *The aftermath of rape: A three-year follow-up*. Presented at the World Congress of Behavior Therapy, 17th Annual Convention, Association for the Advancement of Behavior Therapy, Washington, DC.

Kilpatrick, D. G., & Veronen, L. J. (1983b). Treatment for rape-related problems: Crisis intervention is not enough. In L. H. Cohen, W. L. Claiborn, a& G. A. Spector (Eds.), *Crisis intervention.* (pp. 165-185). New York: Human Sciences Press.

Kilpatrick, D. G., Veronen, L. J., & Resick, P. A. (1979a). The aftermath of rape: Recent empirical findings. *American Journal of Orthopsychiatry, 49,* 658-669.

Kilpatrick, D. G., Veronen, L. J., & Resick, P. A. (1979b). Assessment of the aftermath of rape: Changing patterns of fear. *Journal of Behavioral Assessment, 1,* 133-148.

Kilpatrick, D. G., Veronen, L. J., & Resick, P. A. (1982). Psychological sequelae to rape: Assessment and treatment strategies. In D. M. Doleys, R. L. Meredith, & A. R. Ciminero (Eds.), *Behavioral medicine: Assessment and treatment strategies* (pp. 473-497). New York: Plenum.

Kilpatrick, D. G., Veronen, L. J., Saunders, B. E., Best, C. L., Amick-McMullen, A., & Paduhovich, J. (1987, March). *The psychological impact of crime: A study of randomly surveyed crime victims.* Final report for the National Institute of Justice Grant No. 84-IJ-CX-0039.

Koss, M. P. (1988, August). *Criminal victimization among women: Impact on health status and medical services usage.* Paper presented at the American Psychological Association Annual Meeting, Atlanta.

Koss, M. P., Gidycz, C. A., & Wisniewski, N. (1987). The scope of rape: Incidence and prevalence of sexual aggression and victimization in a national sample of higher education students. *Journal of Consulting and Clinical Psychology, 55,* 162-170.

Meyer, C. B., & Taylor, S. E. (1985). Adjustment to rape. *Journal of Personality and Social Psychology, 50,* 1226-1234.

Miller, W. R., Williams, M., & Bernstein, M. H. (1982). The effects of rape on marital and sexual adjustment. *American Journal of Family Therapy, 10,* 51-58.

Murphy, S. M., Amick-McMullan A. E., Kilpatrick, D. G., Haskett. M. E., Veronen, L. J., Best, C. L., & Saunders, B. E. (1988). Rape victims' self-esteem: A longitudinal analysis. *Journal of Interpersonal Violence, 3,* 255-370.

Perloff, L. S. (1983). Perceptions of vulnerability to victimization. *Journal of Social Issues, 39,* 41-61.

Peterson, C., & Seligman, M. E. P. (1983). Learned helplessness and victimization. *Journal of Social Issues, 39,* 103-116.

Resick, P. A. (1988, September). *Reactions of females and male victims of rape or robbery,* Final report, NIJ Grant No. 85-IJ-CX-0042.

Resick, P. A., Calhoun, K. S., Atkeson, B. M., & Ellis, E. M. (1981). Social adjustment in victims of sexual assault. *Journal of Consulting and Clinical Psychology, 49,* 705-712.

Resick, P. A., Jordan, C. G., Girelli, S. A., Hutter, C. K., & Marhoefer-Dvorak, S. (1988). A comparative outcome study of behavioral group therapy for sexual assault victims. *Behavior Therapy, 19,* 385-401.

Riger, S., & Gordon, M. T. (1981). The fear of rape: A study in social control. *Journal of Social Issues, 37,* 71-92.

Rothbaum, B. O., & Foa, E. B. (1988, September). *Treatment of PTSD in rape victims.* Paper presented at World Congress of Behavior Therapy, Edinburgh, Scotland.

Russell, D. E. H. (1984). *Sexual exploitation: Rape, child sexual abuse, and workplace harassment.* Beverly Hills, CA: Sage Publications.

Sales, E., Baum, M., & Shore, B. (1984). Victim readjustment following assault. *Journal of Social Issues, 40,* 117-136.

Schepple, K. L., & Bart, P. B. (1983). Through women's eyes: Defining danger in the wake of sexual assault. *Journal of Social Issues, 39*, 63-81.

Silver, R., & Wortman, C. (1980). Coping with undesirable life events. In J. Garber & M. Seligman (Eds.), *Human helplessness* (pp. 279-340). New York: Academic Press.

Turner, S. M. (1979, November). *Systematic desensitization of fears and anxiety in rape victims*. Paper presented at the Association for the Advancement of Behavior Therapy, San Francisco.

Veronen, L. J., & Kilpatrick, D. G. (1983). Stress management for rape victims. In D. Meichenbaum & M. E. Jaremko (Eds.), *Stress reduction and prevention*. New York: Plenum Press.

Wolff, R. (1977). Systematic desensitization and negative practice to alter the aftereffects of a rape attempt. *Journal of Behavior Therapy and Experimental Psychiatry, 8*, 423-425.

Chapter 5

DOMESTIC VIOLENCE
The Criminal Justice Response

LUCY N. FRIEDMAN
MINNA SHULMAN

The pressures exerted today on the law enforcement and criminal justice system's response to victims of domestic violence reflect a complicated and controversial history. In the 1970s, before the battered women's movement, domestic violence was rarely treated as criminal conduct except in the most brutal cases.[1] Advocates for battered women sought to reverse this practice and assure that domestic violence was treated by the police and courts as crimes rather than as family matters, and thus be handled as seriously as crimes committed by strangers. This straightforward formula, sound on the surface, has turned out to be inadequate in protecting battered women, their children, and society both because of the powerful dynamics of the victim/offender relationship and the ingrained attitudes and misconceptions at the root of the traditional police and court response to domestic violence. An adequate response for domestic violence cases requires not equal, but special, treatment.

The factors that historically led the police and court system to treat violence between intimates differently than violence between strangers are useful to review because they are many of the same factors that

AUTHORS' NOTE: *The authors are grateful to John Feinblatt, who thoughtfully and with insight reviewed earlier drafts of this chapter.*

support today's belief that special policies should be developed for domestic violence cases. These include

1. the belief in the sanctity of the home and the family;
2. the observation that, in those few cases where an arrest was made, the woman often refused to cooperate and usually remained with or returned to her spouse/partner;
3. the belief that calming down or mediating the dispute was a better solution than arrest because arrest might incite the offender and cause more violence to the victim and the police officer; and
4. the fact that the reported incident often did not appear serious when viewed as a single event rather than as part of a chronic situation.

BACKGROUND

Although references to wife abuse appear in law documents written hundreds of years ago, domestic violence was not considered a crime by our criminal justice system until recently. State statutes began to criminalize wife abuse in the late 1800s but society, as reflected in criminal justice practices, continued to consider domestic violence to be a family matter; little effort was made to enforce criminal laws against wife abusers, and few batterers were brought before the courts.

The focus on women's rights during the early 1970s brought attention to the realities of domestic violence. Researchers began to focus on this hidden crime and reported that married women were not the only ones subjected to such violence; women in common-law and dating relationships and divorced women were subjected to violence by their partners and ex-partners. Studies conducted on the incidence of domestic violence indicated that violence within our homes was not only widespread but often escalated into serious assaults and homicides (Breedlove, Kennish, Sandker & Sawtell, 1976).

In the 1970s, police departments around the country also began to adopt a crisis intervention approach to domestic violence. This approach relied on the belief that mediating the situation would calm the offender and create less risk of violence to the responding officer and the victim. An added factor contributing to this crisis intervention approach was the fact that in most states police were not authorized to make probable-cause, warrantless, misdemeanor arrests when the crime did not occur in their presence. Victims of domestic violence in 36 states who suffered from simple assault or battery at the hands of their partners (the most common form of criminal offense in domestic cases) and who wanted their offenders arrested were forced to initiate their own criminal proceedings.

Advocates for battered women realized that the accepted law enforcement response of crisis intervention or mediation of domestic violence incidents legitimized the battering. Such tactics imposed no consequences on the offender for the violence and approached the problem as a family issue rather than as a crime committed by the batterer. The process of requiring victims to seek arrest warrants also demonstrated little or no understanding of the plight of domestic violence victims, leaving them vulnerable to future attacks and escalated violence. And the effort to provide safety for the battered women and their children through secretly located houses or shelters, while responding to their immediate danger from the batterer, placed the burden of stopping the violence on the victim.

In an effort to ensure that criminal action would be taken against the batterer, battered women and their advocates began to press state legislatures to give police greater authority to make warrantless, probable-cause arrests and file complaints for misdemeanor assaults. As these lobbying efforts were mounted, three lawsuits were brought against police departments alleging that women assaulted by men to whom they were married or with whom they were involved were denied police protection: *Bruno v. Codd* in New York City (1976), *Scott v. Hurt* in California (1976), and *Thomas v. Los Angeles* (1979). As a result of these cases police departments in question agreed to treat domestic violence as a crime.

Efforts to increase the police power to arrest in domestic violence cases were highly successful. Only the state of West Virginia has failed to pass legislation that authorizes the police to make warrantless, probable-cause arrests and file complaints in domestic violence cases. But despite the legislative reforms that established the framework for systematic changes, the law enforcement and criminal justice systems remained locked into written and unwritten policies that not only failed to stop the violence, but also communicated a tolerance for the violence.[2]

Three events in 1984 spurred many law enforcement executives to reject the traditional police response to family violence cases. The first was a landmark court decision, *Thurman v. City of Torrington* (1984), which established the police liability for injuries to battered women when officers failed to respond seriously to a victim's calls for help. The victim, Tracey Thurman, was awarded $2.3 million in compensatory damages against 24 police officers. The second event was the publication of *The Minneapolis Domestic Violence Experiment* (Sherman & Berk, 1984), which showed that arrest was more effective in reducing subsequent violence than traditional police practices of mediation and separation. And the third event was the *Final Report* of the Attorney General's Task Force on Family Violence (1984), which encouraged law enforcement agencies to publish written, operational procedures that establish family violence as a priority call, as well as recommending that arrest be the preferred response in cases of family violence.

The changes in court procedures have not been as dramatic as those in law enforcement; however, some of the lawsuits addressed court process which, combined with recommendations of the Attorney General's *Final Report*, has led to some court reforms. These reforms include procedures that mandate special treatment, not just equal treatment, for domestic cases.

Law enforcement and criminal justice policies that mandate special treatment for domestic violence cases recognize that violence between intimates *is* different than violence between strangers. These policies take into account that the dynamics of the intimate relationship may inhibit domestic violence victims from initiating and cooperating with the criminal justice process. Unlike victims of most other serious crimes, domestic violence victims not only know their offender, but they often live with their offender and share a variety of items and relationships, including property, bank accounts, children, friends, and other family members. And unlike other victims, battered women are rarely subjected to a single incident, rather they experience ongoing and escalating abuse. These policies recognize that fear of retaliation looms large for battered women; the opportunity for intimidation is great; and the need for intervention is imperative.

Today, by understanding the dynamics of this intimate relationship and integrating this understanding into special policies and guidelines, the criminal justice system is becoming responsive to the needs of victims of domestic violence and increasing its effectiveness in handling these complicated cases. In just five years, there have been enormous reforms in policies and attitudes that reflect a growing consensus on how best to handle family violence.

THE POLICE

The police are the "gatekeepers to the criminal justice system" (Goolkasian, 1986), and reforms in the criminal justice response to domestic violence have centered on the police role. Recognizing the significance of the 1984 events described above, police departments have begun to develop policies on family violence that are guided by two principles: (1) domestic violence is a crime; and (2) victims of domestic violence require special consideration.

Domestic Violence Is a Crime

"An assault is a crime, regardless of the relationship of the parties" (Attorney General's Task Force on Family Violence, 1984). Past police practices of treating domestic violence as a family squabble or domestic disturbance left victims unprotected, offenders in control, and police feeling inadequate and resentful. Not only is domestic violence a crime, it is a serious crime. One-third of the domestic violence incidents reported in the National Crime Survey are classified as felony crimes; the remaining two-thirds are misdemeanors, but as many as one-half of these misdemeanors involved bodily injury as serious or more serious than 90% of all rapes, robberies, and aggravated assaults (Langan & Innes, 1986). And the *FBI Uniform Crime Reports*, (United States Department of Justice, 1983) showed that nearly a third of female homicide victims are killed by their husbands or boyfriends.

Police are beginning to realize that the domestic violence calls they traditionally viewed as a nuisance—as non-police work—require them to act not as social workers, but as highly trained law enforcement officers who protect life and property, detect and arrest offenders, prevent crime, enforce the law, and preserve the peace. The Lincoln, Nebraska, Police Department Policy (1986) on domestic violence says:

> When violence has occurred or been threatened, irrespective of the victim's wishes, the primary responsibility of the responding police officers is to investigate a crime, and if probable cause exists, to arrest the person responsible.

In the police world, the elevation of domestic violence from a family matter to a crime is also demonstrated by recent police policies that emphasize on-scene investigation. Through policy and training, police officers are being directed to thoroughly investigate and document all available evidence in domestic violence cases, including the physical condition of the victim, offender, and residence; statements from the victim and witnesses; and household items that may have been or were threatened to be used as weapons. The domestic violence policy of the police department in Carbondale, Illinois (1988), states:

> In *all* cases of domestic violence it is important to collect as much physical evidence as possible . . . including color photographs of any injury/injuries sustained by the victim as well as photographs of the crime scene . . . every reasonable effort should be made to collect statements from the victim and potential witnesses.

The increased use of arrest, the cornerstone of domestic violence policies that emerged from the events of 1984, directly communicates to the victim, offender, and community that domestic violence is a crime. Arrest guarantees immediate safety to the victim, takes control away from the offender, and increases the police officer's ability to carry out the law enforcement mission.

Domestic Violence Victims Require Special Consideration

To be effective, law enforcement policies must not only acknowledge that domestic violence is a crime, but must incorporate special treatment for the victims of domestic violence. In most other crimes, the arrest of the offender is contingent upon the victim's signing of a complaint. "Understandably, battered women often fear that being an active party in an arrest will bring increased retaliation and violence when the offender is released." (Goolkasian, 1986). Policies that predicate the officer's power to arrest on the victim's willingness to sign a complaint, request, or agree to an arrest fail to provide special treatment for battered women. Again, the policy of the Lincoln, Nebraska, Police Department (1986) states that domestic violence calls are:

> "different than non-domestic cases and that . . . irrespective of the victim's wishes . . . if probable cause exists (the responding officers should) arrest the person responsible."

Policies that directly address the officer's determination of probable cause in domestic violence cases are also necessary to ensure special treatment for victims. In the past, officers have made decisions as to whether or not to arrest based largely on the willingness of the victim to prosecute, rather than on the evidence. The battered woman's actions or lack of actions to stop the violence have often confused the responding officer. The victim's behavior, her previous involvement in the criminal justice system, as well as prosecutorial practices, have been incorrectly taken into account by officers when determining whether probable cause exists. New York City Police Deparement Interim Order 17 (1988) simply states that the probable cause standard applied in domestic violence cases should be no different than the standard applied in all other cases. In Stamford, Connecticut (1986), the police chief has gone as far as stating factors that are *not* to be considered when determining probable cause, including whether the parties are married or living together; the victim has sought or obtained a legal restraining or vacate order; the victim has instituted divorce proceedings; the officer prefers to reconcile the parties; or the victim has called for police protection previously and has withdrawn the criminal complaint against the abuser.

Unlike victims of most other crimes, victims of domestic violence feel trapped in the violent relationship. Their offenders have threatened further violence if they attempt to leave or seek assistance; they are unaware of resources available to them; and they may not know that domestic violence is a crime. Most police departments have established procedures (such as securing medical treatment and providing the victim with information regarding legal rights and shelters) to assist victims of domestic violence regardless of whether an arrest is made. Arrest, however, is probably the most significant assistance officers can provide when responding to domestic calls because arrest provides immediate safety to the victim.

Although there is apparent consensus that mandatory, probable-cause arrests for felony domestic violence crimes is appropriate, controversy regarding misdemeanors remains. Police chiefs who are reluctant to require arrests for misdemeanor domestic violence assaults cite the benefits of police discretion, the difficulty of pressing charges with a reluctant complainant, and the crushing volume of cases that would be produced by mandatory misdemeanor arrests. Battered women and their advocates are divided on this issue as well. Those advocates who are reluctant to call for mandatory arrest are concerned about the possibility that both parties will be arrested (as has occurred in several states that instituted mandatory misdemeanor arrest policies),[3] that taking away the victim's choice to press charges will undermine the goals of empowering battered women, that battered women only want the violence to stop (they do not want the abuser to go to jail), and that women of color and undocumented women will be reluctant to call for police assistance for fear of police brutality and deportation, respectively. The discussion on the advisability of mandatory arrests in misdemeanors will be enlightened soon by the results of a six-city study, which replicates the Minneapolis experiment (Garner and Visher, 1988).

All factions agree that law enforcement's goal in responding to domestic violence should be to stop the violence and protect the victim. They also agree that past police practices accomplished neither. Mandatory probable-cause arrest for felonies and misdemeanors communicates to the victim, offender, and community that all domestic violence is criminal behavior and will not be tolerated. Mandatory arrest places immediate consequences on the offender for his violence. And mandatory arrest forces the courts to bring more offenders to prosecution, provide more offenders with court supervision, and order more offenders to treatment.

THE COURTS

Court response to domestic violence has not evolved as far as the law enforcement response. There has been less litigation and research to help articulate the issues, and the interplay of the executive and judicial branches of government discourages the creation of uniform policies.

The history of the court response to domestic violence does, however, parallel that of the police response. A Vera Institute of Justice study (1977), for example, found that, in a sample of assaults in which the victim and offender had a prior relationship, there were no offenders sentenced to prison, compared to 5% in stranger assaults. In a study conducted jointly by Vera and New York City's Victim Services Agency (Davis, Russel, & Kunreuther, 1980), it was discovered that victims were more likely to be consulted by prosecutors in cases where there was a prior relationship between the victim and the offender and the victim's desire for leniency in these cases contributed to "softer" dispositions. The findings of these, as well as other research studies (Ford,

1983, and Gayford, 1977), are confirmed by the observations of prosecutors, judges, and victim advocates that domestic violence cases are more likely to be dismissed than other cases.[4] The explanations from judges and prosecutors for this phenomenon echo the arguments previously heard from police for not making arrests: prosecuting these cases depletes scarce resources; the victim does not follow through; she often refuses to testify against her husband; she rarely is a convincing witness; she may lose her financial support if her husband is imprisoned; the incident is not serious (ignoring the chronic nature that characterizes abusive relationships); and a person who assaults his wife is not a threat to society.

In proposing reforms, advocates for battered women first called for equal treatment in the court system, as they did with law enforcement. But, as with law enforcement, advocates have come to realize that both the history of the court response and the nature of the battering relationship require a differential response from the court system. This differential response should incorporate four components: two are similar to those that guide police policy, and two are practical steps.

Domestic Violence Is a Criminal Offense

The threshold of an effective court response is the unqualified acceptance by prosecutors and judges that domestic violence is a crime against both the victim and the state. Many factors contributed to the historic devaluation of domestic violence cases: they were riddled with evidentiary problems (the only witness was typically the complainant, except for possibly the children); the victim was reluctant to testify either because of fear or ambivalence; and, perhaps most important, society's attitude was that domestic violence is a family and private matter, not a criminal and public one, better resolved by social workers, clergy, or the family than by the courts. (This view was assumed to be held by the jury, and was indeed often held by the prosecutor, judge, and victim.)

As police policies on domestic violence improve, particularly investigatory procedures, evidentiary problems have diminished. And while many women are hesitant to press charges, the finding that "the probability of victim cooperation is in fact better predicted by the conduct of the prosecutor than by the conduct of either the victim or defendant" (Lerman, 1981) underscores the responsibility of prosecutors toward this particular group of victims and the powerful influence they have over such victims. Society's attitudes are the greatest hurdle to overcome, but legislative and regulatory changes and public education, combined with an increased number of women among the ranks of prosecutors and judges, are slowly shifting beliefs about family abuse.

One condition mitigating against judges considering domestic violence as a crime is that, in most states, a woman has a choice between civil and criminal relief in seeking an order of protection. Many women harbor reservations about proceeding in criminal court, particularly if it is the first time they have gone to court and/or if their partner has no criminal record. A woman's reluctance stems from some of the same factors that should have led courts to handle domestic cases differently than stranger cases: she may not want the source of her financial support and/or the father of her children incarcerated. Her reservations may also stem from fear of retaliation, fear of how she will be treated by the courts, or the hassle associated with the criminal court. Many victims feel that if a restraining order[5] achieved through a civil court could stop the abuse, it would be the best route (Pence, personal communication, March, 1989). Women who first go to civil court should have the backup option of criminal court if the violence continues or escalates. To make it work, however, prosecutors and judges need to understand that a woman's less aggressive first response should not be interpreted as a sign that the abuse is not criminal, it is instead a sign that the problem is ongoing and that the victim has taken serious steps to stop it.

The diversion of batterers to educational or counseling programs is another part of the court response, a response that may send a confusing message to the judge, prosecutor, victim, and batterer. Diversion programs for batterers are directly responsive to what many women are seeking from the criminal justice system—teaching the abuser alternatives to violence. However, programs for batterers may reinforce the view that domestic violence is a social issue rather than a criminal one. Research on the effectiveness of batterers programs in reducing subsequent violence has been inconclusive (Pirog-Good & Stets-Kealey, 1985).

(The Institute of Social Analysis has an evaluation underway that compares the behavior and attitudes of 100 men who are attending a 12-week, court-mandated, educational group with those of 100 men who are not referred to the group.)

Programs for batterers may have been readily embraced because they appear to address some troubling aspects of domestic cases: they respond to the woman's desire to have the violence stop without sending the abuser to jail; they are attractive to the judge and prosecutor because they are relatively easy dispositions to achieve; and they do not consume expensive jail resources (judges and prosecutors who are not fully convinced that domestic violence is a crime may more easily embrace batterers programs than jail sentences).

Although few domestic abuse cases currently go to trial,[6] as more do, other issues will emerge. For example, the appropriateness of judges inquiring during *voir dire* about a juror's attitude toward family abuse or about their own abuse history will need to be considered. Another factor for judges and jurors is whether the offender's history of abusing his partner can be introduced into evidence.

Because guilty pleas to felony counts or convictions on such charges are still rare for domestic cases, there is only a small body of research or experience to guide decisions regarding sentencing batterers to jail or probation, and making decisions about parole. However, it can be surmised that judges and probation officers are subject to the same conflicting forces that shape the response to domestic violence at earlier stages in the process.

Relieve Battered Women of the Prosecution Burden

Understanding the dynamics of battering leads to the recognition that requiring the woman to shoulder the responsibility of prosecution is counterproductive: it plays into her very fears and qualms about prosecuting. Thus, prosecutors with progressive policies have taken some of these decisions away from the battered woman by:

a) instituting policies that set guidelines for or stipulate under what conditions charges are filed. For example, San Diego's domestic violence protocol says, "Charge may be filed without victim cooperation if there is deemed to be sufficient independent corroboration of the crime to prove charges without the victim's full involvement" (Witt, 1988);

b) not requiring the victim to sign the complaint (the usual procedure for most crimes). This procedure has been adopted by many jurisdictions including Seattle, Denver, Boulder, Baltimore County, and San Diego;[7]

c) prohibiting the victim from dropping charges or requiring her first to receive counseling before dropping charges.[8] For example, Denver, Boulder, and Anchorage, which require the woman to cooperate, issue subpoenas for her to testify; and

d) not referring cases to mediation. Mediation, which is based on the assumption that both parties are culpable and are negotiating from an equal
power base, seems particularly inappropriate for a situation where a
man has violently assaulted a woman.

Taken together, these measures communicate to the victim as well as
the abuser[9] that the criminal justice system considers these cases criminal, that the state has an interest in prosecuting these cases regardless
of the victim's views, and that the victim is not responsible for how the
court responds to the batterer's actions.

Procedures and policies which deprive the victim of control over the
course of the case are not founded on a philosophy of equal treatment,
but rather "special" treatment. At the root of the victim movement was
the goal to give victims a voice in court proceedings and to encourage
prosecutors to consult with victims before proceeding with the case.
And, indeed, research showed that prosecutors were more likely in
cases where there was a prior relationship between victim and offender
to consult with the victim than in stranger cases, (Davis et al., 1980).
However, as a deeper understanding of domestic abuse is reached, it has
become evident, as it has with police policy, that the victim should not
be laden with the burden of stopping the violence; therefore, she should
not be responsible for how the case is prosecuted. The effectiveness of
prosecution policies that relieve the woman of decision-making is being
evaluated in Indianapolis through a controlled research study (Ford,
personal communication, February, 1989).

The extent to which the victim's desires should govern the process
raises issues at the heart of the special treatment controversy. Pressing
a woman to testify may be coercive and may be perceived as re-victim-
ization. The proposal that a battered woman should have less say than
other victims—that her influence on the criminal justice processing of
her case be limited—seems in direct contradiction to the domestic
violence movement's goal of empowering victims. But rather than send
the message that the victim is incompetent to make decisions, this
proposal of special treatment of battered women demonstrates the
court's understanding of the powerful intimidation that the victim of
domestic violence experiences from the offender.

Domestic Violence Advocates

Whereas advocates are desirable for all types of victims, they are
particularly needed for battered women because: (1) court processing

of domestic abuse cases are in flux in many jurisdictions; (2) domestic violence victims face more choices than "stranger" victims; (3) these victims have more reasons to be fearful or ambivalent about cooperating; and (4) they have been treated shabbily in the past. Advocates (not necessarily lawyers) who work as part of a prosecutor's office or for an independent organization can help the female victim by explaining the system, outlining her options, and advocating for her with the clerk, prosecutor, or judge. The advocate helps ensure that the system treats the case seriously, that the victim knows her rights, and that she understands why a certain process (such as a no-drop policy) has been instituted. The advocate also advises her about services and connects her with them.

Some junctures at which the battered woman needs specific guidance or advocacy are when to obtain a restraining order (should she pursue a case in criminal court or seek relief from a civil or family court); how to affect bail (should she press for high bail if the offender has a history of intimidating her and to ensure that the prosecutor and judge know about past incidents, particularly if the current offense is not the most brutal); whether to permit the offender to be diverted to a batterer's program instead of or in conjunction with a plea; and, in the rare cases that go to trial, whether to prepare a statement on the impact of the abuse on her for the probation officer, sentencing judge, and parole officer.

Services and Protection

Before the court system encourages a woman to come forward—report the crime to the police and cooperate with the prosecutor—it needs to assure her that if her husband/partner responds to her action with violence, the community will support and protect her with shelters or extra police patrols; enforce restraining orders, and impose severe sanctions if restraining orders are violated or the violence continues.[10] Without this type of assurance, the system is asking the woman to put herself at risk, usually considerably more so than the victim of a stranger crime because the batterer knows how to find her.

While some victims of non-domestic crimes are justifiably concerned that the defendant or his family may find and harm them, this is a haunting reality for most battered women. Because detainment of the offender (through high bail) is rare, the community needs to provide the victim access to information about whether the offender has been released; safe shelter for her and her children; an Order of Protection;

and such services as a change of locks, an unlisted phone number, and advocacy for job and school transfers. Other services that can encourage her to follow through are counseling, support groups, vocational and educational assistance, day care, and housing.

An excellent summary of the challenges the criminal justice system faces in responding to domestic violence was expressed by a city attorney:

> When I look back at how it used to be with battered women, I can see that it was a self-fulfilling prophecy. We'd file if she really wanted us to, but we knew that she'd want us to drop charges later . . . we may have even told her so. Then we sent her back home, often back to her abuser, without any support or protection at all. Sure enough, she wouldn't follow through and we'd think, 'It's always the same with these cases.' (Goolkasian, 1986.)

CONCLUSION

Past practices have left us with the bleak picture that nothing can be done to stop family abuse. The staggering, but probably conservative, statistics that indicate 2.1 million women are beaten each year (Bureau of Justice Statistics, 1984), 3,000 die and 20% of homicides are committed within the family (FBI Uniform Crime Reports, 1983) demand that law enforcement and criminal justice agencies develop special responses to domestic violence cases to counteract years of reverse practices.

Ironically, domestic violence may be more amenable to law enforcement and criminal justice intervention than most other crimes. It is ironic because domestic violence is a crime that has been avoided, devalued, and joked about by police, prosecutors, and judges. It is amenable because data and experience are showing that, unlike drug dealers, burglars, and muggers (criminals who are notorious recidivists), batterers may change their behavior in response to sanctions—warrants issued, arrests made, and jail time served. While the goals of sentencing—deterrence, rehabilitation, and retribution—elude the system for the most part, they appear attainable in domestic cases: offenders respond to arrests and jailing (specific deterrence), some abusers learn to be non-violent (rehabilitation), and the victim feels justice is done (retribution). Therefore, rather than perceiving domestic cases as a millstone, criminal justice practitioners should perhaps view family cases—if treated as a crime and handled with special procedures—as cases that can burnish their image, and show the promise, not the frailties, of the system.

NOTES

1. Although the authors recognize that men are sometimes abused by women, the most common set of events that the police and courts respond to are repeated assaults, threats, or harassment of a women by her male partner. Accordingly, in this chapter victims are referred to as female and abusers as male.

2. Connecticut, Iowa, Louisiana, Nevada, New Jersey, Oregon, Washington, and Wisconsin have passed legislation that mandates the police to arrest in all domestic violence cases. The enactment of mandatory arrest laws for domestic violence offenses (from 1977 through 1988) highlights the seriousness that state legislatures now ascribe to family violence crimes (Victim Services Agency, 1988).

3. A study of dual arrests occurring during the first ten months of Connecticut's mandatory arrest law found they fit into four categories: violence by both parties, use of self-defense, insufficient investigation, and false arrest (Epstein, 1987). Through training and policy directives, the Dallas Police Department reduced its dual arrest rate from 7% in September, 1987, to an average of 1.9% from November, 1987, through July, 1988, (City of Dallas Domestic Violence Task Force, *Annual Report*, 1988).

4. Some researchers have questioned this observation and cite the paucity of rigorous data to back up their skepticism (Mederer & Gelles, 1989).

5. Also called a stay away order, or an Order of Protection.

6. More common (or celebrated) than men on trial for battering their partners have been cases in which battered women are on trial as defendants because they have fought back and injured or killed their husband or lover.

7. Some states, such as New York, do not permit this.

8. In Kings County (New York), this procedure has reduced dismissals. A Victim Services Agency evaluation of the impact of case-by-case advocacy and the requirement that a woman talk to a counselor before dropping charges reduced the rate of cases dismissed because of complainant non-cooperation from 12% to 3% (1987).

9. It should be noted that judges can be particularly influential regarding batterers because batterers are often people who hold extraordinary respect for authority figures. The judge is perceived as a powerful figure who, according to their belief system, should be obeyed.

10. Although data as to whether or not going to court provokes more violence are scarce, there are anecdotal observations of women who further enrage the offender by taking such action.

REFERENCES

Attorney General's Task Force on Family Violence (1984). *Final Report*. Washington, DC: U. S. Department of Justice.

Breedlove, Kennish, Sandker, & Sawtell (1976). *Domestic violence and the police: Studies in Detroit and Kansas City*. Washington, DC: The Police Foundation.

Bureau of Justice Statistics (1984, April). *National crime survey*: (Family Violence, NCJ-93449). Rockville, MD: Author.

Carbondale Police Department Policy #88-03, issued February, 1988.

City of Dallas Domestic Violence Task Force (1988, September). *Annual Report*. Dallas, Texas.

Davis, R. C., Russel, V., & Kunreuther, F. (1980, July). *The role of the complaining witness in an urban criminal court*. New York: Vera Institute of Justice/Victim Services Agency.

Epstein, S. D. (1987, October). *The problem of dual arrest in family violence cases*. Prepared for the Connecticut Coalition Against Domestic Violence.

Ford, D. A. (1983, October). Wife battery and criminal justice: A study of victim decision-making. *Family Relations, 32*, 463-475.

Garner, J. H., & Visher, C. A. (1988, September/October). Policy experiments come of age. *NIJ Reports, 211*, 2-8. Washington, DC: National Institute of Justice.

Gayford, J. J. (1977). The plight of the battered wife. *Journal of Environmental Studies, 10*, 283-286.

Goolkasian, G. A. (1986). *Confronting domestic violence: A guide for criminal justice agencies*. Washington, DC: National Institute for Justice.

Langan, P. A., & Innes, C. A. (1986). Preventing domestic violence against women. *Bureau of Justice Statistics Special Report*. Washington, DC: U. S. Department of Justice.

Lerman, L. G. (1981). Criminal prosecution of wife beaters. *Response to Violence in the Family, 4*, 1-19.

Lincoln Police Department Policy #024044, issued June, 1986.

Mederer, H. J., & Gelles, R. J. (1989, March). Compassion or control: Intervention in cases of wife abuse. *Journal of Interpersonal Violence, 4*.

New York City Police Department Interim Order 17, issued March, 1988.

Pirog-Good, M., & Stets-Kealey, J. (1985, Summer). Male batterers and battering prevention programs: A national survey. *Response*.

Sherman, L., & Berk, R. A. (1984). *The Minneapolis domestic violence experiment*. Washington, DC: The Police Foundation.

Stamford Police Department Domestic Violence Policy, issued February, 1986.

U.S. Department of Justice (1983). *FBI uniform crime reports*. Washington, DC: Author.

Vera Institute of Justice (1977). *Felony arrests: Their prosecution and disposition in New York City's courts*. New York City: Author.

Victim Services Agency (1987, November 4). *Some preliminary findings of the family violence intervention project study*. Internal memo.

Victim Services Agency (1988, September). *A state by state guide to family violence legislation: The law enforcement response to family violence*. New York City: Author.

Witt, J. W. (1988, July 26). *City of San Diego Domestic Violence Prosecutions Bulletin, Appendix 2*. San Diego: Author.

CASES

Bruno v. Codd 47 N.Y.2d 582 (1979).
Scott v. Hurt C76-2395 WWS. Oakland, CA (1976).
Thomas v. Los Angeles (1979).
Thurman v. City of Torrington 595 F.Supp. 1521, USDC Conn. (1984).

Chapter 6

THE ADJUDICATION OF CHILD SEXUAL ABUSE CASES

BARBARA E. SMITH

The adjudication of child sexual abuse cases has had a profound effect on law enforcement, prosecutors, and our nation's criminal courts. It is a well accepted fact that investigating and prosecuting child sexual abuse cases is often a time-intensive and difficult task (Whitcomb, Shapiro, & Stellwagen, 1985, Goldstein, 1987; Smith, Bulkley, & Jackson, 1988). Although the sexual abuse of children is not new, the criminal justice system has been faced with large numbers of these cases only within the last two decades. Media and other reports of such abuse range from the more common cases of sexual abuse by parents and other family members to the more bizarre accounts of ritualistic abuse in out-of-home settings, such as the McMartin pre-school case in Manhattan Beach, California. As a result of increasing numbers of reports of child sexual abuse, the public and officials have been forced to deal with these cases. Child sexual abuse is no longer the hidden event it often was in the past (Bulkley, 1981; Boerma, 1985; Finkelhor, 1985; Goldstein, 1987; Toth & Whalen, 1987).

Child sexual abuse cases may be problematic from several perspectives. Previous research has provided evidence that child sexual abuse cases comprise a large proportion of both criminal and appellate court calendars and, as a result, they consume a large portion of very scarce criminal court resources. In addition, these cases are often traumatic for the children involved and their families thereby representing considerable human suffering. Substantial evidence supports the conclusion that they are difficult to prosecute successfully and problematic for sentencing judges. Such cases also often require special attention. Criminal courts have been confronted with the reexamination of basic due process tenets in responding to these cases, and a considerable evolution has occurred in recent years.

How has the criminal justice system coped with these cases, and how is the system likely to respond in the future? These are the key questions addressed in this chapter. Given the number of these cases and the proportion of resources consumed to adjudicate them, these are important questions for those concerned with criminal justice issues.

DIFFICULTIES IN ADJUDICATING
CHILD SEXUAL ABUSE CASES

It is well recognized that cases of child sexual abuse are difficult to adjudicate for criminal justice officials and are traumatic for the victims involved. Several, often interrelated, factors combine to make these cases problematic, including (1) the age of the victim, (2) the number of agencies potentially involved in the investigation, (3) the media attention generated by such cases, (4) the time involved to conduct a thorough investigation, and (5) the psychological and emotional trauma the victims may experience as a result of the investigation (Goodman, Golding, & Haith, 1984; Whitcomb et al., 1985; Boerma, 1985; Goldstein, 1987; Rockell, 1988).

It is important to consider that child sexual abuse, by definition, is abuse of children. Yet criminal court procedures were designed with adults in mind and are not amenable to the testimony of very young victims. An adversary system of confrontation may be especially confusing and frightening to young children, and there is evidence that jurors are less likely to give credence to testimony of young children (Goodman et al., 1984). Because child sexual abuse often occurs without witnesses and with limited physical evidence in many cases (especially cases of fondling without penetration), the child's testimony is often the only evidence available to prosecute the abuser. Indeed, "the need for the child victim's testimony in a sexual abuse case may be critical since the availability of other admissible evidence is often scarce, if not non-existent. The child, therefore, becomes the prosecutor's most valuable resource" (American Bar Association, National Legal Resource Center, 1983). But as a National Institute of Justice study argued, "children are not merely miniature adults," although the American justice system traditionally has treated them as such and expected them to perform as if they had the capabilities of adults (Whitcomb et al., 1985). Prosecutors, therefore, are often caught in a bind in which their only evidence is the child, who may not be found competent to testify or whose credibility will be seriously challenged by defense attorneys. As a result, they may be hesitant to file charges and anxious to plea-bargain these types of cases—practices that have sparked criticism by both the Attorney General's Task Force on Family Violence (1984) and the President's Task Force on Victims of Crime (1982).

Reports of child sexual abuse may trigger the intervention of a variety of agencies, including child protective agencies, law enforcement, the juvenile justice system, criminal courts, and the medical and mental health communities. The number of agencies involved may complicate the investigation and result in unnecessary, multiple, and traumatic interviews with the child victim (Goldstein, 1987). In addition to the potential harm to the child from countless number of interviewers, each of the various agencies have different goals, philosophies, rules, regulations, and staff, each with different abilities and expertise guiding its response. As a consequence, there is great potential for conflict, disagreement, overlap, general confusion, and contamination of the evidence.

Child sexual abuse cases, especially ones involving multiple victims and ritualistic and sadistic abuse, generate considerable media attention. Such attention excites the community and instills a sense of panic and frenzy, which often result in a call for quick conclusions and premature closure of investigations. This can hinder a thorough and professional response by criminal justice and social service officials.

Child sexual abuse investigations are often time consuming. Children, especially very young children and those abused by loved ones, are frequently reluctant to reveal the details of the abuse and are slow to trust other adults. Therefore, investigators need to spend considerable amounts of time with the child and allow the details of the abuse to emerge during the conduct of several interviews. This type of fact-finding usually results in time-intensive investigations (Boerma, 1985; Goldstein, 1987; Toth & Whalen, 1987).

Interviewing children about sexual abuse may prove very traumatic for the victim. Criminal justice officials are often forced to weigh the amount of trauma caused by the interview and courtroom testimony of children against the probable outcome of the case. This may result in a "bottom-line" determination by officials or the victim's parents as to whether it is worth putting the child through the strain of the criminal justice process. Concern about the potential trauma to the child may lead police and prosecutors, with the best of intentions, to shield the child from official action (Bulkley, 1985; Melton, 1981, Whitcomb et al., 1985).

There is, however, growing contrary evidence that children may not suffer as much trauma from testifying in court as was originally feared. In fact, some researchers and theorists have now suggested that such testimony may actually prove therapeutic for these victims by reassuring them that their accounts of the abuse are believable and that others do care that they were abused (Melton & Lind, 1982; Melton, 1983; Thibaut & Walker, 1978). But the evidence is still mixed, and police, prosecutors, and judges continue to be concerned about the effects of the criminal court process on children. This concern sometimes, or even often, translates into a reluctance to file formal charges or to take some cases to trial; such a concern is likely to remain a consideration in the future (Ginkowski, 1986).

As a consequence of the difficulties involved in prosecuting child sexual abuse cases, it was reported that over 90% of all child abuse cases are not prosecuted (Whitcomb et al., 1985). There is disagreement about whether prosecution is the best course of action. Finkelhor (1985) has noted that there is considerable disagreement about the wisdom of prosecuting such cases, with some arguing that prosecution only causes further damage to the child, while others contend that punitive action earmarked for the offender is necessary and beneficial for the child.

The feminist movement was instrumental in changing attitudes toward a variety of cases, including the prosecution of domestic violence cases, sexual assault cases, and child abuse cases. Courts have responded by prosecuting more of these cases in recent years. Attitudes are not changed easily, however, and there remains active and heated debate about how best to handle cases of child sexual abuse. Given these mixed messages, how are courts responding?

THE CRIMINAL JUSTICE SYSTEM'S CURRENT RESPONSE

Criminal courts today are facing cases of child sexual abuse in record numbers. There are no national statistics available on the proportion of child sexual abuse cases comprising criminal court dockets. Estimates are high. According to the American Prosecutor's Research Institute, these cases constitute a considerable part of prosecutors' caseloads initially, and they are increasing in number (personal communication with Patricia Toth, J.D. Director, National Center for the Prosecution of Child Abuse). In one large urban county—Los Angeles, California—the district attorney's office reported that one-third of its sex crimes involved child victims (Goldstein, 1987). Appellate courts are also grappling with the complexities of child sexual abuse cases in record numbers (Myers, 1987).

The response of the police. Police are increasingly being called upon to investigate allegations of child sexual abuse. How are they responding? Chapman and Smith (1988) examined the response of the police in two jurisdictions: Fairfax County, Virginia, and Santa Cruz, California. Completed police investigative reports were sampled in 106 child sexual abuse cases in Santa Cruz and 99 cases in Fairfax. "Founded" cases were those in which the investigating officer determined that the abuse had occurred. Even among these founded cases, the study found that only 51% of the cases resulted in the arrest of the abuser. Reasons for not arresting the perpetrator were varied, including insufficient evidence to prosecute, the victim was too young to qualify as a witness, the victim's parents refused to cooperate in prosecuting the case, the perpetrator's identity was unknown, and the perpetrator fled the jurisdiction. While many valid reasons may explain the lack of an arrest by the police, it is important to emphasize that no arrest was made in nearly half of the cases in which the police believed sexual abuse had occurred. This attrition continued as the cases proceeded to the prosecutor. Of the 51% of the cases in which an arrest occurred, the prosecutor rejected 13% of the cases (attrition between the arrest and prosecution stage was fairly minimal in these two jurisdictions because it was the policy for police to consult with prosecutors prior to an arrest and to arrest only when prosecution appears likely; still, 13% of the cases dropped out of the system at this stage).

The response of the criminal courts. How are criminal courts responding to the large number of child sexual abuse cases that fill their dockets? This issue was also addressed by Chapman and Smith in the 1988 study. In three jurisdictions, the response of the criminal justice system was compared to cases in which sexual abuse was alleged to have taken place against children rather than adults. The study grew out of a concern that the criminal justice system was responding less seriously to allegations of sexual abuse when the victim was a child than when the victim was an adult. Evidence was found to support that concern.

Criminal court outcomes in three selected counties were examined: Fairfax County, Virginia; Mercer County, New Jersey; and Santa Cruz County, California. In each of these three counties, information was extracted on a sample of all disposed sexual offense cases involving child and adult victims over a period of several years. In total, 296 completed felony sexual assault cases were examined: 55 child and 48 adult cases in Fairfax County, 52 child and 45 adult cases in Mercer County, and 52 child and 44 adult cases in Santa Cruz County.

The research found that those who sexually assaulted children either pled guilty or were found to be guilty about as often as those who sexually assaulted adults: 73% compared with 67%. However, those who were convicted of sexual abuse of children were incarcerated *less often* and for shorter periods of time than those who sexually abused adults. While 89% of those who assaulted adults received some incarceration, only 69% of those who assaulted children received jail or prison terms. Even more striking, child sexual abusers received considerably shorter periods of incarceration than those who targeted adults as their victims. Slightly over one third of the child sexual abusers were sentenced to five months or less and 10% received less than one month in jail. In sharp contrast, only 33% of those who sexually assaulted adults received sentences as short as one year or less, while almost 40% were given ten years or more of imprisonment.

Probation was used far more extensively for those who abused children as opposed to adults: 68% of those convicted of sex crimes against children were placed on probation, as compared with only 29% of those convicted of sex against adults. Orders of probation for child sexual offenders were frequently accompanied with a condition that the offender receive some counseling or therapy: 48% of the child offenders were given such orders compared with just 13% of the adult sexual offenders (Chapman & Smith, 1988).

One explanation for the sentencing disparities between those convicted of sex crimes against children as opposed to adults lies in the nature of the relationship between the defendants and the victims. Most of the child sexual abusers knew their victims in the cases sampled for study. Only 12% of the child victim cases involved strangers, compared with almost 50% of the cases involving adult victims. In addition, in most of the child cases, the abuser was either a parent or step-parent, whereas for adult victims, the relationship was more often a fairly distant one, such as a friend or acquaintance. Therefore, some of the sentencing disparities may have resulted more from the nature of the relationship than from the fact that the victim was a child. Other studies have found that courts sentence defendants who are related to their victims less severely than those who victimize strangers (Smith, 1983; Vera Institute of Justice, 1977). However, there were too few cases in the sample of stranger molestation of children to statistically document the effects of relationship on sentences. Further research is needed with a larger number of cases to accurately assess whether relationship explains the differences found in the study or whether the age of the victim is the most salient factor.

In summary, research has found that those who chose children as their victims in sexual assault crimes were less often sentenced to periods of incarceration, were less often given long periods of incarceration, and were more often placed on probation with the condition that they receive counseling or treatment in the three counties studied. Whether this trend would apply to other counties remains untested. But it appears courts are responding differently to child sexual abuse cases than to adult sexual assault cases in terms of sentences. What else are they doing differently? A major response to these cases has been the establishment of innovative and "special" techniques designed to improve the handling of child sexual abuse cases by the criminal justice system and to reduce the trauma on the child. We now turn to a discussion of this response.

INNOVATIONS IN THE
CRIMINAL JUSTICE SYSTEM'S RESPONSE

To improve the processing of child sexual abuse cases and reduce the trauma to the victim, jurisdictions across the country have experimented with innovative approaches and techniques. The extent to which these innovations intrude upon and alter the traditional processing of criminal cases varies. Less obtrusive "special" techniques, such as improved interviewing skills, have sparked less controversy, but as the reforms become more intrusive, so have the defense challenges.

One of the most comprehensive responses—and one of the most highly endorsed innovations advocated by many experts in the field—is the use of interdisciplinary teams to investigate cases of alleged sexual abuse. The American Bar Association's *Guidelines for the Fair Treatment of Child Witnesses* (1985) recommended that multidisciplinary teams, including the prosecutor, police, and social service resource personnel, be utilized in the investigation and prosecution of all child abuse cases in order to reduce the number of interviews with the child.

This idea has been widely supported by many practitioners in the field as an effective strategy for combining resources in these cases, eliminating overlap, and reducing trauma to the child; at the same time, it does not take away basic due process rights of defendants (see, for example, Goldstein, 1987; Ginkowski, 1986; Schmitt, 1978; Whitcomb et al., 1985; Rockell, 1988; Laszlo & Romano, 1989).

Multidisciplinary teams sometimes also employ other "special" techniques, such as the use of anatomically correct dolls and drawings, videotaping, and the altering of the courtroom environment (e.g., using screens, closing the courtroom to observers, and allowing the child to testify in the judge's chambers). Before discussing these special techniques, we consider the interdisciplinary team approach and its effect on the response of criminal justice officials.

Joint investigations of child sexual abuse. In a recently completed study, Smith et al. (1988) examined four sites that use a coordinated multidisciplinary approach to respond to reports of child sexual abuse. Based on a total of 46 interviews with police, prosecutors, and child protective workers in the four sites, the rationale and the nature of the joint response to these cases as they impact on case processing were explored. While each of the four sites in the study employed some type of joint multidisciplinary response, the dynamics and the nature of that response varied. Before discussing some of the common experiences of these jurisdictions, a brief description of the coordinated response in each of the sites is presented. The sites included Denver, Colorado; Greenville, South Carolina; Montgomery County, Maryland; and Nashville, Tennessee.

In Denver, Colorado, when a report of child sexual abuse is received by either the police or the child protective service agency, one immediately notifies the other and arranges to conduct a joint interview with the child. After the initial joint interview, the police and child protective worker each conduct their own investigation. Throughout their investigation, the police and child protective worker continue to provide feedback to each other on their progress. A prosecutor from the sexual abuse unit goes to the police station daily to consult with officers on ongoing investigations of child sexual abuse cases to determine whether to file criminal charges.

In Greenville, South Carolina, by law, all cases of child abuse (sexual as well as physical) reported to either the police or the child protective service agency are cross-reported to the other agency within 24 hours. Usually the initial interview with the child is conducted jointly by the police and the child protective service worker. Police and child protective service staff share case progress information with one another during team meetings (also at the team meetings are representatives from the victim witness program, guardian *ad litems*, and mental health professionals). At these meetings, key case decisions are discussed, including the decision as to whether to file criminal charges, and a consensus is reached by majority vote.

In Montgomery County, all child sexual abuse cases are jointly investigated by the child protective service agency and the Montgomery County Police Department. By Maryland law, joint reporting between the police and the child protective service agency is mandated. Montgomery County has gone one step further by requiring a joint initial interview with the child by the police and the child protective worker. After the initial interview, however, there is little interaction between the two agencies.

In Nashville, as in all of Tennessee, state law mandates that a team be established to respond to all cases of child sexual abuse and serious physical abuse. The team must have a representative from the police, the prosecutor's office, the child protective service agency, the victim witness program, and the mental health community. After any agency receives a report of sexual or serious physical abuse, the other team members are notified within 24 hours. A joint interview between the police and the child protective service agency is supposed to be scheduled, but there is a shortage of officers assigned to the police child abuse unit in Nashville. As a result, the child protective worker often does the initial interview alone, and the police are called out to interview the child if the case is founded. This second interview is a joint interview between the police and the child protective worker assigned to the case. Each week, the team meets to discuss new cases and recent developments in ongoing cases. A vote is taken as to whether to arrest and prosecute the offender and whether counseling is indicated: the majority vote rules.

In each of the four sites, 46 staff from the child protective service agency, the police, and the prosecutor's office were interviewed about the rationale for responding to child sexual abuse reports with a coordinated system and the advantages and disadvantages of using a coordinated response. Everyone interviewed concurred that the primary rationales were to save the child victim from unnecessary multiple interviews and to share skills and resources in responding to these often difficult cases. Not one person interviewed advocated that a unilateral response from just one agency would be the preferable method. However, many respondents did point out that while a coordinated response was ideally the best possible way to handle child abuse cases, it has difficulties and problems associated with it. When it works well, the child and his/her family are spared undue numbers of interviews, and the investigation benefits from bringing together professionals with different skills, training, knowledge, and resources. When it breaks down, however, the investigation is jeopardized and the child's needs are not adequately served. How can jurisdictions guard against this type of breakdown and make the coordinated system function smoothly? Respondents were asked to address this question in terms of which agencies should be involved, how extensively they should coordinate their response, how a coordinated response can be established, and how to maintain a coordinated system.

Which agencies should be involved in a coordinated system? The answer depends on state laws and local policies. State legislation usually mandates which agency in the state is responsible for investigating child sexual abuse. Local policies may further define the roles and responsibilities of the various agencies involved. Who may be included in a coordinated response is dictated by this legislation and those policies. In addition to the legal constraints dictating which agencies may be involved in a coordinated response system, policies of local agencies and the philosophies of those who set those policies will affect which agencies participate in a coordinated response. It may only be feasible, or desirable, in some localities to include two agencies in a coordinated response, or several agencies may be involved. For example, in Montgomery County, the joint response is between the police and the child protective service agency and involves primarily an initial joint interview, followed by straight investigations. In contrast, in Nashville, the team is more broadly comprised of law enforcement, the prosecutor, the child protective service agency, the victim witness program, and the mental health community. Key decisions are reached by majority vote of the team members, each of whom has an equal vote regarding the arrest and prosecution of the offender, and the counseling service recommended for the child.

Sites may choose to coordinate the initial interview with the child only and then proceed with largely independent investigations, or they may select to respond with a joint team approach, which begins with the initial investigation and continues until the case is disposed. This too will depend in part on local policies and practices and state laws regarding reporting, investigation, and the confidentiality of that investigation.

How can sites develop a coordinated response to child sexual abuse cases? Approaches vary from the most formal system wherein the joint response is mandated by law, to the most informal system wherein the joint response is mandated only by unwritten policy. Among the four sites studied, Nashville had the most formalized system, with the team approach being dictated by state-wide legislation. In contrast, Greenville had the most informal system, with the coordination established among the agencies by unwritten policies. Denver and Montgomery County fell in between the two approaches. They have written procedures and/or protocols that defined the nature of the coordinated response.

Once a site establishes a coordinated system, how can it make the system work smoothly? Without exception, the 46 practitioners interviewed reported that it requires *constant* work and attention. It is not something to be set up once and then ignored, nor should sites expect that the system will always work smoothly. The keys to maintaining a viable coordinated system, according to those we interviewed, were simply good commonsense guides to making any interaction between two agencies work effectively. The following suggestions were made by those interviewed.

1. *Maintain open communication.* It was stressed that staff members between the agencies openly discuss differences of opinion while trying to understand the perspective of other agencies within the system. Any problem areas should be brought to the attention of supervisory staff and early action undertaken to clear up misunderstandings because these conflicts will only worsen over time if they are not resolved.

2. *Conduct joint training.* As a means of establishing good communication, many of our respondents discussed the value of conducting joint training for staff among those agencies participating in the coordinated system. Joint training was cited as an excellent way to build rapport, while at the same time educating one another on their various roles and responsibilities. The need to clearly define roles and responsibilities of the staff involved from the various agencies was frequently mentioned by those we interviewed. Joint training can be very helpful in addressing that need.

3. *Conduct interagency staff retreats.* Several of the sites in our case studies hold interagency staff retreats on an annual basis. Like joint training retreats can serve to build rapport and trust among staff from the various agencies.

4. *Conduct regular interagency meetings.* All of the sites had institutionalized some type of regular meetings for staff from the various agencies to discuss issues of mutual concern. Most respondents reported that the more frequent the meeting schedule and the more staff involved, the better it was for maintaining a smoothly operating coordinated system.

5. *Establishing specialized units.* All four of the sites had established specialized units in the child protective service agency, the police, and the prosecutor's office to respond to child sexual abuse cases. One of the benefits of specialization is that staff receive special training on handling these kinds of cases. Another important benefit is that the specialization had resulted in relatively few numbers of individuals in each agency being responsible for responding to these cases. This allowed the staff from the various agencies to know each other well; in most instances, it led them to trust the responses of the others. Of course, if personality conflicts among the small number of staff arise, this could be disadvantageous, but such conflicts had not occurred among the four sites studied.

6. *Balance the number of staff among the coordinated agencies.* Because a coordinated response requires the staff of two or more agencies to communicate with one another and to conduct some type of joint investigation, it is important that the agencies involved have comparable number of staff. Otherwise, coordination and scheduling interviews together may prove very difficult.

7. *Exercise patience.* A constant theme emerging during the interviews with staff in the four sites was that a coordinated response takes patience and understanding. All of the respondents were quick to note that their coordinated system is by no means perfect, nor does it work smoothly all of the time. But they were also quick to add that there is really no other choice. Child sexual abuse cases involve a number of agencies and are often complicated to investigate. The seriousness of the abuse and the gravity of the consequences for the victim and other potential victims requires agencies to work together.

In summary, coordinated multidisciplinary team approaches to child sexual abuse have been implemented in some jurisdictions to improve the response of the criminal justice and child protective service systems to reports of child sexual abuse. From the experiences of practitioners operating in such systems, such approaches appear to hold substantial promise, but their ultimate effectiveness in reducing the trauma for the child victim and increasing the effectiveness of the police, prosecutors, and the courts remains to be empirically tested.

The use of "special" techniques. As discussed earlier, child sexual abuse cases may prove difficult to prosecute for a variety of reasons, including the age of the victim, the number of agencies involved, the media attention generated by such cases, the time-consuming nature of the investigations, and the trauma caused to the child victim. Recognizing that criminal courts may be especially intimidating for young children and designed in light of the capabilities of adults to testify, the criminal justice system in recent years has responded by modifying some aspects of traditional case processing. One innovation has just been discussed: the use of coordinated multidisciplinary teams responsible for investigating child sexual abuse cases. Coupled with, or isolated from, this joint response are "special" interviewing and cross-examination procedures designed to reduce the trauma to children and to elicit more detailed accounts of the alleged abuse. These techniques include the use of videotape for investigative and court hearings; the use of drawings and/or anatomical dolls for investigation and courtroom testimony; the use of closed circuit television; the limitations of confrontation of defense attorneys through the redesign of the courtroom and the use of such devices as screens to shield the victim from the defendant and closing the courtroom to spectators; hearsay exceptions; the use of expert witnesses, and expedited case processing (Whitcomb et al., 1985; Toth & Whalen, 1987).

The most recent study to examine legislation regarding the use of special techniques by criminal courts was a 1985 study by Whitcomb et al. They found the following, as of 1985 (other states have undoubtedly enacted or modified their legislation since):

- Twenty states had laws that excluded some observers from the courtroom while child sexual abuse victims were testifying.
- Nine states had statutorily enacted a special hearsay exception in child sexual abuse cases. Twenty states ruled that all persons are competent if they meet the standard in Federal Rule 601; 13 states presume that all persons are competent, as long as they can understand the oath and their obligation to testify truthfully; 13 states have ruled that a child over the age of 10 is presumed competent to testify; five states have declared a child is competent to testify if he or she understands his or her responsibility to testify truthfully, and 5 states use the common law standard, which holds that a child over 14 is presumed competent to testify.
- Several states have ruled on the use of videotape testimony. Eleven states mandate that the defendant be present during the taping; six states require that the defendant be allowed to cross-examine the child when videotape testimony is introduced; two states necessitate that the videotape testimony

be administered under the Rules of Evidence, and eight states require that videotapes only be used under limited specified circumstances.

- Closed-circuit television and expedited case processing had been authorized in only three states.

The use of these special techniques, however, has been the subject of considerable concern in regard to their potential interference with the due process rights of defendants and has received significant attention by the courts. There is concern that these techniques are easing the burden on child victims by taking away the basic rights of defendants. Constitutional challenges to their use have been, and are currently being, brought in appellate courts around the country and in the U.S. Supreme Court. Their future use will be an important development to monitor. (For a discussion of the constitutional challenges to these cases, see Myers, 1987.)

THE FUTURE OF THE
CRIMINAL JUSTICE SYSTEM'S RESPONSE

Police, prosecutors, and judges are becoming more involved in the processing of child sexual abuse cases. Two decades ago, it was rare to see a child sexual abuse case on our nation's criminal court dockets. Things have changed dramatically. More cases are entering the criminal courts, but research findings suggest that courts are adjudicating these cases by accepting minor misdemeanor pleas and bestowing sentences that rely heavily on the use of probation conditioned on the abuser receiving treatment. The wisdom of such pleas and sentences depends largely on the effectiveness of available treatment programs for child sexual abusers. Unfortunately, little is known about their effectiveness or the ability of a probation department to effectively monitor child sexual abusers.

Criminal justice officials have responded to the special problems posed by child sexual abuse cases by modifying traditional investigative and prosecution techniques. Multidisciplinary team approaches have been developed to improve the response of the criminal justice and social service systems and are operating in many jurisdictions. Special techniques to help these systems respond better to these cases and their child victims are being tried, and much has been accomplished to make the system more sensitive to the needs of children and their ability to function in an adversary justice system. However, there are serious limitations as to how far the system can go to accommodate the special needs of child sexual abuse victims. Important due process issues are likely to limit the practice of at least some techniques that might reduce the trauma to the child because of sometimes competing concerns about the protection of basic constitutional rights of the defendant. Courts are likely to move cautiously and conservatively in changing traditional processing. While this is essential in protecting a defendant's rights, it may prove to be a major obstacle to rendering the system maximally responsive to the needs of child victims. Therefore, child sexual abuse cases, especially those involving very young victims, will likely continue to be difficult to adjudicate.

REFERENCES

American Bar Association (1985). *Guidelines for the fair treatment of child witnesses in cases where child abuse is alleged.* Washington, DC.

Attorney General's Task Force on Family Violence (1984). *Final Report.*

Boerma, L. S. (1985). In J. Bulkley (Ed.). *Papers from a national policy conference on legal reforms in child sexual abuse cases.* Washington, DC: National Legal Resource Center for Child Advocacy and Protection, American Bar Association.

Bulkley, J. (Ed.). (1981). *Innovations in the prosecution of child sexual abuse cases.* Washington, DC: National Legal Resource Center for Child Advocacy and Protection, American Bar Association.

Bulkley, J. (1985). *State legislative reform efforts and suggested future policy directions to improve legal intervention in child sexual abuse cases.* Washington, DC: National Legal Resource Center for Child Advocacy and Protection, American Bar Association.

Chapman, J., & Smith, B. (1988). *Child sexual abuse: An analysis of case processing.* Washington, DC: Criminal Justice Section, American Bar Association.

Ginkowski, R. (1986). The abused child: The prosecutor's terrifying nightmare. *Criminal Justice Magazine,* American Bar Association, *1*(1), 30-45.

Goldstein, S. L. (1987). *The sexual exploitation of children: A practical guide to assessment, investigation and intervention.* New York: Elsevier.

Goodman, G. S., Golding, J. M., & Haith, H. H. (1984). Jurors' reactions to child witnesses. *Journal of Social Issues, 40*(2), 139-156.

Laszlo, A. T., & Romano, L. J. (1989). *Child sexual assault: Confronting the crisis (Vol. 2). A trainers' guide for multidisciplinary team investigations of child sexual assault in out-of-home care setting.* Alexandria, VA: National Sheriffs' Association.

Melton, G. B. (1981). Children's competency to testify. *Law and Human Behavior, 5,* 73-85.

Melton, G. B. (1983). Decision making by children: Psychological risks and benefits. In G. B. Melton, G. P. Koocher, & M. J. Saks (Eds.), *Children's competence to consent* (pp. 21-40). New York: Plenum Press.

Melton, G. B., & Lind, E. A. (1982). Procedural justice in family court: Does the adversary model make sense? In G. B. Melton (Ed.), *Legal reforms affecting child and youth services* (pp. 64-83). New York: Haworth Press.

Myers, J. E. B. (1987). *Child witness law and practice*. New York: John Wiley and Sons.

President's Task Force on Victims of Crime (1982). *Final Report*.

Rockwell, B. A. (1988). *The investigation and prosecution of crimes against children in New York State*. Office of Justice Systems Analysis, New York State Division of Justice Services.

Schmitt, B. D. (1978). *The child protection team handbook*. New York: Garland and STPM Press.

Smith, B. E. (1983). *Non-stranger violence: The criminal courts' response*. U.S. Department of Justice: The National Institute of Justice.

Smith, B. E., Bulkley, J., & Jackson, J. A. (1988). *Improving the coordinated response of agencies to child abuse in out-of-home care settings*. Washington, DC: Criminal Justice Section, American Bar Association.

Thibaut, J., & Walker, L. (1978). A theory of procedure. *California Law Review, 66*, 541-566.

Toth, P. A., & Whalen, W. P. (1987), Eds., *Investigation and prosecution of child abuse*. Alexandria, VA: American Prosecutors Research Institute.

Vera Institute of Justice (1977). *Felony arrests: prosecution and disposition in New York City's courts*. New York: Vera Institute of Justice.

Whitcomb, D., Shapiro, E. R., & Stellwagen, L. D. (1985). *When the victim is a child*. Washington, DC: U.S. Department of Justice.

Chapter 7

FAMILIES AND FRIENDS
Indirect Victimization by Crime

DAVID S. RIGGS
DEAN G. KILPATRICK

During the past few years, the legal and mental health professions have begun to examine and respond to the needs of crime victims. It appears that people who are emotionally close to the victims of crime also experience problems as a result of the incident. These "indirect victims" of crime appear to experience difficulties and symptoms similar to those of the direct victims. This chapter will discuss the phenomenon of indirect victimization, summarize the data available on the problems of indirect victims, and discuss theoretical and practical reasons why indirect victimization may lead to psychological difficulties.

PSYCHOLOGICAL DISTRESS AMONG THE VICTIMS OF CRIME

The National Crime Survey (NCS) estimates that there were approximately 35 million criminal victimizations during 1986. This figure represents almost 6 million violent crimes, including over 20,000 murders. The monetary cost of these crimes totals well over 10 billion dollars. The emotional toll of criminal victimization has only lately become the topic of research (see Lurigio & Resick, this volume; Resick, this volume).

Recently, there has been an increased awareness of the psychological and emotional impact of crime (American Psychological Association Task Force on Victims of Crime and Violence, 1984; Attorney General's

Task Force on Family Violence, 1984; Frieze, Hymer, & Greenberg, 1987; President's Task Force on Victims of Crime, 1982). Frieze, Hymer, and Greenberg provided a summary of the problems experienced by the victims of crime. They report that victims experience problems that can be categorized loosely as immediate, short term, and long term in nature. The immediate reactions include shock, denial, anxiety, anger, depression, and feelings of vulnerability. These symptoms usually last for a period of hours to days. In the weeks and months that follow a criminal act the victims may experience mood swings, variously feeling fearful, angry, sad, or elated. Victims often experience guilt, loss of self-esteem, vulnerability, anxiety, and depression, and they may reexperience the traumatic event in the form of nightmares or flashbacks. During this period, victims often report increased fears of being alone or abandoned, as well as concern that the traumatic event will occur again. Although most of these symptoms dissipate over time, many victims appear to suffer long-term reactions, including low self-esteem, depression, anxiety, and difficulties in intimate relationships.

While much of the work examining the psychological functioning of crime victims has focused on rape and sexual assault victims, there are indications that other types of criminal victimization may lead to psychological distress (Kilpatrick, Saunders, Veronen, Best, & Von, 1987). Over 75% of the 391 women in the above-mentioned Kilpatrick et al. study had been victims of crime, and the average time since the last criminal victimization was 15 years. Criminal victimization was associated with increased psychological distress and symptomatology. Of 295 women who had experienced a criminal victimization, almost 28% had evidenced symptoms of Post-Traumatic Stress Disorder (PTSD) at some time since the crime. Nearly 10% of the victims were experiencing symptoms of the disorder at the time of the assessment. Further, psychological distress and PTSD could be found among victims of each type of crime identified (i.e., sexual assault, aggravated assault, robbery, and burglary). Further analyses with this sample (Kilpatrick, Saunders, Amick-McMullan, Best, Veronen, & Resnick, 1989) suggested that PTSD is more common among victims of a completed rape, victims who perceived a threat to their lives, and victims who suffered a physical injury as a result of the crime. Although few studies to date have examined the association of various types of criminal victimization with psychological distress, it appears that the experience of any criminal victimization may result in such distress.

INDIRECT VICTIMS OF CRIME

Surviving Family Members of Homicide Victims

In recent years, researchers have begun to study the impact of criminal victimization on individuals who do not experience the crime directly, but who are close to the person who is victimized. Most of this research has focused on two particular groups: family members of homicide victims and intimate partners of rape victims.

It has long been believed that the families of homicide victims suffer as a result of the victim's death. Until recently, the focus of the problem has been on the stress resulting from the loss of a family member and the grief associated with such a loss (Burgess, 1975; Doyle, 1980). These issues are clearly important, but additional factors, which have been neglected, are also related to the loss of a loved one to criminal victimization. The experience of a traumatic event, such as a crime, may have an impact beyond that of the grief associated with death. Recent evidence suggests that the surviving family members experience problems similar to those experienced by crime victims in general (Amick-McMullan, Kilpatrick, Veronen, & Smith, 1989; Amick-McMullan, Kilpatrick, & Resnick, 1988; Amick, Kilpatrick, Resnick, & Saunders, 1989).

Burgess (1975) described a two-stage model of response to homicide that she termed the Homicide Trauma Syndrome. Phase One was characterized by grief and preoccupation with details of the death, funeral plans, and the police investigation. Phase Two involved reorganization, bereavement, and coping. Survivor reactions differed from typical grief responses in that horror, rage, desire for revenge, and fear were present. Bowman (1980) and Doyle (1980) also reported that homicide survivors experienced feelings of fear, anger, and vengefulness that differed from normal bereavement. All three (Bowman, Burgess, and Doyle) found that extensive contact with the criminal justice system interfered with the reorganization process.

Poussaint (1984) examined the reactions to homicide among ten low-socioeconomic status minority families. He reported responses, such as rage, desire for revenge, and terror, among the family members. He also noted that heightened levels of anxiety were present at later stages of the grieving process. Finally, he suggested that the normal grieving process was impeded by the continued and prolonged involvement with the criminal justice system.

Shanfield and Swain (1984) administered the SCL-90-R, a brief assessment instrument used to identify psychological symptoms, and the Beck Depression Inventory to the parents of adults killed in traffic accidents. They reported that the survivors showed intense grieving and elevated levels of psychiatric symptoms. Similarly, Lehman, Wortman, and Williams (1987) reported that the spouses of victims of automobile accidents were more depressed, reported more psychiatric symptoms, and had more difficulties in social functioning when compared to a control group that was matched for age, sex, income, education, and number and ages of children. The parents of children killed in a motor vehicle accident showed, but less pervasive, difficulties in comparison to a matched control group.

In a small sample (N = 19) of homicide survivors, Amick-McMullan and her colleagues (Amick-McMullan, Kilpatrick, & Veronen, 1989) found high frequencies of intrusive thoughts and feelings related to the homicide. Indirect victims also reported attempts to avoid cues associated with the homicide. A majority (64%) of the sample had at least two elevated scales on the SCL-90. They were most likely to have elevated scores on the depression, anxiety, somatization, and phobic anxiety scales of the SCL-90. The survivors' anxiety and depression scores, as well as a total symptom score from the SCL-90, were correlated negatively with the survivors' satisfaction with their treatment within the criminal justice system. Specifically, about two-thirds of the variance in current symptoms was accounted for by one question that assessed the family member's level of satisfaction with the justice system.

Many of the existing studies in the area of indirect victimization suffer from methodological problems similar to those found in studies of criminal victimization in general (see Kilpatrick et al., 1987). One problem is the procedure used to obtain the samples for the studies. Most of the studies regarding surviving family members of homicide relied on clinical referrals (e.g., Burgess, 1975; Poussaint, 1984) or victim service agencies (e.g., Getzel & Masters, 1984) as a source of subjects. This is problematic because researchers found that many victims of crime do not seek help from health care or victims service agencies (Kilpatrick et al., 1987; Skogan, 1981; Sparks, 1982). The resulting samples are not likely to be representative of the total population of indirect crime victims. In addition, most of the studies used small samples of subjects, further limiting the generalizability of the results. Much of the research also is hampered by the lack of standardized assessment tools (see Kilpatrick et al., 1989; Veronen, Saunders,

& Resnick, 1988). Finally, few of the existing studies used non-victimized comparison groups (Lurigio & Rosenbaum, in press).

A more recent project, funded by the National Institute of Justice (Kilpatrick & Amick-McMullan, 1987), gathered data about the prevalence of indirect victimization due to the homicide death of a family member or close friend among a national probability sample of adults (age 18 or older) in the United States. Data were collected via a random digit-dialing telephone survey conducted by a national survey research firm. In the first stage of the project, 12,500 respondents were screened for incidents of either criminal homicide or alcohol-related vehicular homicide. Screening indicated that 2.8% of the sample were immediate family members of either criminal homicide (1.6%) or alcohol-related vehicular homicide (1.2%) victims. Another 3.7% of the sample were distant relatives of homicide victims, and 2.7% said that they lost close friends to homicide. Overall, 9.3% of the sample was comprised of either family members, more distant relatives, or close friends of homicide victims. These researchers estimated that about 5 million adults are family members of homicide victims, about 6.6 million have lost other relatives, and about 4.8 million have lost close friends to homicide (Amick et al., 1989). Of these, 6.7 million have lost family members, other relatives, or close friends to criminal homicide, while 9.7 million lost someone due to alcohol-related vehicular homicide (Amick et al.).

The second stage of the Kilpatrick and Amick-McMullan (1987) project gathered information about the experience of surviving family members with the criminal justice system and the psychological impact of the homicide. Overall, 23.4% of all family member survivors met the DSM-III-R criteria for homicide-related PTSD at some time following the death. Over 40% met diagnostic criteria for at least one aspect of PTSD (i.e., reexperiencing, avoidance, or arousal). Even though, on the average, these homicides occurred more than ten years prior to the time of the assessment, 5.1% of the family member survivors met full PTSD criteria within the six weeks prior to their assessment in the study (Amick et al., 1989). Over 20% of those surveyed had experienced some PTSD symptoms during the last six weeks. With respect to current PTSD symptoms, 3.3% of the survivors met the full diagnostic criteria, and 18.7% reported some PTSD symptoms. There were no differences in the rates of PTSD symptoms between the criminal homicide and alcohol-related vehicular homicide survivors. From these figures, the authors concluded that over 1.1 million adults have developed PTSD following the homicide of a family member, and about 165,000 have homicide-related PTSD at the time of this writing (Amick et al.).

Partners of Rape Victims

The second form of indirect victimization that has received empirical attention is the impact of rape on the intimate partners of the victims. Two effects of rape on the victim's partners have been examined: the impact of the victimization on the relationship between victims and their intimate partners, and the psychological functioning of the partners themselves. Stone (1980) studied seven partners of rape victims. These men described feelings of powerlessness, vulnerability, anger, and guilt. They also reported feeling that they had failed to protect their partners, suggesting a lowered sense of self-worth and self-esteem. Guilt over this failure appears to lead to withdrawal from the victimized partner. All of the men in the Stone sample reported intrusive thoughts related to the attack. In addition, they reported a number of relationship difficulties following the rape, including communication problems and the fear that they would remind their partners of the attack. This fear appears to contribute to difficulties in the expression of affection and sexual interactions.

Miller, Williams, and Bernstein (1982) studied the marital and sexual adjustment of 43 rape victims and their partners. Nearly 60% of the sample experienced major to moderate maladjustment following the rape, while only 28% of the couples were exhibiting moderately good to very good adjustment. As in the Stone (1980) study, the couples reported problems with communication, concerns about sexual interactions, and difficulties with the expression of emotion, including control of anger. Although these studies suffer from some methodological problems, they suggest that rape can have a considerable impact on the psychological functioning of the partners of the victims.

Holmstrom and Burgess (1979) describe a two-stage reaction based on their study of 16 couples. Initially, the partners experience such feelings as disbelief, concern, anger, shame, guilt, and betrayal that are similar to those described by Stone (1980). Following this, the couple begins to cope more constructively with the trauma through a more open discussion of the assault and the victim's fears. There is some indication that the person's reaction may have an effect on the victim's ability to adjust following the assault (McCahill, Meyer, & Fischman, 1979; Ruch & Chandler, 1983).

A more recent investigation, conducted by Veronen and Saunders (1985), compared victims of rape and their partners to a comparison group of non-assaulted women and their partners. The groups were matched for age, race, neighborhood of residence, relationship status, and length of relationship. Victims, their partners, and control group participants were assessed several times during the year following the rape. The groups of men were compared on a number of self-report measures to assess symptoms of psychopathology, fear, and PTSD, as well as a variety of couple functioning measures. Partners of rape victims scored worse than the partner comparison group on measures of psychological symptoms, including interpersonal sensitivity, depression, anxiety, and hostility (Veronen, Saunders, & Resnick, 1988). Differences were found throughout the first year following the rape. Structured diagnostic interviews conducted within one year after the rapes with a small subset (N = 9) of the sample found that partners of rape victims experienced symptoms of PTSD (Resnick, Veronen, & Saunders, 1988). Also, the symptoms of PTSD among the partners were correlated with symptoms of the victims. Preliminary analyses of the couple functioning data (Veronen & Saunders, 1988) suggested that the experience of rape has a significant detrimental effect on the relationships of a substantial subset of the sample, and this effect appears approximately six months after the rape. Communication between the partners was most disrupted by the rape, although feelings of commitment and emotional cohesion were also negatively affected (Veronen & Saunders).

The impact of other types of criminal victimization on the psychological functioning of those close to victims has not been examined. However, the existing literature indicates that one could also expect to find increased levels of distress among these indirect victims. Kilpatrick et al. (1988) found that criminal victimization of any type may lead to increased levels of distress to indirect victims. There are a number of practical and theoretical explanations as to why indirect victimization of any type may lead to psychological stress and symptomatology.

THEORETICAL MODELS FOR
THE EFFECT OF CRIME ON INDIRECT VICTIMS

Criminal victimization is clearly stressful and often quite traumatic. It is not surprising that crime victims experience psychological distress and symptoms. The processes through which indirect victims develop such problems are more difficult to elucidate because such victims do not experience directly the trauma and stress associated with the criminal act. There are three major theoretical perspectives, however, that may help explain the process through which indirect victims of crime may develop psychological problems: grief theory, attribution theory, and stress and social learning theory.

Grief Theory. Grief theory is most applicable to the indirect victims of homicide as it describes the emotional and behavioral reactions to the death of someone to whom the survivor is emotionally attached. Theorists (e.g., Bowlby, 1980; Lindermann, 1965; Parkes, 1972) identified stages through which people pass as they grieve a loss. The progression through these stages is used to determine the potential pathology of the grieving process. However, grief theorists do not agree as to the number of stages through which survivors must pass. The existing literature suggests that, as a group, surviving family members of homicide victims suffer more complex and difficult grief reactions than people who have lost others through natural causes or accidents (Lehman, Wortman, & Williams, 1987). Because grief theorists have focused primarily on describing the process of grief rather than explaining why certain reactions occur, grief theory is not likely to be the most useful theoretical perspective for understanding why the indirect victims of crime experience particular types of problems.

Attribution Theory: Attribution theorists have contributed understanding of why the victims of crime, both direct and indirect, experience difficulties (e.g., Frieze, Hymer, & Greenberg, 1987; Janoff-Bulman & Frieze, 1983; Perloff, 1983; Wortman, 1983). Attribution theorists argue that any attempt to understand and protect human behavior must take into account the attributions, or reasons, that people ascribe to events. Therefore, to understand why certain reactions occur among both direct and indirect victims of crime, it is important to examine what actually happened to the person, their attributions for why it occurred, and what they think it means. Research has found that the surviving family members of homicide victims search for a meaning to the event, and the extent to which the searching process continues is related to increased levels of psychological distress (Veronen, Amick-McMullan, & Smith, 1986).

With respect to criminal victimization, Janoff-Bulman and Frieze (1983) argue that being the victim of a crime changes one's basic attributions about the safety and just nature of the world, often creating intense feelings of vulnerability. Perloff (1983) distinguished between "universal" and "unique" vulnerability. Universal vulnerability is the extent to which one believes that all people are vulnerable to crime, while unique vulnerability is the perceived risk of one's own future victimization. Perloff argued that those victims who subsequently feel that they are more at risk than others for future victimization (increased unique vulnerability) are more likely to experience such problems as anxiety, depression, and lowered self-esteem than are victims without elevated feelings of unique vulnerability. Most relevant to the current chapter, it has been found that the victimization of a friend or relative can alter perceptions of vulnerability (Perloff).

Another attributional process of potential importance to understanding indirect victimization is equity theory (e.g., Walster, Walster, & Berscheid, 1978), which posits that people feel uncomfortable and experience distress if a state of inequity exists. Criminal victimization clearly puts the victim in an inequitable position vis a vis the assailant and thus can create feelings of anger and distress. The primary source for reestablishing equity is through the legal system. Thus, feelings of equity probably are closely related to the victim's perception of his/her treatment by the legal system vis a vis the system's treatment of the criminal. This is also likely the case with indirect victims. For the most indirect victims, feelings of inequity are probably less intense than among direct victims because they are not directly victimized. In the case of family survivors of homicide victims, though, the indirect victims are likely to experience great feelings of inequity due to the loss that was brought about by the criminal act. Data support the contention that psychological distress experienced by homicide survivors is closely related to their perceived treatment by the legal system (Amick-McMullan, Kilpatrick, & Veronen, 1989).

Stress and Coping. The concept of stress has been researched widely (see Cohen & Wills, 1985; Depue & Monroe, 1986, Monroe & Steiner, 1986). Various theorists have offered models to describe the role of stress in the development of psychological and behavioral problems. Theoretically, the ability of an individual to cope effectively with a stressful event will decrease as a person's perception of the level of stress associated with that event increases. Thus, one would expect more severe problems among both direct and indirect victims as the severity of the crime increased. This is apparently the case for direct victims where the seriousness of the crime (e.g., completed rape), physical injury, and perceived life threat are important predictors of

PTSD symptoms (Kilpatrick et al., 1989). Cohen and Wills (1985) suggested that social support can help "buffer" individuals from the effect of stress by reducing the appraised level of the stress. Social support also can serve to improve the psychological well-being of individuals who are in stressful situations by providing generally positive reinforcement. In the area of criminal victimization, it has been shown that social support is important in the long-term emotional recovery of rape victims following their assault (Sales, Baum, & Shore, 1984).

In general, when coping strategies and social support after a stressful event prove ineffective, it is possible that the individual will develop a chronic stress disorder, such as Post-Traumatic Stress Disorder. As discussed earlier, the rates of PTSD among crime victims are quite high (Kilpatrick et al., 1987). Symptoms of PTSD also are reported by indirect victims of crime, such as the surviving family members of homicide victims (Amick-McMullan, Kilpatrick, & Resnick, 1988) and the partners of rape victims (Resnick, Veronen, & Saunders, 1988).

Learned Helplessness Theory. Learned helplessness theory is used typically to explain symptoms of depression (e.g., Abramson, Seligman, & Teasdale, 1978), but it has also been applied to the problems experienced by victims (Peterson & Seligman, 1983). According to this theory, an individual subjected to an unexpected and uncontrollable aversive event, or series of events, will learn the futility of trying to escape the situation. If this same individual is faced with a similar aversive situation in the future, he or she will not attempt to escape. Rather, the individual will likely appear passive, withdrawn, sad, anxious, and depressed. Learned helplessness theory argues that high deficits are due to a cognitive expectation that escape from an aversive situation is not contingent on the responses of the individual. Having learned this lesson, an individual will fail to act in a future situation that is potentially controllable.

Following a crime, many victims report feeling helpless, vulnerable, and depressed. Researchers (Kilpatrick, Veronen, & Resick, 1982; Peterson & Seligman, 1983; Wortman, 1983) have argued that these responses might best be understood within the context of learned helplessness theory. The crime is conceptualized as the initial learning situation. Additional feelings of helplessness and lack of control may be elicited by the victim's experience with the criminal justice system (Kilpatrick & Otto, 1987). These feelings generalize to the point where they may interfere with a wide variety of daily activities. Wortman argues that the perception of control is one of the most important factors in understanding the emotional and psychological difficulties of crime victims.

As mentioned earlier, indirect victims of crime may also experience feelings of vulnerability, particularly when the direct victim is injured or killed. Indirect victims are quite likely to view the crime as an event beyond their control. Like direct victims of crime, indirect victims will be exposed to the criminal justice system to some degree and experience continued feelings of helplessness. This is particularly true for the surviving family members of homicide victims. The inability to control the judicial process may even be greater for indirect victims who, with the exception of homicide survivors, must rely on decisions made by the direct victim to provide any input into the system. These feelings may generalize and contribute to the difficulties experienced by the indirect victims.

Learning Theory. The learning principles of classical conditioning, second order conditioning, operant reinforcement and vicarious learning have been used to explain the reactions of direct victims (Kilpatrick, Resick, & Veronen, 1981; Kilpatrick, Veronen, & Resick, 1982). Physical stimuli, thoughts, or memories of the crime may become conditioned to elicit emotional responses similar to those activated during the crime (Kilpatrick et al., 1982). Thus, a victim who recounts his or her victimization experience to the police, lawyer, or counselor is likely to experience feelings of anxiety regardless of the presence of physical cues.

Whether physical or cognitive in nature, conditioned stimuli can produce intense feelings. When such a state of arousal is elicited, the emotions can become associated with internal and external stimuli in the situation. These new stimuli can become conditioned to produce emotional arousal through second order conditioning. Through this process, a variety of external and internal cues, seemingly unrelated to the crime itself, may become cues for emotional arousal. For example, a victim who becomes anxious while relating the events of his or her victimization to a therapist may associate those feelings with physical stimuli in the therapist's office. Characteristics of the office or of the therapist may evoke feelings of anxiety in the future. Similarly, contacts with the criminal justice system may become aversive and anxiety provoking through the principles of classical and second order conditioning (Veronen, Kilpatrick, & Resick, 1979).

Avoidance of anxiety-provoking situations is one of the major ways that people attempt to decrease the anxiety. Avoidance is effective in the short-term reduction of anxiety. Thus, a crime victim is likely to avoid anxiety by avoiding stimuli that elicit responses similar to the crime. These could include contacts with the criminal justice system and with therapists. The avoidant behaviors are reinforced by the immediate reduction of the anxiety and are therefore often difficult to overcome. However, the continued avoidance may maintain the anxiety problems in the future.

The importance of learning theory to the problems of direct victims of crime appears clear, but to apply these principles to indirect victims is less straightforward. The principles of modeling (Bandura, 1977), or vicarious learning, are helpful in understanding the process through which indirect victims develop problems. Vicarious learning proposes that people can learn, not only from direct experience, but also from observing others and modeling their behavior. Researchers found that individuals exhibited greater levels of fear after observing another person undergo an aversive event (Bandura, Blanchard, & Ritter, 1969). A person may develop anxiety in response to crime-related stimuli as a result of knowing someone who has been victimized. Studies examining fear of crime found that one need not be a direct victim to become fearful of victimization (Riger & Gordon, 1981).

As with the conditioning model of anxiety in direct victims, indirect victims can model anxiety reactions to both cognitive and physical stimuli. For example, a direct victim may tell another individual about the crime. The direct victim is likely to exhibit elevated levels of anxiety in response to aspects of the story. The indirect victim listening to the description of the crime may model the anxiety felt by the direct victim. The indirect victim also may observe the direct victim's anxiety response to physical cues and, over time, begin to model these reactions. Thus, vicarious learning may account for much of the anxiety and fear experienced by indirect victims.

While vicarious learning may explain many of the symptoms of anxiety experienced by indirect victims, the principles of classical conditioning, stimulus generalization, and second order conditioning mentioned above offer alternative explanations for the development of these problems. For example, the indirect victims of crime are likely to experience strong emotional responses, such as anxiety, fear, and anger, when told of the crime by the direct victim or police, regardless of the emotional state of the person relating the story. This heightened arousal is likely to become associated with stimuli linked with both the crime situation being described and environmental stimuli present when the indirect victim is told. In a process similar to that described above for the direct victims, these stimuli acquire the ability to elicit these emotional responses in indirect victims in the future. Stimulus generalization and second order conditioning can then work to develop anxiety responses in various other situations.

Amick-McMullan and her colleagues (Amick-McMullan, Kilpatrick, Veronen, & Smith, 1989; Amick-McMullan, Kilpatrick, and Veronen, 1989) applied learning theory and behavioral models to grief and PTSD symptoms among the family survivors of homicide victims. They noted changes in reinforcement patterns associated with the loss of a significant other (Averill & Wisocki, 1981). While the behavioral explanation is able to account for many of the reactions found among indirect victims, Amick-McMullan, Kilpatrick, Veronen, and Smith (1989) noted the problems that this formulation encounters when attempting to explain the attributional changes that take place among indirect victims.

PRACTICAL CONSIDERATIONS REGARDING THE INDIRECT VICTIMS OF CRIME

While researchers are only beginning to examine and understand the problems faced by victims of crime, it does appear that direct victims are not the only people who may develop problems following a crime. In a survey of homicide victim survivors, Amick et al. (1989) found that 74% of the respondents believed the legal system should be responsible for providing psychological counseling to the family members of homicide victims, but only 17% felt they had received adequate access to psychological services.

There are many complex issues facing the mental health and legal professions when dealing with the indirect victims of crime. Many of these issues are similar to those involved in dealing with direct victims. However, there are aspects to the indirect experience of crime that make the problems faced by these individuals unique. Steps taken to assist these individuals must take into account the particular nature of their situation.

With respect to the mental health difficulties faced by indirect victims, these individuals are placed in a difficult position. Friends and family members constitute the central social support network for direct victims; as such, they can play an important role in helping to alleviate some of the victim's psychological distress. However, for the reasons outlined above, this supportive contact with direct victims may result in psychological problems for the indirect victims. Data suggest that individuals who are emotionally close to crime victims, particularly those of violent crime, should be assessed for psychological problems and counseled about the difficulties they may face.

The development of the psychological problems that are likely to appear among indirect victims of crime may exacerbate the symptoms of direct victims. For example, a husband faced with the news that his wife has been raped may respond with feelings of guilt, anger, and desire for revenge. These feelings are likely to make it more difficult for him to provide the emotional support that his wife needs to deal with her own response to the rape. In addition, the husband's reaction may contribute to the wife's avoidance of the crime-related stimuli that provoke her anxiety because she now has to worry about her husband's reaction as well. The husband's inability to offer support to his wife also may elicit new feelings of guilt, characterized by statements such as, "I couldn't protect her when she needed it, and now I can't even help her when she needs me."

The recognition by mental health professions that indirect victims may suffer psychological problems following a crime is an important step in assisting direct victims and indirect victims. When counseling a crime victim, it appears important to assess the functioning of individuals who serve as the victim's social support, rather than to simply assume that the support system will help the victim cope. It may be necessary to provide separate individual counseling for the indirect victims and/or allow them to participate in counseling sessions provided for the victim.

Indirect victims of crime are also in a unique position with respect to the legal system. With the notable exception of family members of homicide victims, indirect victims generally have little direct contact with the legal system, but many of the frustrations experienced by victims are shared by close friends and relatives. Improved understanding, within the legal system, of the psychological problems and needs of both direct and indirect victims may lead to more cooperation by the victims, a more favorable perception of the legal system, reduced trauma as a result of contact with the legal system, and more effective testimony by victims (Kilpatrick, 1986). In many ways, the needs of indirect victims are similar to those of direct victims with respect to the legal system.

Indirect victims may be even less able to control aspects of the legal system than direct victims. The potential importance of this sense of lack of control in the development of psychological problems was discussed earlier (see also Kilpatrick & Otto, 1987). Providing information to victims can reduce these feelings of helplessness (Kilpatrick, 1986). Information of importance to both direct and indirect victims includes information about the status of the case, the structure and functioning of the justice system, and specific plans for their case. Other issues related to the criminal justice system that can contribute to problems faced by indirect victims of crime include, but are not limited to, the manner of notification that a crime has taken place, the depiction of a loved one as a terrible person by a defense attorney attempting to shift the blame for the crime, and concern over the possible release of the assailant on bail, parole, or probation. Indirect victims also witness their loved one suffer the stress associated with a victim's experience in the criminal justice system.

Among homicide survivors, over 80% felt that the criminal justice system should provide them with more information on the status of the legal case and with legal assistance if necessary (Amick et al., 1989). Only 30 to 35% of the participants felt that they had received adequate services in these areas. Over 80% of the homicide survivors felt that the system should provide a court/police advocate, as well as personal protection for family members. Again, only a small percentage (27% for the advocacy, 10% for personal protection) felt that they were adequately served in these areas.

In conclusion, while the percentage of indirect victims of crime who experience psychological problems is apparently somewhat smaller than in the case of direct victims, the problems they suffer are just as real. These symptoms typically include anxiety, depression, fear, and anger. Indirect victims also report symptoms of Post-Traumatic Stress Disorder, including intrusive thoughts and memories of the crime, attempts to avoid cues related to the crime, and increased levels of arousal. A variety of theoretical formulations may assist us in understanding these difficulties, and it is likely that a number of these approaches are necessary to understand fully the development of psychological problems among indirect victims of crime. Regardless of the etiological process by which problems develop, indirect victims who develop problems are likely to benefit from counseling. Addressing the problems of the indirect victim also may be important for the future adjustment of the direct victim, as this adjustment process is likely to be complicated by the distress of the indirect victim. Finally, it is important for the criminal justice system to recognize the difficulties faced by the friends and family members of crime victims. Those involved in the criminal justice system should help indirect victims find legal and psychological assistance and prepare them for the stress that might result from contact with the criminal justice system.

REFERENCES

Abramson, L. Y., Seligman, M. E. P., & Teasdale, D. E. (1978). Learned helplessness in humans: Critique and reformulation. *Journal of Abnormal Psychology, 87,* 49-74.

American Psychiatric Association (1987). *Diagnostic and statistical manual of disorders.* (3rd ed., revised). Washington, DC: American Psychiatric Association.

American Psychological Association Task Force on Victims of Crime and Violence (1984). *American Psychological Association task force on victims of crime and violence final report.* Washington, DC: Author.

Amick-McMullan, A., Kilpatrick, D. G., & Resnick, H. S. (1988, October). *Survivors of homicide victims: National prevalence and psychological adjustment.* Paper presented at the Society for Traumatic Stress Studies, Dallas.

Amick, A., Kilpatrick, D. G., Resnick, H. S., & Saunders, B. E. (1989, March). *Public health implications of homicide for surviving family members: An epidemiological study.* Paper presented at the Tenth Meeting of the Society of Behavioral Medicine, San Francisco.

Amick- McMullan, A., Kilpatrick, D. G., & Veronen, L. J. (1989). Family survivors of homicide victims: A behavioral analysis. *The Behavior Therapist, 12,* 75-79.

Amick-McMullan, A., Kilpatrick, D. G., Veronen, L. J., & Smith, S. (1989). Family survivors of homicide victims: Theoretical perspectives and an exploratory study. *Journal of Traumatic Stress Studies, 2,* 21-35.

Attorney General's Task Force on Family Violence (September, 1984). *Attorney General's task force on family violence final report.* Washington, DC: U.S. Government Printing Office.

Averill, J. R., & Wisocki, P. A. (1981). Some observations on behavioral approaches to the treatment of grief among the elderly. In H. Sobel (Ed.), *Behavior therapy in terminal care: A humanistic approach.* New York: Ballinger.

Bandura, A. (1977). *Social learning theory.* Englewood Cliffs, NJ: Prentice-Hall.

Bandura, A., Blanchard, E. B., & Ritter, B. (1969). The relative efficacy of desensitization and modeling approaches for inducing behavioral, affective, and attitudinal changes. *Journal of Personality and Social Psychology, 13,* 173-199.

Bowlby, J. (1980). *Attachment and loss, Vol. III: Sadness and depression.* London: Hogarth Press.

Bowman, N. J. (1980). *Differential reaction to dissimilar types of death: Specifically, the homicide/murder.* Unpublished doctoral dissertation, United States International University.

Burgess, A. W. (1975). Family reaction to homicide. *American Journal of Orthopsychiatry, 45*, 391-398.

Cohen, W., & Wills, T. A. (1985). Stress, social support, and the buffering hypothesis. *Psychological Bulletin, 98*, 310-357.

Depue, R. A., & Monroe, S. M. (1986). Conceptualization and measurement of human disorder in life stress research: The problem of chronic disturbance. *Psychological Bulletin, 99*, 35-51.

Doyle, P. (1980). *Grief counseling and sudden death.* Springfield, IL: Charles C. Thomas.

Frieze, I. H., Hymer, S., & Greenberg, M. S. (1987). Describing the crime victim: Psychological reactions to victimization. *Professional Psychology Research and Practice, 18*, 222-315.

Getzel, G. S., & Masters, R. (1984). Serving families who survive homicide victims. *Social Casework: The Journal of Contemporary Social Work*, March, 138-144.

Holmstrom, L. L., & Burgess, A. N. (1979). Rape: The husband's and boyfriend's initial reactions. *The Family Coordinator, 28*, 321-330.

Janoff-Bulman, R., & Frieze, I. H. (1983). A theoretical perspective for understanding reactions to victimization. *Journal of Social Issues, 38*, 1-17.

Kilpatrick, D. G. (1986). Addressing the needs of traumatized victims. *The Practical Prosecutor, 1986*, 15-18.

Kilpatrick, D. G., & Amick-McMullan, A. (1987). *Criminal homicide and alcohol-related vehicular homicide: A national study of surviving family members* (Grant No. 87-IJ-CX-0017). Washington, DC: National Institute of Justice.

Kilpatrick, D. G., & Otto, R. K. (1987). Constitutionally guaranteed participation in criminal proceedings for victims: Potential effects on psychological functioning. *The Wayne Law Review, 34*, 7-289.

Kilpatrick, D. G., Resick, P. A. & Veronen, L. J. (1981). Effects of a rape experience: A longitudinal study. *Journal of Social Issues, 37*, 105-122.

Kilpatrick, D. G., Saunders, B. E., Amick-McMullan, A., Best, C. L., Veronen, L. J., & Resnick, H. S. (1989). Victim and crime factors associated with the development of post-traumatic stress disorder. *Behavior Therapist, 20*, 199-214.

Kilpatrick, D. G., Saunders, B. E., Veronen, L. J., Best, C. L., & Von, J. M. (1987). Criminal victimization: Lifetime prevalence, reporting to police, and psychological impact. *Crime and Delinquency, 33*, 479-489.

Kilpatrick, D. G., Veronen, L. J., & Resick, P. A. (1982). Psychological sequelae to rape: Assessment and treatment strategies. In D. M., Doleys, P. I. Meredity, & A. R. Ciminero (Eds.), *Behavioral Medicine: Assessment and Treatment Strategies.* New York, Plenum.

Lehman, D. R., Wortman, C. B., & Williams, A. F. (1987). Long-term effects of losing a spouse or child in a motor vehicle crash. *Journal of Personality and Social Psychology, 52*, 218-231.

Lindermann, E. (1965). Symptomatology and management of acute grief. In *Death and Identity* (pp. 186-201). New York: John Wiley & Sons.

McCahill, T. W., Meyer, L. C., & Fischman, A. M. (1979). *The aftermath of rape.* Lexington, MA: Lexington Books, D. C. Heath.

Miller, W. R., Williams, A. M., & Bernstein, M. H. (1982). The effects of rape on marital and sexual adjustment. *American Journal of Family Therapy, 10*, 51-58.

Monroe, S. M. , & Steiner, S. C. (1986). Social support and psychopathology: Interrelations with preexisting disorder, stress, and personality. *Journal of Abnormal Psychology*, *95*, 29-39.

Parkes, C. M. (1972). *Bereavement: Studies of grief in adult life*. London: Pelican Books.

Perloff, L. S. (1983). Perceptions of vulnerability to victimization. *Journal of Social Issues*, *39*, 41-61.

Peterson, C., & Seligman, M. E. P. (1983). Learned helplessness and victimization. *Journal of Social Issues*, *39*, 103-116.

Poussaint, A. F. (1984, August). *The grief response following a homicide*. Paper presented at the annual meeting of the American Psychological Association, Toronto, Canada.

President's Task Force on Victims of Crime (1982). *President's task force on victims of crime final report*. Washington, DC: U.S. Government Printing Office.

Resnick, H. S., Veronen, L. J., & Saunders, B. E. (1988, October). *Symptoms of post-traumatic stress disorder in rape victims and their partners: A behavioral formulation*. Paper presented at the Fourth Annual Meeting of the Society for Traumatic Stress Studies, Dallas.

Riger, S., & Gordon, M. T. (1981). The fear of rape: A study of social control. *Journal of Social Issues*, *37*, 71-92.

Ruch, L. O., & Chandler, S. M. (1983). Sexual assault trauma during the acute phase: An exploratory model and multivariate analysis. *Journal of Health and Social Behavior*, *24*, 174-185.

Sales, E., Baum, M., & Shore, B. (1984). Victim readjustment following assault. *Journal of Social Issues*, *40*, 117-136.

Shanfield, S. B., & Swain, B. J. (1984). Death of adult children in traffic accidents. *The Journal of Nervous and Mental Disease*, *172*, 533-538.

Silver, R. L., Boon, C., & Stone, M. H. (1983). Searching for meaning in misfortune: Making sense of incest. *Journal of Social Issues*, *39*, 81-102.

Skogan, W. G. (1981). *Issues in the measurement of victimization*. Washington, DC: Department of Justice, Bureau of Statistics.

Sparks, R. F. (1981). *Research on victims of crime: Accomplishments, issues, and new directions*. Washington, DC: Department of Health and Human Services.

Stone, K. (1980). *The second victims: Altruism and the affective reactions of affiliated males to their partner's rape*. Ann Arbor, MI: University Microfilms International.

U.S. Bureau of the Census (1987). *Statistical abstract of the United States, 1988* (108th ed.). Washington, DC: U.S. Government Printing Office.

Veronen, L. J., Amick-McMullan, A., & Smith, S. A. (1986). *Impact of criminal homicide on surviving family members*. Unpublished manuscript.

Veronen, L. J., Kilpatrick, D. G., & Resick, P. A. (1979). Treatment of fear and anxiety in rape victims: Implications for the criminal justice system. In W. H. Parsonage (Ed.), *Perspectives on victimology* (pp. 148-159). Beverly Hills, CA: Sage.

Veronen, L. J., & Saunders, B. E. (1985). *Impact of Rape on Dyadic Involvement and Functioning*. (Grant No. MH40360-01). Washington, DC: National Institute of Mental Health.

Veronen, L. J., & Saunders, B. E. (1988). *Impact of rape on dyadic involvement and functioning: Application for continuation*. Application submitted to the National Institute of Mental Health, Washington, DC.

Veronen, L. J., Saunders, B. E., & Resnick, H. S. (1988), November). *Partner reactions to rape*. Paper presented at the 22nd Annual Meeting of the Association for the Advancement of Behavior Therapy. New York, NY.

Walster, E., Walster, G. W., & Berscheid, E. (1978). *Equity: Theory and research*. Boston: Allyn & Bacon.

Wortman, C. B. (1983). Coping with victimization: Conclusions and implications for future research. *Journal of Social Issues, 39*, 195-221.

Chapter 8

THE POLICE: FIRST IN AID?

IRVIN WALLER

On our television screens, cops are heroes, fighting uncaring international drug traffickers and vicious bank robbers. Yet for the victim of a
crime, they are heroes called to help. The police department is the
agency most often and first contacted by victims after a crime. The
police are available 24 hours a day, 7 days a week. They call ambulances
and fire departments. They can separate the parties in a dispute. They
recover property, protect the victim from an aggressor, and arrest the
suspect.

For the police, most crimes involve a victim. Most often it is the
victim who initiates the information that the crime occurred, as well as
describes the details of the crime and the suspect. It is the victim's
cooperation that facilitates an arrest and a conviction. Further, satisfied
victims can be an important source of public support for the police at
budget time.

Given the importance of the victim to the police, one would expect
police leaders to have ensured that victims are treated as "privileged
clients" by implementing the policy of the International Association of
Chiefs of Police (IACP). The association urges police forces to "establish procedures and train personnel" to implement the "incontrovertible
rights of all crime victims," which it defines:

1. to be free from intimidation;
2. to be told of financial assistance and social services available and how to
   apply for them;
3. to be provided a secure area during interviews and court proceedings, and
   to be notified if presence in court is needed;

4. to be provided a quick return of stolen or other personal property when no longer needed as evidence;

5. to a speedy disposition of the case, and to be periodically informed of case status and final disposition; and, wherever personnel and resource capabilities allow, to be notified in felony cases whenever the perpetrator is released from custody;

6. to be interviewed by a female official in the case of rape and other sexual offenses, wherever personnel and resource capabilities allow. (IACP, 1983)

Even though these incontrovertible rights are adopted by the United Nations and most U.S. legislatures, they are largely ignored by police leaders and researchers. Victim advocates in the United States often overlook the importance of the police response to victims.

In this chapter, research and common sense show that police leaders who implement the IACP Crime Victims Bill of Rights will achieve the police mission in ways no other reforms can. Implementing those rights will help victims in ways only the police can.

VICTIMS: IN AID OF POLICING

Today our main response to crime is to have our police and court and correctional systems catch, convict, and punish the offender. The role of the police in this response is to maintain the public peace and enforce the law by discovering crimes and then catching, charging, and helping convict offenders.

Not only have the police, rather than the victim, performed many of these functions, but, in North America, they also enforce fines that are paid to the states rather than redress to the victim. In earlier centuries, it was the victims or their families who pursued the offender in order to obtain redress. As the state took over this responsibility, the victim's role was reduced to that of a witness. In part, this was justified as a way to avoid private retaliation by victims that might have lead to further disorder; in part, it saved victims an expense.

Over time, limits have been set on the powers of the state, which provides explicit rights for both suspects and offenders, as well as responsibilities for police, lawyers, judges, and correctional authorities. These rights are specified in the U.S. Constitution, penal codes, and police acts, and Canada's constitution. Police have to follow rules in relation to offenders, but they have no clear rules as to the right of the victims to redress, protection, or justice.

However, many police officers, prosecutors, and judges perform their duties in the name of the victim. Victims are the reason for incarcerating offenders or asking for longer sentences. They are acting to protect potential victims. Even though the police work for the state and have no clear obligations toward victims, they are working indirectly for victims because, in some limited ways, the state also represents victims.

Information from Victims

One of the basic functions of police in modern societies is to obtain information about crimes and criminals, and to use this to get criminals convicted (Skogan, 1985). However, police leaders and researchers have generally neither recognized the importance of the information that victims can provide to the police nor the ways through which this information can be improved.

The police have instituted many innovative programs to get better information from the general public for these purposes. For instance, neighborhood watch encourages citizens to report more suspicious circumstances to the police, know how to report a crime, and recall characteristics of offenders. Many cities have instituted "911" numbers so that the public can dial the police more easily. "Crime stoppers" programs have been established wherein a recent criminal occurrence is publicized and a reward offered in an effort to get additional information from the public.

Victims are the immediate source of 60% of common crime known to the police; that is, without victims' action, police would only be aware of 40% of the crime that they know of today. These statistics come from the U.S. National Crime Survey, described by John H. Laub in Chapter 2. The survey contacted a representative sample of adults to ask them about such personal crimes as theft, burglary, rape, robbery, and assault (U.S. Department of Justice, 1988, p. 35, 62). Other members of the victim's household report 13% of the crimes with other witnesses reporting 22%. Less than 3% of common crime known to the police is first discovered by the police. Other nations' crime surveys report similar figures.

More than one-third of the robberies, aggravated assaults, burglaries, and rapes reported in the U.S. National Crime Survey were not reported to the police (U.S. Department of Justice, 1988, p. 34), a finding that suggests that substantially more information about crime could be obtained if victims could be persuaded to report more crime to the police.

It is particularly important to encourage victims who saw the offender to report the offense. For every five offenses reported to the police, there is only one arrest (U.S. Department of Justice, 1988, pp. 68-69). The proportion of crimes resulting in arrest and conviction is dependent on the extent to which the victim knew and saw the offender. The clearance rate for such offenses as rape and assault involving confrontation is more than half, whereas the clearance rate for offenses occurring without the victim seeing the offender, such as burglary, is less than 20%. So getting victims to report offenses where they saw the offender would increase the proportion of offenses cleared.

The reasons for not reporting have been discussed in an earlier chapter. Each of these reasons should be the focus of improvements in policing programs.

For instance, victims do not report because they believe that the police will be unable to do anything. Statistics confirm the victims' view: Seventy-five percent of robberies and 85% of burglaries will not be cleared, and an even higher proportion will not result in an arrest (Skogan, 1985, p. 332). The police are becoming more problem oriented, however, using crime analysis and community approaches to crime prevention. These crimes can often be part of a neighborhood pattern that helps police plan and promote prevention strategies or undertake problem-oriented policing to understand the underlying causes (Waller, 1989a; Goldstein, 1987). Police should communicate this to victims so that they would be more likely to report crimes to the police even though they believe the crimes are not serious enough or that they will stymie the police.

Victims also do not report because they consider the matter private. School and public education programs should reinforce the reasons why "private matters" that are crimes should be brought to the attention of the police.

In the case of sexual assault, the reasons for not reporting relate both to fear of reprisal and threats, as well as the reception given by the police. Therefore, the police could improve the way sexual assault testimony is taken, particularly through the use of videotaping in the initial interviews, in order to prevent reprisals from influencing later evidence.

Victims often delay reporting while they discuss what action to take with a family member or neighbor; some even wait until after they have talked to their insurance companies. Only 6% of the persons who call the police are reporting a crime in progress (U.S. Department of Justice, 1988, p. 62). It is only in these cases that the police stand a reasonable chance of identifying and arresting the suspect. The longer the time delay, the more likely that there will be insufficient evidence and that the evidence will be less reliable.

The police can also improve the quality of information they get from victims. When the police officer interviews a victim who has recently been victimized, the victim may be in a state of shock and thus have difficulty giving the police the information they need. It is likely that the speed and quality with which the victim provides information to the police could also be improved if the police were better able to support the victim. This would result in better information for the police and less time spent on the case.

The police not only want to get information, but they want this information to be useful when it gets to court. Many arrests do not result in conviction because the victim does not come to court as a witness. In major cities, 20% or more of cases are dropped by prosecutors because of witness problems. In cases where the offender and the victim know each other, more than 50% of the cases are dropped because of witness problems (U.S. Department of Justice, 1988, p. 73). These problems can be solved in part through victim witness programs, such as that of the Victim Services Agency in New York. It would also be useful, however, to have police-based victim service programs that provide information and support to the victim from the moment the offense is reported until the case is resolved in the criminal justice system.

Satisfied Victims Support Police

In order for the police to maintain public support for their activities, the public must have a good image of them. As stated, 60% of crimes reported to the police come from victims. Therefore, victims are one of the most important members of the public who have contact with the police.

Persons participating in crime prevention programs organized by the police also have contact with the officers, as do children in schools where police make appearances. In addition, the move toward foot patrols and mini-stations creates more public contact with the police. All of these, however, occur in non-crisis situations.

Suspected offenders provide one view of the police as a result of being charged, arrested, or investigated. They talk to their friends and spread their view of the police as well.

Victims tend to be satisfied with the police response in about two-thirds of the cases (Shapland & Duff, 1985; Waller & Okihiro, 1978, p. 46; Drennan-Searson, 1982, p. 133). Those who are dissatisfied most frequently cite a lack of police follow-up, though delays in getting to the scene and lack of a thorough investigation are also mentioned.

In practice, there are many more victims than offenders. Victims are likely to be more concerned about how they are treated than people participating in citizen crime prevention programs. If victims have a positive image of their experience with the police, this positive image will be communicated to their friends and family. Through implementing the IACP Crime Victims Bill of Rights, the police can improve the public support for their activities.

POLICING: IN AID OF VICTIMS

Victims report offenses to the police because they feel it is their civic duty to do so (Waller & Okihiro, 1978). However, they are also looking for certain services from the police.

Two out of five victims report the crime because they want to recover property or make an insurance claim. One in three report to prevent the incident from happening again. Less than 10% report to see the offender punished (U.S. Department of Justice, 1988, p. 35). Therefore, the police could aid victims by giving greater emphasis on returning property to its owners and to crime prevention.

Information, Referral, and Property Return

When the victims call the police, it is often the first time that they have had contact with the criminal justice system. They are also often in need of medical assistance, protection, and crisis services. If they have had property stolen, they want to have it returned.

The police, available around the clock, have sophisticated communications equipment linked to a central dispatcher. This could enable them to get information very quickly on the availability and location of services, such as emergency welfare, rape crisis, transition homes for battered wives, victim support units, or criminal injuries compensation.

Victims are rarely given information regarding social, legal, or practical services and are often too confused to ask for it; some time later, however, they realize how helpful the services could have been.

Victims want information on the offender, when he or she has been freed, and information as to the progress of the police investigation.

At the time an offender is identified, victims may be concerned as to whether the offender is going to retaliate because they called the police. They want to know about the bail hearing and sometimes present their views. They often express considerable surprise when they find out that an offender who has just been caught has also just been released.

Victims can be unfamiliar with the courts and therefore want information as to where to go and what will happen in the court proceedings.

Crime Prevention

Victims often need information on how to prevent crime in the future (for instance, how to make their homes more secure). Consequently, an important service for victims is the presentation of reliable and valid information on measures they could take for crime prevention. Even police departments that have a specialized victim service unit do not ensure that victims get the best crime prevention information.

Victims could also be protected better if the information police were receiving was being used to tackle the situations that breed persistent offending. If the police were using such information as where, when, why, and to whom crimes occur to encourage community agencies (involved in housing, schools, city planning, and social services) to improve their programs, there would be less crime (Waller, 1989a, 1989b).

Victims involved in personal injury offenses, particularly involving suspects who are known to them, are concerned about how to prevent retaliation and may also be worried about threats meant to prevent them from testifying. In exceptional cases, the police may arrange a new identity and address; usually, however, little is done to protect the victim.

In light of these considerations, the IACP statement should also include a commitment to the number one right of every potential victim to have the best prevention and protection programs in place.

Sensitivity to Victims' Trauma

The reaction of telephone dispatchers and patrol officers may have a substantial influence on the adjustment of the victim to the crime. When the police arrive, victims are looking for order to be reestablished and recognition that an offense was committed against them. Case studies suggest that the police can often exacerbate the difficulties of victims by making the victim feel guiltier and more afraid than is necessary.

The emotional trauma, or "invisible wound" (Resick, 1987; Canadian Council on Social Development, 1985) is the least evident and understood, but it is often the most brutal effect of crime, not only on the direct victim, but on the victim's dependents and friends. Further, it is a major part of the anger that is felt by some victims.

People are often surprised that crimes against property can generate this trauma. In one study of victims located from police files, more than 70% of the victims experienced crying, shaking, and fear. In addition, 20% recorded physical upset and memory loss, while 5% recorded longer term residual effects (Waller, 1986; see also Resick, 1987). For the police officer, it is easy to overlook the 5% who are seriously traumatized, because the event seems so rare. However, this is the equivalent of 300,000 households in the United States and 20,000 in Canada.

The reaction of the victim can vary with his or her life situation, which may not be obvious to the police officer, and will vary over time. So, when the police arrive, the victim may be cool and calm, yet a few days later, he/she may be experiencing sadness and anger (see Chapter 2).

In addition, police officers may have difficulty in being sensitive to emotional reaction. In the course of their duties, they deal routinely with crimes and severe accidents in which victims have been physically injured and must handle such situations with a professional detachment.

Being sensitive to the victim's trauma is more than just reporting to the scene and providing some information later. The Detroit police force undertook a special experiment to train police officers in how to treat victims. Though the police learned the theory, victims did not notice any difference between officers who were trained in this special experiment and those who were not (Rosenbaum, 1987). Therefore, improving the immediate police response was not enough.

In another experiment, some Houston police officers were to call back the victims some time after the offense to see if they needed assistance. The experiment did not work because it was too little, too late (Skogan & Wycoff, 1987, p. 500).

It seems that in order for police action to be sensitive to victims' needs, there must be at least a combination of a sensitive immediate response and an effort to give victims information on services. The next section describes more comprehensive approaches to responding to these needs.

POLICING AND VICTIMS: PRESCRIPTIONS

In 1985, the General Assembly of the United Nations adopted the Declaration of Basic Principles of Justice for Victims of Crime and Abuse of Power, which specified how governments, the police, and community agencies could assist and protect the rights of victims. This included ways to provide access to justice and fair treatment, restitution, compensation, and services to victims of crime.

Principle 4 states that "victims should be treated with compassion and respect for their dignity." Bassiouni (1988) provides many detailed proposals about the role that the police must play in meeting this objective. It is more precise than the IACP Crime Victims Bill of Rights, as it specifies the need for "mental first aid" to help victims cope with the psychological trauma, the creation of crisis intervention teams, and the sensitization of the police through peer review teams.

Principle 15 states, "victims should be informed of the availability of health and social services and other relevant assistance, and readily afforded access to them," which clarifies that victims need more than information to have access to such services. Bassiouni (1988) stressed the need for community services to "outreach" to victims as soon as the police have alerted the appropriate service.

The Council of Europe is equally clear on the need for countries to improve their legislation and practice, stressing the same issues as the IACP Crime Victims Bill of Rights. They add an emphasis on the way the police officer treats the victim and the role of the police in preparing a type of victim impact statement. They also want the police to ensure that the victims receive help, prevention information, and details of any victim rights (Bassiouni, 1988, p. 436, 461).

U.S. Legislation Prescribes Police Role

In general, legislation on both the federal and the state levels is consistent with the IACP Crime Victims Bill of Rights, though it is often not very concerned with implementation. Starting with Wisconsin in 1980, 44 states and the federal government have legislated guidelines as to how police and other officials in the criminal justice system should treat victims of crime (National Organization for Victim Assistance, or NOVA, 1988). For the states, these guidelines are contained in "bills of rights" for victims of crime. For the federal system, the 1982 Federal Act provided for standards of fair treatment for victims of crime.

These acts specify that the police are responsible for providing information to victims about emergency, medical, compensation, and other social services. They also specify that the police will return property to victims promptly; in some instances the legislation specifies that the victim be informed about the release of the defendant.

The most impressive enunciation of rights is contained in the Michigan Crime Victim's Rights Act (NOVA, 1988, pp. 169-176), which specifies rights similar to those of the IACP, but stresses that they must be respected "within 24 hours after the initial contact between the victim of a reported crime and the law enforcement agency."

In November 1988, an amendment to the constitution of Michigan enshrined the essence of these principles, though their implementation remains in the hands of the legislature or personal initiative.

Although remedies to ensure the implementation of these bills are still being developed, those states that have created a victim assistance board using money from general revenue or from surtaxes on offenders (such as Massachusetts) are beginning to make the bills a reality.

A few states (NOVA, 1988, p. 25) provide for mandatory training of police officers on the topics of sexual assault, domestic violence, and child abuse. Some even provide for training on the subject of general victim issues. These proposals, however, focus more on pre-service and occasional in-service training than on ensuring that there is a change in how police actually respond to incidents.

The National Organization for Victim Assistance has developed a special training package for patrol officers on how to respond to crime victims. Police departments, such as that of Oxnard County, have taken every police officer through a special training package on how to respond to victims of crime. More and more central police colleges are including material on crime victims in their courses. Police departments in the United States have set up other programs to respond to the needs of victims. These often involve crisis units that evolved out of the concern with domestic violence response teams in the 1970s, such as those operating in Phoenix and Glendale. Others involve the work of a central victim advocate, such as can be found in Rochester and Indianapolis.

CANADIAN POLICE FORCES AID VICTIMS

More than any other country, Canada has established police programs for victims of crime. For several years, the large police forces, such as the Royal Canadian Mounted Police and the Metropolitan Police forces in Montreal and Toronto, have been concerned about how police officers respond to cases of wife assault and sexual assault. As a result of particular police chiefs, however, the police forces in cities like Edmonton and Calgary are the world leaders in implementing the Crime Victims Bill of Rights of the IACP.

While more and more police departments are establishing units, not all have ensured that the patrol officer is an integral part of the program. Consequently, the crime victim is not systematically given information about existing services or how to get information out of the police department.

Undoubtedly, the most impressive model of services for victims from a police department is that of Edmonton. Their program involves each patrol officer and uses a central victim assistance unit to outreach to particular victims who are identified on the police computerized information system. This approach assists 3,000 victims a month in a city of 600,000 that has approximately 1,200 police personnel. The contacts vary from correspondence and telephone calls to "outreach" visits by volunteers. One indicator of the program's effectiveness is that it doubled the number of claims to the Alberta Victims Compensation Board in the first year of operation.

A major reason for its success was the personal commitment of the chief of police to create a program for victims in the late 1970s. Two other reasons are that the patrol officer *must* (not *may*) give the victim a special victim services card, and the victim assistance unit has full access to all police incident reports (Pullyblank, 1986). More recently, this unit has been placed in the four district stations.

Special efforts are made to train and provide guidelines for the individual patrol officers so that they respond to the victim in a more sensitive manner and link the victim to the central unit.

The central unit has more than 100 victim advocates who may be called in on a 24-hour basis to assist with victims suffering "severe trauma," such as deaths, sexual assaults, armed robberies, break-ins, and disasters, particularly where there are no family or friends to provide support (Edmonton Police, 1989). Ten thousand hours are volunteered each year.

Another important model project is the London, Ontario, police department, which, as early as 1972, established mental health worker crisis intervention teams within the police department to respond to domestic violence cases (Jaffe, Finlay, & Wolfe, 1984). In simple terms, the police officer was there to control the crisis and make law enforcement powers available. The mental health workers could follow up on the case to make sure that long-term solutions were found. The evaluation supports the conclusion that "families were found to be better adjusted and functioning at a higher level three months and three years after the family consultant intervention had begun."

In 1978, the Restigouche Project was started in a rural area with similar objectives (Bragg, 1986). Such projects are similar to projects in the United States. Like their U.S. counterparts, they remain success stories in the communities where they were started, but they have not been adopted by other police departments.

Despite this progress, many major police departments have not established any policies for patrol and investigative officers or for the establishment of a central victim assistance unit. The Canadian government could provide leadership by training Canadian police leaders and establishing public guidelines for the RCMP. These guidelines could specify how patrol and investigative officers would give the victim information on available services and remedies as well as how the victim will be informed as the investigation continues.

TOWARD POLICE FIRST IN AID

The first three sections of this chapter have established that (1) the police can get more information and public support by assisting victims,

(2) victims need the police because they are the first to respond and have the communications equipment to refer, and (3) international and U.S. legislation specifies that police should be implementing the IACP Crime Victims Bill of Rights. How can police leaders better provide such assistance?

Make Police Patrol Responsive

The police are well situated to initiate crisis support to victims. Because they are often the first officials to talk to the crime victim, they are able to reassure and refer the victim to appropriate services in the community. Therefore, the training of all police officers should include how to reassure and refer victims so that victims receive not only emergency medical care, but information and social support.

The police could improve their support for crime victims by requiring the responding officer to provide the victim with a card that identifies the key telephone numbers of such services as the local distress center, locksmiths, criminal injuries compensation, the crime prevention unit, and a service that could help or refer the victim to other community services. Ideally, this card would identify both the file number of the case as well as the name of the police officer.

Much greater use could be made of modern technology to ensure that the individual patrol officer can inform the victim of available services by being able to check with the dispatcher while the patrol officer is with the victim. In crisis situations, the dispatcher could also patch the victim directly through to the patrol car as it responds to the victim.

Establish Police Crisis Unit

Mental health crisis units provide a cost-effective way to reduce police time and frustration in dealing with repeat calls, while providing a lasting service to the victims, especially in hours when social service providers are not available.

> Domestic disputes grave enough to require police intervention do not keep office hours—but, unfortunately, most of the social work agencies that can help people in those situations do. (Jaffe et al., 1984)

Special crisis units deal with family disputes and the care and management of children. They also deal with depressed and suicidal individuals, as well as the elderly. Their uniqueness comes from their ability to cope with people in crisis and link them with agencies that can provide longer term care.

Provide Information

Victims appear to require several things from the police investigator and prosecutor: to be kept informed of the progress of the investigation and to have their property recovered as soon as the police identify it. They sometimes want to present their views at bail hearings or talk to the prosecutor before the trial. They want separate waiting rooms from accused persons.

Police could require that property be returned to its owner on recovery; doing so may require the development of procedures for photographing or videotaping the victim with his property. Further, detectives could be required to inform victims from time to time of their actions or explain their inaction on an investigation. This can be done relatively easily by individualizing form letters.

Police procedures must also be coordinated with the work of any program that schedules or assists witnesses in criminal trials. These agencies provide significant savings in police overtime by taking responsibility for scheduling police witnesses, as well as victims and other civilian witnesses. In New York City, the Victim Services Agency in 1978 saved the police department more than 8 million dollars in police overtime, thereby providing savings that exceeded its own budget for all activities by 2 million dollars.

Victim Impact Statements and Reparation

Because the police obtain information as to what is lost or stolen for the purposes of establishing whether or not a crime has occurred, they are in a good position to prepare a full up-to-date report on the financial, social, psychological, and medical impact of the crime on the victim. These "victim impact statements" are used to assist in sentencing, particularly for financial reparation by the offender to the victim.

In Canada, several police departments have been preparing these reports, though agencies in the States that are less involved with the victim (such as probation officers) are used. The police officer will update the report by checking with the victim near the time of the sentencing decision.

In the Netherlands, police officers are also involved in ordering restitution in cases involving less than $1,000.

Crime Victim Support Units

Every community could identify or organize a crime victim support unit (Reiff, 1979), which would have two roles. The first would be to work with individual crime victims to ensure they get appropriate assistance from available services. Second, it would engage in training, sensitizing, and working for improvements in those services.

The unit could provide support and assistance for the victim in obtaining help from such agencies as the hospital emergency room, welfare, legal aid, and the police. This unit would also work with the police to identify cases where victims were likely to need "outreach" services. Many victims do not feel they can be helped and are not aware that they can be. A telephone call, letter, or personnel visit can encourage victims to seek help and find out what services are available.

The second function of the unit would be to improve services for crime victims. They could promote better coordination between existing services and make the public more aware of existing services and the need for improvements.

For instance, hospital emergency rooms, local doctors, and psychiatric services could be better organized to assist victims to recover from Post Traumatic Stress. Another example of assistance is where a door has been damaged as a result of a burglary and there is a need to get a carpenter or locksmith. (The Victim Services Agency in New York established its own program, SAFE, comprised of locksmiths who were available on 24-hour call for elderly victims of residential burglary.) With training, a tradesman fixing the door could serve as a counselor of sorts, who could talk to the victims and help them feel safer, which would help them recover from any trauma.

For these community services to focus better on victims, the victim assistance unit must play the essential role in promoting the need for these agencies to take responsibility for responding to the needs of victims.

CONCLUSION

Relative to overall police budgets, the above-mentioned initiatives need not be costly. They do, however, require police leaders to make personal commitments. If they chose to emphasize assistance to crime victims as one of their ways of responding to the community, many of the necessary changes in attitudes of police officers would follow.

It is in the interest of the police to aid victims; it is in the interest of victims to be helped by the police. International bodies and U.S. legislation call for this change in the police role. We have identified the specific tasks that police need to fulfill. But will these ever happen?

Police in the United States are fighting some fierce "alligators"—drugs, gangs, corruption, gun-related violence, and even some riots. The factors that lead to levels of crime unknown in any other rich democratic society lie in major part beyond the control of the police. Yet, Americans expect police officers to mop up after the failures of policies in areas such as housing, early childhood, race relations, and schools. They are given cars, computers, communication gadgets, and firepower and are told to solve the crime problem.

Given this, how could the police find time to take brochures out of trunks, refer victims to social agencies, and get property returned, let alone try to "drain the swamp" by promoting more effective crime prevention policies in cities? How could they learn from their counterparts in Canada, who face smaller alligators, often with better pay, better training, higher morale, and more coordination?

Effective police leaders are interested in better community relations. Community policing is an emerging trend. Police officers are being moved onto foot patrol. Mini-stations are being established in neighborhoods (see, Waller, 1989a; Greene & Mastrofski, 1988). Reform *is* possible. Indeed, many of the recommendations of this chapter are fully in line with the general philosophy of community policing. Therefore, one way to introduce the improvements that are needed is to include the issue of the victim in the context of community policing.

The costs of implementing the IACP recommendations, even when improved to meet the additional requirements set out in this chapter, represent a fraction of a percentage of the costs of operating a police agency. Changes in police procedures require only the printing of the card, modification of forms, and the commitment to make it happen. Victim support centers require the funding of a few core staff or the redeployment of existing staff. The training of personnel in general services does not need to cost extra amounts. Instituting procedures to keep the victim informed can be facilitated through the use of word processing equipment and obliging the victim to give his or her name and address if he or she wants the information. Scheduling civilian witnesses can be combined with that of police witnesses so that there are savings in police overtime.

It is medium-sized police agencies in such Canadian cities as Edmonton, Calgary, London (Ontario), and Vancouver that lead the world in ensuring that the first agency to respond to the victims of crime is indeed there to help them in the crisis and to provide physical and psychological first aid, as well as referral assistance. The time has come for police leaders across North America to "establish procedures and train personnel toward the recognition and implementation" of the "incontrovertible rights of all crime victims" (IACP, 1983). It is in the interest of police to find the personnel, resources, and commitment to provide justice and assistance—even for the victim—on the streets and in the homes of North America.

REFERENCES

American Psychological Association (1984). *Final report of the Task Force on the Victims of Crime and Violence.*

Bassiouni, M. C. (1988). International Protection of Victims. Special issue *Nouvelles Etudes Pénales*, special issue, VII.

Bragg, C. (1986). *Meeting the needs of victims: Some research findings.* Ottawa: Solicitor General of Canada.

Canadian Council on Social Development (1985). *Mental health assistance to victims of crime and their families.* Ottawa.

Drennan-Searson, P. (1982). *Crime victim needs and services: Ottawa.* Ottawa: University of Ottawa, Department of Criminology.

Edmonton Police Department (1989). Victim services unit: A Summary.

Goldstein, H. (1987). Toward Community Oriented Policing: Potential, Basic Requirements and Threshold Questions. *Crime and Delinquency. 33:1*:6-30.

Greene, J. R., & Mastrofski, S. D. (1988). *Community policing: Rhetoric or reality.* New York: Praeger.

Jaffe, P., Finlay, & Wolfe. (1984). Evaluating the Impact of a Specialized Civilian Family Crisis Unit Within a Police Force on the Resolution of Family Conflicts. *Journal of Preventive Psychiatry. 2:1*:63-73.

International Association of Chiefs of Police (1983). Crime Victims Bill of Rights. Board of Officers. Arlington: Policy Center.

National Organization for Victim Assistance (1988). *Victim Rights and Services: A Legislative Directory.* Washington, DC: NOVA.

Pullyblank, J. (1986). *The victim services unit of the Edmonton police department: An evaluation.* Ottawa: Solicitor General.

Reiff, R. (1979). *The Invisible Victim.* New York: Basic Books.

Resick, P. A. (1987). Psychological effects of victimization: Implications for the criminal justice system. *Crime and Delinquency, 33*, 4, 468-478.

Rosenbaum, D. P. (1987). Coping with victimization: The effects of policy intervention on victims' psychological readjustment. *Crime and Delinquency, 33*:4, 502-519.

Shapland, J., & Duff, J. W. P. (1985). *Victims in the criminal justice system* (pp. 175-194). London: Gower.

Skogan, W. G. & Wycoff, M. A. (1987). Some unexpected effects of a police service for victims. *Crime and Delinquency, 33*:4, 490-501.

Skogan, W. G. (1985). Making better use of victims and witnesses. In W. Geller (Ed.), *Police leadership in America*, (pp. 332-339). New York: Praeger.

United Natios General Assembly (1985). *The declaration on basic principles of justice for victims of crime and abuse of power.* (40/34)

U.S. Department of Justice (1988). *Report to the nation on crime and justice.* Washington, DC: U.S. Government Printing Office.

Waller, I. (1989a). *Crime prevention in a community policing context.* Ottawa: Report for Solicitor General Canada.

Waller, I. (1989b). *Current trends in European crime prevention.* Ottawa: Justice Canada.

Waller, I. (1986). Crime victims not to be orphans of social policy: Needs, services and reforms. In Miyazawa, K., & Ohya, M. *Victimology in comparative perspective* (pp. 302-322). Tokyo: Seibundo.

Waller, I. & Okihiro, N. (1978). *Burglary: The victim and the public.* Toronto: University of Toronto Press.

Chapter 9

VICTIM SERVICE PROGRAMS

ROBERT C. DAVIS
MADELINE HENLEY

The growth of service programs in the United States has been nothing short of phenomenal. Whereas 20 years ago there were none, today experts estimate the number of programs to be in excess of 5,000.[1] Thanks, in part, to federal funding through the Victims of Crime Act (VOCA), victim service programs have developed a secure niche for themselves both within and outside of the criminal justice system.

This chapter traces the origins of service programs in both government and private initiatives. It then looks at where service programs are today and where they are heading. Finally, it asks some hard questions about whether the services victim programs offer meet the needs of their clientele.

THE ORIGINS OF VICTIM PROGRAMS

Early Government Initiatives

During the late 1960s, a series of victimization surveys was launched by the President's Commission on Law Enforcement and the Administration of Justice and later by the Law Enforcement Assistance Administration (LEAA). The results of these studies were considered alarming because they showed that, as high as reported crime was, the actual

AUTHORS' NOTE: *We would like to thank the following people for sharing their thoughts with us and for offering us much useful information: Lucy Friedman, John Stein, Cheryl Tyiska, Janice Lord, Shelley Neiderbach, Constance Noblett, Sherry Price, Deborah Spungen, David Wertheimer, and Nancy Ruhe.*

crime rate was much higher: Many people were failing to report crimes to the police.

At about the same time, it was becoming evident that even when victims did report crimes and police did make arrests, the victims and other witnesses frequently did not cooperate in prosecuting the defendants. As a result, many cases that might have resulted in conviction had victims cooperated more fully with prosecutors were eventually dismissed. As early as 1967, the President's Commission on Law Enforcement and Criminal Justice noted that:

> In recent years there has been growing concern that the average citizen identifies himself less and less with the criminal process and its officials. In particular, citizens have manifested reluctance to come forward with information, to participate as witnesses in judicial proceedings, and to serve as jurors. The causes of these negative attitudes are many and complex, but some aspects of the problems may be traced directly to treatment afforded witnesses and jurors.

The reluctance of victim/witnesses to attend court and the consequences of their failure to do so were soon highlighted in other studies. The Courts Task Force of the National Advisory Commission on Criminal Justice Standards and Goals (1973) reported that the failure of victim/witnesses to attend court proceedings was a significant contributor to dismissal rates. At about the same time, a study in Washington, D.C., revealed that nearly half of felony arrests were being rejected for prosecution at the prosecutor's initial screening because victim/witnesses were uncooperative (Hamilton & Work, 1973).

In an influential paper, Ash (1972) attributed victim/witness noncooperation to the high costs that citizens suffer as a result of their involvement in the prosecution of criminals:

> In the typical situation the witness will several times be ordered to appear at some designated place, usually a courtroom, but sometimes a prosecutor's office or grand jury room. Several times he will be made to wait tedious, unconscionable long intervals of time in dingy courthouse corridors or in other grim surroundings. Several times he will suffer the discomfort of being ignored by busy officials and the bewilderment and painful anxiety of not knowing what is going on around him or what is going to happen to him. . . . In sum, the experience is dreary, time-wasting, depressing, exhausting, confusing, frustrating, numbing and seemingly endless. (p. 390)

In response to the reluctance of citizens to become involved in the criminal justice system, the Law Enforcement Assistance Administration (LEAA) began a Citizens' Initiative Program in 1974. The purpose of the program was to encourage citizens to cooperate in the apprehension and conviction of criminals. As part of this effort, the Citizen's Initiative Program planned to fund 19 victim/witness projects during its first year. The funding of these projects marked the formal beginning of what Stein (1977) has referred to as the "victim movement."

By 1978, more than 90 victim/witness projects had been funded by LEAA. Many were located within, or worked closely with, prosecutors' offices in order to encourage victim/witnesses to cooperate in the conviction of criminals. Projects created reception centers to provide comfortable and secure places for victim/witnesses to wait while in court, aided them in collecting witness fees from prosecutors, assisted with the prompt return of stolen property that had been recovered, and encouraged officials to take strong action in instances when victim/witnesses were threatened by defendants. A number of projects began or expanded the use of standby telephone "alerts" to keep victim/witnesses from having to appear in court unless it was determined on the day of a scheduled hearing that the victim/witness was actually needed. These projects also distributed brochures, explained court procedures, and notified victim/witnesses of upcoming court dates in order to provide victim/witnesses with a clearer understanding of the court process.

Initiatives by Private Citizens

At the same time that the federal government was supporting programs for victims, private initiatives were developing. In contrast to the federal interest, which was largely motivated by a desire to improve the justice system, private, or grass-roots, efforts were prompted by the simple humanitarian conviction that society has an obligation to treat victims fairly. This is an important philosophical distinction, and one that has guided programatic and legislative changes in the 1980s.

The first grass-roots programs were established between 1972 and 1976. Of the first three, all begun in 1972, two were rape crisis centers that grew out of the impetus of the women's movement. Such centers "in time set the model of crisis response to all victims" (Young, 1988: p. 320). The feminist ideology that guided these first programs was incorporated by grass-roots philosophy; grass-roots victim service programs allied themselves with the victim, defining themselves as clear alternatives to existing flawed structures. They resisted joining established systems and rejected the possibility of working within the criminal justice system to achieve justice for victims. During the early years, grass-roots programs were even reluctant to pursue federal or state money since doing so would require them to meet codes and regulations mandated by the system.

Most grass-roots victim service programs were founded by former victims; they were—and still are—run predominantly by laypeople. Typically, grass-roots programs were begun by victims who, in seeking recourse or assistance, discovered that needed services were lacking or inadequate. In addition, as victims found that family and friends were not able to help them, and in fact sometimes stigmatized them for their victimization, they frequently turned to other victims for the validation and encouragement they needed. For example, Parents of Murdered Children (POMC), which now has 256 chapters in the United States and Canada, was begun by a couple whose daughter was murdered. They had contacted crisis intervention agencies, as well as professionals, and found neither to be sufficiently helpful. Finally, they were put in touch with three other families who had experienced similar losses and discovered empathy from peers to be essential to their recovery.

Grass-roots victim service programs have diverse agendas, which may include either legislative change, public education, or long-term or crisis counseling, or all of these. Mothers Against Drunk Driving (MADD) was founded in 1981 by the mother of a young woman killed by a drunk driver. She examined existing laws, discovered that drunk driving was not a crime in the penal codes, and began to work for legislative reforms on her own. While MADD has clearly been successful in encouraging legislative reform—4000 drunk driving laws have been changed—it now also offers support services for victims. At POMC, providing crisis intervention and support groups for victims are priorities. Unfortunately, service programs are often restricted by limited funding as to how many and what types of services they can offer.

Recent Legislative Initiatives

During the 1980s, government, prodded by grass-roots groups, has regained center stage in the victim service movement. Recent legislative activity has greatly altered the standing of victims in the courts.

Victims finally have the right to fair treatment and have begun to emerge as participants in the legal system.

In 1981, President Reagan proclaimed an annual National Victims of Crime Week which was designed to focus attention on victim issues. In April 1982, he established the President's Task Force on Victims of Crime, which made 68 recommendations for addressing the problems of victims. Then, in 1984, the Attorney General's Task Force on Family Violence presented 63 recommendations for combating violence within the family and for aiding its victims.

In addition, Congress passed several laws promoting victims' rights. The 1982 Omnibus Victim and Witness Protection Act requires victim impact statements to be considered at sentencing in federal criminal cases. This also provides for greater protection of federal victims and witnesses from intimidation by defendants or their associates, restitution by offenders to victims of federal crimes, guidelines for fair treatment of victims and witnesses in federal criminal cases, and more stringent bail laws.

The 1984 Victims of Crime Act established a Crime Victims Fund to aid state compensation and victim assistance programs, as well as victims of federal crimes. The fund, which supported nearly 1,500 programs during fiscal year 1986, draws its revenues from fines, penalty assessments, bond forfeitures, and literary profits from federal offenders. Priority in funding is given to programs serving victims of sexual assault, spouse abuse, and child abuse. VOCA represents a renewal of the early federal commitment to fund victim programs. It has become a key component in the overall picture of victim assistance in the United States.

Led by Wisconsin in 1980, states have also been active in establishing victims' rights. Since then, at least 35 states have passed comprehensive legislation protecting the interests of victims, and at least 43 states have given victims the right to prepare victim impact statements prior to sentencing defendants.

Most recently, victim rights activists have lobbied for amendments to state constitutions in order to guarantee victims and family members the right to be present during court proceedings and the right to be notified of significant developments in their cases. As of November 1988, such amendments have been passed in California, Rhode Island, Michigan, and Florida.

CURRENT TRENDS

In their 20-year history, service programs have grown and evolved rapidly. In this section we will look at some developments and issues that we believe are important to understanding where service programs are heading.

Integration of Grass-roots Programs with the Justice System

Founders of service programs for victims of rape and domestic violence were frequently critical of the criminal justice system, which they felt tolerated, and therefore encouraged, violence toward women. In turn, criminal justice officials wanted little to do with such "extremists." Consequently, early grass-roots programs operated largely outside the established criminal justice structure (Friedman, 1985).

Operating with close ties to the community rather than to the criminal justice system did have some advantages. Grass-roots programs were tied into service networks within the community. Being outside of the criminal justice system, the programs had the credibility to work with victims distrustful of the system, including those who didn't report crimes to the authorities.

Working outside the system, however, could also be problematic. Because community-based programs had little access to victims involved in the criminal justice system, they had limited opportunity to improve the system's handling of victims (Finn & Lee, 1987). Eventually, grass-roots victim service providers came to acknowledge that they must in some manner reconcile themselves with the criminal justice system in order to better aid victims in the court process. Grass-roots service programs did not embrace the criminal justice system, but were instead determined to work to reform it.

Criminal justice agencies, too, saw reasons to cooperate with community-based programs. Changing public opinion and several key lawsuits made it clear that criminal justice agencies had to modify the way they dealt with rape and domestic violence. The 1984 report of the Attorney General's Task Force on Domestic Violence threw the weight of the federal government behind reform and boosted the credibility of rape and domestic violence advocates.

Thus, the system began to respond and to institute reforms. Many service programs that began outside the establishment now work to educate law enforcement, prosecutors, and judges about victimization, running training programs to teach these groups to identify and be more responsive to victims' needs. Instead of excluding the police, the programs now bring their concerns to them. Rape crisis centers, for example, now often expect the police to make a referral and to support a woman through the system. Victim advocates are getting involved at all stages of the court process, even at corrections.[2]

Qualifications of Crisis Intervention Workers

The current concern of grass-roots victim service programs with demonstrating their credibility influences not only their attitude toward the criminal justice system, but also their internal policies. Their desire to increase levels of professionalism in service provision has caused them to examine the questions of who should be responsible for giving psychological support to victims and what should be the requisite qualifications for victim counselors.

Historically, the leaders of victim services support groups have been predominantly lay people: volunteers and former victims. Peer-led support groups are the most common, and many people believe that those who have themselves experienced the feelings of victimization can best help others. Yet, as knowledge about the extensive, long-term psychological trauma of victims of serious violent crimes has grown, it has become clear that mental health professionals might be better equipped to deal with the emotional effects of victimization. Some funding sources determined to fund only those programs with mental health professionals on staff, a position endorsed by the 1982 President's Task Force on Victims of Crime.

However, having a degree in the field of mental health does not guarantee knowledge of issues specific to crime victims. Indeed, mental health professionals have been said to be "strangely passive in the area of victim services" (Kiresuk & Lund, 1981: p. 40).

Many programs seem to have struck a balance by using a combination of laypeople and trained professionals to counsel victims. At Mothers Against Drunk Driving (MADD), for example, telephone crisis intervention is generally conducted by peers. During the intervention, the worker tries to connect victims to families who have experienced a similar loss. But, if the victim is thought to need professional care, crisis intervention workers are trained to refer such victims to professionals in the community. Group counseling sessions are co-facilitated by a former victim and a professional. At Parents of Murdered Children, crisis intervention and monthly support groups are conducted by people who have lost a family member to homicide. Crisis intervention workers are carefully screened and then receive training from a mental health professional.

These approaches are variations on a theme that calls for a combination of the skills and experience both laypeople and professionals have to offer. There is general agreement that minimal standards of qualifications for both groups need to be established to ensure quality care for crime victims. Mental health professionals need to be trained in trauma counseling, an essential service for crime victims who suffer from Post-Traumatic Stress Disorder. Conversely, lay service providers need training in order to identify trauma cases and, if necessary, make the appropriate referrals.

Community Crisis Intervention

Historically, community services have been targeted to individual victims. Recently, however, the concept of "victim" has been expanded to include entire communities affected by tragedy. In 1986, NOVA organized a Crisis Response Team (CRT) to assist communities beset by such disasters as plane crashes, bus and car accidents, shootings, electrocutions, and forest fires. The CRT is a nationwide network of volunteers who have attended NOVA-sponsored training sessions throughout the country.

When a community requests help, NOVA staff members contact network members in the vicinity of the stricken community. Typically, a specific team consists of a NOVA coordinator, member of the clergy, mental health professional, law enforcement representative, medical specialist, and press liaison. The community pays for transportation and lodging, but team members do not receive pay for their work.

Upon arrival, team members discuss strategy and interview community leaders to gain an understanding of the scope and effects of the disaster. Team members work with natural helpers—firemen, policemen, school counselors, and so forth—to help them develop strategies for dealing with the trauma inflicted by the crisis. Finally, the team advertises and holds community debriefing sessions, during which they discuss the disaster with affected residents. Within 48 hours, CRT volunteers are on their way home, and the community's natural helpers take over.

DO SERVICE PROGRAMS HELP?

It is clear that victim service programs have multiplied rapidly. They have also begun to mature: The questions of how to become integrated with the criminal justice establishment and the extent to which counselors ought to possess professional credentials suggest a social movement no longer in its infancy. As programs become more established and sophisticated, it becomes reasonable to ask whether they are doing a good job of serving the needs of their target population. That is the focus of this third section: (1) Are programs providing the services victims need? (2) Are they reaching the people they seek to serve? and (3) Are the services that programs provide effective in healing the trauma of victimization? Although data are limited, some research results are available to help answer each of these questions.

Are Programs Meeting People's Needs?

A study by Friedman, Bischoff, Davis, and Person (1982) of victims who reported crimes to the police in New York City provided the most comprehensive look at specific victim needs. The researchers tallied the proportion of victims who needed each of 12 different forms of assistance, from borrowing money, to psychological counseling, to finding a temporary place to stay. However, the primary interest of the Friedman et al. study was to look at informal social support received by victims after the crime. Recognizing that it does not make good public policy sense for service programs to supplant natural support systems, the researchers looked at the proportion of people who needed, but did not receive, each of the 12 kinds of assistance through informal sources. That group of victims would be the ones whose needs could only be met by service programs.

Friedman et al. found that improving security (repairing or upgrading locks and doors) and borrowing money were the types of help most needed by victims in their sample after informal support was discounted. A study of English crime victims by Maguire and Corbett (1987) came up with relatively similar conclusions with respect to the proportion of victims who needed help with improving security and making ends meet but did not get assistance from friends, family, or neighbors.

The importance of security assistance and emergency financial aid in these studies is interesting when contrasted with results of a recent study by Roberts (1987). Roberts surveyed 184 victim assistance programs throughout the United States. He found that security and financial assistance were among the *least* common services that programs offered: Only 13% offered the former service, and 24% the latter. Moreover, Roberts noted that most programs do not intervene immediately but do so days or weeks after the crime. By that time, it may be too late to help victims resolve urgent practical problems, such as repairing broken doors, windows, or locks or buying groceries.

This discrepancy between what victims need and what programs offer may result from an historical emphasis in victim services on the mental and emotional needs of victims. The field has been strongly influenced by mental health professionals (see, for example, Salasin, 1981; Symonds, 1975; Bard & Sangrey, 1979) and clinical researchers studying rape victims (e.g., Burgess & Holmstrom, 1974; Sutherland & Scherl, 1970) who have documented the serious emotional needs that some victims may have.

The limited information available suggests that there may be significant victim needs that are not now being met. It might be worthwhile for programs as a whole to consider placing greater emphasis on practical forms of help like security assistance and emergency financial aid.

Are Programs Reaching All Those in Need?

Again, there is little information available with which to answer this question. However, the scant evidence that does exist suggests that service programs reach only a small fraction of persons victimized by crime. For example, a study of Milwaukee residents found that few persons who reported being victims of crime sought aid from service organizations (Knudten, Meade, Knudten, & Doerner, 1976). The study of New York City crime victims by Friedman et al. (1982) found that only 15% sought aid from service organizations, including welfare, the housing authority, Social Security Administration, senior citizens groups, or the state's crime victims compensation program. Less than 1% sought assistance from the city's Victim Services Agency. An unpublished study by the Victim Services Agency also reported that only 2 to 10% of the persons who filed criminal complaints with the police used services at the agency's community offices, even when they were sent outreach letters describing the assistance available through the agency.

The fact that victim service programs seem to serve a small proportion of victims may not be distressing if they are serving the neediest victims. There is some indication that this is so. For example, the study by Friedman et al. (1982) showed that victims who went to service organizations for help tended to be poorer, to have been victimized more often, and to report more crime-related problems than victims who did not seek formal assistance. Another study conducted by New York's Victim Services Agency (Davis, 1987) also found that persons who used agency services were more traumatized by crime than a sample of victims who reported crimes to the police (few of whom used agency services). This study suggested further that service users tend to suffer from greater life stress (domestic, employment, and health problems) when compared to non-service users.

We know very little about why victims fail to utilize victim service programs. Knudten's study suggested that many simply don't know that help was available. Nonetheless, in the New York experiment with outreach letters, victims were made aware of services, yet still very few sought help.

There is a need in the victim services "industry" for basic market research to find out what forms of aid people seek when they come to service programs and whether those needs are being met. Conversely, we need to know whether those who don't come for assistance are aware of available programs, whether the victims have a need for services, and whether their needs correspond to the services offered by programs. That kind of research would go a long way toward determining whether it would be worthwhile for programs to engage in more strenuous outreach efforts or to rethink the mix of services they offer.

Are Service Programs Effective?

While crisis intervention has been widely applied to the treatment of crime victims, there is relatively little data on whether it is effective in helping victims to recover. In a 1981 survey of victim assistance programs, Cronin and Bourque decried the lack of evaluative data on crisis intervention services: "No studies have yet examined whether project clients suffer less trauma, either in the short or long run, than victims who go without help" (1982: p. 100). When the American Psychological Association's Task Force on the Victims of Crime and Violence issued its final report in 1984, they found that the situation had changed little. The Task Force report states bluntly, "Both those who seek help and those who pay for services deserve interventions for which the efficacy is known or is under systematic study. Little is known about the effectiveness of services currently being offered to victims" (p. 100).

Recently, some studies on the effects of counseling have begun to appear in the literature. Most, however, have not focused on the crisis intervention model that most victim programs use. Rather, they have examined the effects of cognitive-behavioral therapies on rape victims (e.g., Kilpatrick & Veronen, 1984; Frank & Stewart, 1984; Becker, Skinner, Abel, & Cichon, 1984). Even within this limited domain, these studies have not shed much light on the broad question, "Does counseling help?" (For an expanded discussion, see Davis, 1987).

The first study to examine the crisis intervention model was conducted by the Institute for Social Analysis (ISA). ISA's study (Harrell, Smith, & Cook, 1985) was of the Pima County Victim/Witness Advocate Program in Tucson, Arizona, a program that provides on-site crisis intervention services to victims of all types of crimes when summoned to the crime scene by the police. ISA's study compared victims for whom the police had summoned a victim caseworker to the scene to those for whom they had not requested a caseworker. The authors concluded that "despite the victims' feelings that the program helped them considerably, the measures of emotional trauma did not indicate any substantial effects" (p. 103). However, the authors noted that the program service and control groups were not, in fact, very comparable because the police called in the victim assistance crisis unit only for the most severely traumatized victims.

Another large study of the effectiveness of crisis intervention services was conducted at New York's Victim Services Agency by Davis (1987). That study randomly assigned 249 victims of robbery, burglary, and assault to either a crisis counseling treatment or a control treatment. Victims on the crisis counseling condition received material crisis assistance (help with practical problems, such as document replacement, filing state compensation claims, and relocation information) and psychological counseling. Victims in the control condition received no assistance. Victims' recovery was assessed three months following treatment, using measures of material adjustment and standardized psychological scales. No effects of counseling were evident.

The New York study noted that the three-month follow-up interval used was relatively long. It may be that victims who had received program services showed an initial advantage over those who did not get services. But by the end of three months, control victims may have recovered on their own to the point where they were indistinguishable from those who received counseling. This argument suggests that future research should either examine counseling outcomes on a shorter term basis or study only victims likely to experience serious, long-lasting trauma (for example, rape victims or homicide survivors).

So, overall, there is little indication from research to date that counseling of any sort is effective in reducing postcrime trauma.[3] Given the infancy of the field, that indication is hardly surprising; the situation is little better in other areas of crisis intervention (see, for example, the discussion of crisis counseling outcome research in the fields of suicide prevention, acute psychiatric crises, and surgical patients in Auerbach & Kilmann, 1978). It has only been in recent years that the weight of evidence has begun to suggest that even long-term psychotherapy for neuroses is more effective than no treatment (Smith, Glass, & Miller, 1980). The effects of counseling are simply not easy to measure, and the methodological problems involved in trying to measure them are substantial. Still, much money is being spent on crisis intervention services for victims, and—as the American Psychological Association's Task Force suggested—those who receive services and pay for them certainly have a need to know which forms of treatment work and which do not.

NOTES

1. Based on the number of programs in the directory of the National Organization of Victim Assistance and upon a study by the Office for Victims of Crime, U.S. Department of Justice.

2. In June 1988, the American Corrections Association Task Force on Victims of Crime made 15 recommendations to the Department of Corrections concerning its handling of victims' needs.

3. Maguire and Corbett (1987) composed a small sample of British robbery and burglary victims who used services with a similar sample of victims who had not used services. They report that victims who had been through counseling felt better adjusted than those who hadn't, but the difference was not statistically reliable.

REFERENCES

American Psychological Association (1984). Final report to the Task Force on the Victims of Crime and Violence.

Ash, M. (1972). On witnesses: A radical critique of criminal court procedures. *Notre Dame Lawyer, 48*, 386-425.

Auerbach, S. M., & Kilman, P. R. (1978). Crisis intervention: a review of outcome research. *Psychological Bulletin, 84*, 1189-1217.

Bard, M. B., & Sangrey, D. (1979). *The crime victim's book.* New York: Basic Books, Inc.

Becker, J. B., Skinner, L. J., Abel, G. G., & Cichon, J. (1984). Time limited therapy with sexually dysfunctional sexually assaulted women. *Journal of Social Work and Human Sexuality, 3*, 97-115.

Burgess, A. W., & Holmstrom, L. L. (1974). *Rape: Victims of crisis.* Bowie, MD: Robert J. Brady Co.

Cronin, R. C., & Bourque, B. B. (1981). *Assessment of victim/witness assistance projects, Phase I report.* Final report of the American Institutes for Research to the U.S. Department of Justice.

Davis, R. C. (1987). *Providing help to victims: A study of psychological and material outcomes.* Final report of Victim Services Agency (New York) to the National Institute of Justice.

Finn, P., & Lee, B. (1987). *Serving crime victims and witnesses.* Washington, DC: National Institute of Justice.

Frank, E., & Stewart, B. D. (1984). Physical aggression: Treating the victims. In E. A. Blechman (Ed.), *Behavior modification with women.* New York: The Guilford Press.

Friedman, K., Bischoff, L., Davis, R., & Person, A. (1982). *Victims and helpers: Reactions to crime.* Washington, DC: U.S. Government Printing Office.

Friedman, L. (1985). The crime victim movement at its first decade. *Public Administration Review,* November 1985, 790-794.

Hamilton, W. A., & Work C. R. (1973). The prosecutor's role in the urban court system: The cases for management consciousness. *Journal of Criminal Law and Criminology,* 183-189.

Harrell, A. V., Smith, B. E., & Cook, R. F. (1985). The social psychological effects of victimization. Final report to the National Institute of Justice.

Kilpatrick, D. G., & Veronen, L. J. (1984). Treatment of fear and anxiety in victims of rape. Final report to the National Institute of Mental Health, Grant No. MH29602.

Kiresuk, T. J., & Lund, S. (1981). Knowledge transfer for victim services. In S. Salasin (Ed.), *Evaluating victim services.* Beverly Hills, CA: Sage Publications.

Knudten, R. D., Meade, A., Knudten, M., & Doerner, W. (1976). *Victims and witnesses: The impact of crime and their experience with the criminal justice system.* Washington, DC: U.S. Government Printing Office.

Maguire, M., & Corbett, C. (1987). *The effects of crime and the work of victims support schemes.* Hampshire, England: Gower House.

National Advisory Commission on Criminal Justice Standards and Goals (1973). *Courts.* Washington, DC; U.S. Government Printing Office.

Roberts, A. (1987). "National survey of victim services completed." *NOVA Newsletter, 11*(9), 1-2.

Salasin, S. (1981). Services to victims: Needs assessment. In S. Salasin (Ed.), *Evaluating victim services.* Beverly Hills, CA: Sage Publications.

Smith, M. L., Glass, G. V., & Miller, T. I. (1980). *Psychotherapy.* Baltimore: Johns Hopkins University Press.

Stein, J. H. (1977). *Better services for crime victims: A prescriptive package.* Unpublished manuscript.

Sutherland, S. & Scherl, D. (1970). Patterns of response among victims of rape. *American Journal of Orthopsychiatry, 40*, 503-511.

Symonds, M. (1975). Victims of violence: Psychological effects and after-effects. *The American Journal of Psychoanalysis, 40*, 503-511.

Young, M. (1988). The crime victims' movement. In F. Ochberg (Ed.), *Post-Traumatic Therapy and Victims of Violence*. New York: Brunner-Mazel.

Chapter 10

VICTIM PARTICIPATION IN THE CRIMINAL JUSTICE SYSTEM

DEBORAH KELLY

It was not long ago that attention to victims was limited to sensation-alized reports of lurid crimes. During the late 1970s and early 1960s, various organizations worked to change that emphasis and to increase public awareness of how insensitively victims were being treated by the criminal justice system. These "consciousness-raising" efforts resulted in administrative changes within police departments and the courts, and more recently in legislation to increase victims' rights within the criminal justice system. As most states have now adopted some type of victim reforms, the time is right to review these changes and assess whether they actually benefit crime victims or are instead undelivered promises.

This chapter will focus on reforms that seek to increase victims' participation in the criminal justice system. I will therefore: (1) summarize what led to a focus on increased rights to participation; (2) briefly describe the various forms of victims' participation adopted by federal and state legislatures, including victim-impact statements, rights of allocution, and rights to attend the trial of the accused; and (3) consider the impact of these reforms and the related debate over whether such reforms have gone too far or not far enough.

A CONCISE HISTORY OF VICTIMS' REFORMS

As recently as the early 1970s, attention to crime victims was virtually nonexistent. Efforts to change this were initiated by feminists, who mobilized to increase public awareness of callous treatment to which rape victims were subjected by the criminal justice system, and "law and order groups," who argued that fewer criminals were prosecuted and convicted as a result of this poor treatment. During this time, victim advocates often sought to publicize the personal trauma of victimization in an effort to elicit sympathy for crime victims and thereby increase public attention to their needs.

Once attention turned to victims, the next step was to change criminal justice procedures to be more sensitive to their concerns. Administrative reforms were adopted to notify victims when hearings were scheduled so that they would not be kept waiting unnecessarily. In many courthouses, separate waiting rooms were established for defense and state witnesses. Police departments also responded by providing training to their officers to educate them about the special needs of rape victims and to minimize victim-blaming behavior.[1]

Such reforms were not motivated primarily by a newfound compassion for victims. Rather, studies suggested that the criminal justice system itself would directly benefit by "being nicer to victims." National Crime Survey revealed that, at best, 50% of crimes were reported to the police.[2] A major reason for nonreporting was victims' apprehension as to how they would be treated[3] and whether they would be believed.[4] Others studies showed that although prosecutors blamed high dismissal rates on victim and witness noncooperation, victims and witnesses were not generally uncooperative—just intimidated by the criminal justice system and uninformed as to what they were expected to do.[5] Accordingly, victim-witness units were designed to address the victims' need for better treatment and more information, as well as the state's need for cooperative witnesses.

Although these attitudinal and administrative changes were certainly welcome, crime victims wanted more than pity and politeness. They wanted rights to participate in the criminal justice system. This prospect of victim participation, however, met with resistance because it threatened to disturb established patterns within the courthouse. Studies showed that within the judicial branch, prosecutors, defense attorneys, and judges operated as a "work group," sharing the mutual goal of disposing of cases as fast as time and justice would allow.[6] To introduce the victim as a fourth party in decision-making would be to upset the efficiency of this work group and slow down an already overloaded docket. As researchers concluded after studying a project promoting victim involvement in Brooklyn Criminal Courts:

> Prosecutors are particularly likely to resist consideration of the victims' point of view because it is prosecutors' control that would be most eroded if the victim were given a greater voice. . . . [C]ourthouse professionals have a substantial interest in processing cases in summary fashion and . . . may tend to become insensitive to human suffering involved in the "normal crimes" they process.[7]

The work group, however, also needed cooperative victims and witnesses to function smoothly. As Congress stated in enacting the Victim Witness Protection Act of 1982 (VWPA),[8] "The Congress finds and declares that . . . without the cooperation of victims . . . the criminal justice system would cease to function." Rights to victim participation were also endorsed by the National Judicial College[9] and the President's Task Force on Victims of Crime.[10] Even the Supreme Court took notice that victims could only be pushed so far. As it stated in *Morris v. Slappy*, 461 U.S. 1, 14 (1983):

> The court wholly failed to take into consideration the interest of the victim of these crimes in not undergoing the ordeal of a third trial in this case . . . . [I]n the administration of criminal justice, courts may not ignore the concerns of victims. Apart from other factors such a course would hardly encourage victims to report violations to the proper authorities. Precisely what weight should be given to the ordeal of reliving such an experience for the third time need not be decided now but that factor is not to be ignored by the courts.

The Court reaffirmed this view in *U.S. v. Hasting*. As Chief Justice Burger wrote, "The Court of Appeals failed to give appropriate—if indeed any—weight to these relevant interests. It did not consider the trauma the victims of these particularly heinous crimes would experience in a new trial, forcing them to relive harrowing experiences now long past" (461 U.S. 419, 507, 1983).

Findings of researchers and victim advocates substantiated this link between how well victims were treated by criminal justice personnel and how likely victims were to cooperate with them. Those victims who were satisfied with their treatment expressed more willingness to cooperate with the criminal justice system in the future. This satisfaction was in turn related to perceived levels of participation. Research indicated that victims' satisfaction increased if they perceived that they had influenced the criminal justice process, regardless of whether they really had.[11] For example, victims who believed they were able to speak with prosecutors and judges were more satisfied with the criminal justice system than those who believed they were not able to do so.[12] Indeed, studies revealed that a sense of participation was more critical to victims' satisfaction with the criminal justice system than how severely the defendant was punished.[13]

In short, studies suggested that in spite of the fact that victims were outsiders to the work group, or perhaps because of it,[14] victim satisfaction ultimately benefited the work group. Participation increased levels of satisfaction, which increased the likelihood that victims would cooperate. More cooperative witnesses would in turn increase prosecutors' efficiency as fewer witness conferences would have to be rescheduled, fewer police officers brought back to court, and fewer cases dismissed because of witness noncooperation.

Victim participation not only affected potential cooperation with the criminal justice system, but it also promoted victims' recovery from the aftermath of crime by helping them reassert a sense of control over their lives. As psychologist Dean Kilpatrick noted, "the perception-of-control variable has been identified as a key factor in understanding the impact of victimization . . .[15] a criminal justice system that provides no opportunity for victims to participate in proceedings would foster greater feelings of helplessness and lack of control than one that offers the victim such rights."[16]

Additionally, victim participation was thought to increase accuracy in the judicial process by providing judges with facts that would otherwise be lost in the bureaucracy of criminal courts.[17] As Prof. Goldstein wrote "By the time a file is closed, it may not be clear to anyone what a conviction or dismissal stands for . . . by the time such matters are presented to a court, defense counsel and prosecutor are in agreement and have a considerable stake in blurring the underlying facts."[18]

As victim advocates began their successful campaign to persuade state and federal legislators to establish statutory rights to victim participation, they armed themselves with these three tools of persuasion: administrative efficiency, compassion for victims, and accuracy in the judicial process.

LEGISLATIVE REFORMS

In this section, I will provide an overview of three kinds of statutory reforms designed to increase victim participation in the criminal justice system: victim participation in plea bargaining; victim involvement in sentencing, including victim-impact statements and rights of allocution; and victim attendance at trial.

Plea Bargaining

Plea bargains and dismissals are the most common ways to dispose of cases. National estimates indicate that between 83 and 90% of all cases that remain in the system are plea bargained.[19] Until recently, however, the victim's role in plea bargaining was rarely considered. Indeed, a noted expert on plea bargaining, Alan Alschuler, once described the victim's opinion of plea bargaining as "extraneous."[20]

The prosecutor's discretion in plea bargaining is paramount; the usual role for victims in plea bargaining is as a weapon or weakness in the prosecutor's arsenal. An articulate victim, who would make a good courtroom appearance, could be used as leverage against the defense. The reverse is also true. An inarticulate, easily rattled state's witness could work in favor of the defense in plea negotiations. The irony is that the better witness the victim is, the less likely she or he would ever be called upon to testify. Since testifying had traditionally been the only method for victims to participate in the judicial process, plea bargaining excluded them completely.

In the early 1980s, that began to change. Many organizations endorsed some form of victim participation in plea bargaining. In the Victim Witness Protection Act of 1982, Congress stated that prosecutors should consult victims about the terms of a plea. The American Bar Association approved Guidelines for Fair Treatment of Crime Victims,[21] which recommended that victims have an opportunity to consult with a prosecutor before the plea is filed and be notified when the prosecutor submits a plea. The ABA Standards Relating to Pleas of Guilty state that prosecutors "should make every effort to remain advised of the attitudes and sentiments of victims . . . before reaching a plea agreement," and the court "may require or allow any person including the alleged victim . . . to appear or testify before approving a plea."[22] Victim participation was also endorsed in the Attorney Generals' Guidelines for Victim and Witness Assistance,[23] by the National Judicial College, and the President's Task Force on Victims.[24]

Such approval has fostered legislative changes. The number of laws allowing victims to have a say before a plea is finalized has doubled since 1985. Twenty-three states now allow or mandate some form of victim participation in plea bargains.[25] As of 1987, seven states allowed victims to participate in plea bargaining by giving them the right to speak to the prosecutor or to address the court.[26]

The extent to which victims are permitted to be involved in deliberations varies considerably. In Nebraska, for example, prosecutors must make a "good faith" effort to consult with victims about negotiations. In Arizona, rights to participation extend only to surviving families of homicide victims. Minnesota law requires the prosecutor to notify the victim about the planned disposition and then allows the victim to file an objection. No state, however, gives victims a veto over plea bargains.

Fear that such victim participation would result in harsh pleas has not been realized. Early experiments suggested that victim participation in deliberations helped victims without harming defendants. In Pima County, Arizona, for example, starting in 1973, defendants in property crime cases were not admitted to county diversion programs without the victim's approval. A preliminary study of the program's early years indicated that less than 5% of victims vetoed their offender's participation in this program.[27] A pilot program in Dade County, Florida, in which victims were allowed to participate in pretrial negotiations, was later replicated nationwide. Researchers found that victims did not routinely recommend that prosecutors "throw the book" at defendants; rather, they generally agreed to the prosecutor's recommendation for proper disposition.[28] Similarly, researchers with the Institute for Law and Social Research (INSLAW) found that victim participation did not result in increased sentences for defendants overall.[29] A recent study of jurisdictions allowing victim participation in plea bargaining again concluded that "victim participation in plea bargains would advance various interests of the victim and of society without any significant detrimental impact to the interests of prosecutors and defendants."[30]

Victim Involvement at Sentencing

Sentencing is one of the most important stages to crime victims because it provides an end to their long ordeal. Ironically, while sentencing is one of the most important to the victim, it occurs at a time when the victim is least important to the state. The victim's crucial role in providing evidence is no longer needed. The defendant has been convicted. The state has won.

Because of these conflicting perspectives, as recently as 1982, victims were routinely excluded from sentencing deliberations. Times have changed. Victim participation in sentencing has been endorsed by the American Bar Association,[31] the National Judicial College,[32] and the President's Task Force on Victims of Crime.[33] In part, these endorsements recognized that victim participation in sentencing clearly benefits victims. In one study, for example, 200 victims were interviewed right after the offender was charged and again after disposition. Results showed that merely attending court during sentencing improved victims' evaluations of sentencing decisions.[34]

As of August 1987, about 96% of the states allowed some form of victim involvement at sentencing.[35] The two most common methods are the victim-impact statement (VIS) or victim statement of opinion (VSO). Victim-impact statements are now required in the federal system under the Victim Witness Protection Act of 1982.[36] Forty-seven states also allow VIS to be introduced at sentencing.[37]

The VIS allows victims to detail the medical, financial, and emotional injuries that resulted from the crime. This information is usually provided to a probation officer, who then writes up a summary that is included in the defendant's presenting packet.[38] The report then goes to the judge, who may give it as little or as much weight as he or she likes.

In contrast, the VSO is considered more subjective. VSO allows victims to tell the court their opinion on what sentence the defendant should receive. This can be accomplished by speaking in court (allocution) or by a written statement to the judge. Currently, about 35 states provide for the direct introduction of victims' opinion at sentencing.[39]

These methods of participation have not been without critics. Some legal scholars question whether victim participation in sentencing blurs the lines between civil and criminal courts. As Prof. Yale Kamisar is quoted as saying, "I wince when I hear that the victim ought to testify at the sentencing or before the parole board. This is not a tort, this is a crime against society."[40] Others express concern that victim-impact statements "have the potential to obfuscate the objectivity of the sentencing judge and parole board."[41] Prof. Henderson has argued that victim-impact statements are a thinly disguised means to wreak vengeance on the defendant, and are further evidence that the victims' movement is actually part of a conservative movement that exploits victims for its own agenda.[42]

Although there is virtually no empirical evidence to back up the assertion that victim-impact statements hurt defendants,[43] nonetheless, a similar argument was raised when Maryland's victim-impact law was successfully challenged in the Supreme Court. In *Booth v. Maryland*,[44] the Court held that victim impact statements were unconstitutional when applied to capital cases. It reasoned that only the defendant's "personal responsibility and moral guilt" may be considered in capital sentencing. In the Court's view, the effect on victims (in this case, survivors of homicide) was irrelevant to the defendant's culpability[45] and served to inflame the jury and divert attention away from the crime and the defendant.[46] This view was narrowly adopted by the Court in a 5-4 decision, in which the dissenters underscored the skewed image such a ruling reflected.[47] As Justice Antonin Scalia noted in his dissent:

> Many citizens have found one-sided and hence unjust the criminal trial in which a parade of witnesses comes forth to testify to the pressures beyond normal human experience that drove the defendant to commit his crime, with no one to lay before the sentencing authority the full reality of human suffering the defendant has produced—which (and *not* moral guilt alone) is one of the reasons society deems his act worthy of the prescribed penalty.[48]

Justice White adopted a similar view in his dissent when he wrote ". . . at bottom, the Court's view seems to be that it is somehow unfair to confront a defendant with an account of the loss his deliberate act has caused the victim's family and society."[49]

Recently, a trial judge in Minnesota afforded a victim rights that were more extensive than those created by victim-impact laws. Minneapolis Trial Judge William Posten allowed a 65-year-old rape victim to choose her assailant's sentence. Her options were to accept the defendant's guilty plea and attached 54 months incarceration, or to have the case go to trial and expose the defendant to the 108-month sentence advocated by the prosecutor. Because the defendant would have been free while awaiting trial, the victim chose the lesser sentence.[50]

Court Attendance

The defendant's right to remain in the courtroom is guaranteed by the Sixth Amendment to the Constitution. Crime victims have no such right. They are lumped together in the category of "state's witnesses." Yet, the trial has special importance for the victim. It is the moment the victim has both waited for and dreaded. Not only will the defendant's fate be determined, but the victim's reputation and character may also be attacked.

If so, unlike the defendant, victims will not be in the courtroom to defend themselves and consult with the prosecutor. In most jurisdictions, the rule of sequestration applies. Victims are excluded from court before and after they have testified. While the trial is in progress, victims wait outside the courtroom. For many victims, to be relegated to a hallway or waiting room represents both the ultimate insult and the ultimate loss of control. Their exclusion from trial proceedings sends the clear message, "This case belongs to the state and the defendant, not you. We will call you only if and when we need you." In a study of 100 rape victims, 80% singled out this practice as "unfair to victims." As one respondent commented, "Since I became a witness, I have no rights."[51]

This sense of injustice at being excluded from trial proceedings was a constant theme heard by the President's Task Force on Victims of Crime during the year it received testimony. Family and friends of victims recounted instances wherein they were called as witnesses merely so they could be included in sequestration rules and excluded from court. As a result of this testimony, the Task Force recommended in its Final Report that the Sixth Amendment be amended to guarantee a victim's right "to be present and to be heard at all critical stages of judicial proceedings."[52]

Alabama, the first state to act on this recommendation, passed a law in 1983 that allowed victims to sit at the prosecutor's table during the trial, as well as to attend bench conferences and motions hearings just as the defendant would.[53] Fourteen other states have passed statutes allowing victims to remain in court, subject to the judges' discretion.[54] In four of these states, victims have an absolute right to be present throughout the criminal trial, even if they are witnesses; and in ten states, they have a conditional right to be present after they have testified and at the judge's discretion.

Prof. Hagan's research revealed that such participation was critical to the victim's satisfaction with case outcomes. Merely being notified of sentences was not enough. In fact, Hagan found that information on case outcome often increased the victims' perceptions that the sentence was too lenient, whereas victims who attended hearings were less likely to think that the sentence was too easy.[55]

Inspired by the belief that the victim's attendance at the trial is critical, a national movement was formally organized in 1987. The Victims Constitutional Amendment Network (VCAN) works for state constitutional amendments to allow victims to be present and heard at all stages of the criminal justice system.

ASSESSING THE EFFECT AND REFORMING THE REFORMS

While the above summary of developments may create the impression that victims' rights are omnipresent in most criminal courts, merely counting the number of statutes is misleading. Statutory changes may be a prerequisite for substantive reform, but the ultimate test is whether victims ever receive the benefits of these reforms.

Preliminary research indicates they do not. For example, while VIS have been widely adopted, studies suggest that most victims are either unaware of this right or choose not to use it. In 1982, California enacted Proposition 8 of the Victims' Bill of Rights, which allowed victims "to attend all sentencing proceedings . . . and to reasonably express his or her views concerning the crime, the person responsible, and the need for restitution.[56] Yet, a recent National Institute of Justice study found that less than 3% of eligible victims actually do so.[57] Similarly, a survey of 165 probation offices from thirty-three states concluded that,

> Victims seldom employ these participation options. Overall, fewer than 18% of victims attend sentencing; only 15% of crime victims submit written statements. Where allocution is a statutory right, oral statements are presented by just over 9% of victims. Those victims most likely to participate are sexual assault and violent crime victims.[58]

Results from a Texas study support these findings. The Texas Crime Victim's Bill of Rights[59] requires the Board of Pardon and Parole to notify victims about pending parole hearings. The only way the board learns the names and addresses of victims is through the impact statements that are to be sent to the Board by the prosecutor's office. As Kilpatrick reports,

> [t]he Board received only 106 of the 5850 impact statements (1.8%) obtained by prosecutors. Furthermore, only 6 of the 106 victims whose impact statements had been received were notified by the Board about pending parole hearings.[60]

In addition to the ignorance or disuse of newfound rights, many statutory rights are conditional—they only apply when something else happens first. For example, the use of victim-impact statements in presentencing reports only applies if there is a presentencing report. Rights to allocution are virtually irrelevant in plea bargains. Victims' rights to attend the trial of their assailants only apply to the fraction of cases that go to trial. In effect, many victims reforms are little more than undelivered promises.

If these reforms are not reaching their intended audience, does it matter? Psychologist Dean Kilpatrick, for example, argues "yes" and cautions that there is great danger in promising victims what will not be delivered. "Providing rights without remedies would result in the worse of consequences, such as feelings of helplessness, lack of control, and further victimization. . . . Ultimately, with the crime victims' best interests in mind, it is better to confer no rights at all than 'rights' without remedies."[61]

Many believe victims' "rights" are really privileges that operate at the mercy of the police, prosecutor, or judge.[62] Such sentiments have prompted new efforts to reform the reforms. One proposal is to expand the scope of victim impact statements. Currently, questions arise as to whether VIS should be restricted to those crimes to which the defendant pled guilty or expanded to include all the crimes with which the defendant was charged.[63] The difference can be significant, since restitution to the victim may be tied to the plea.[64]

How this issue is resolved depends on how one views the purpose of victim-impact statements. If it is to learn the full extent of the harm the offender has caused and allow the victim to be a full participant in decision-making, then it does not make sense to limit a victim's description of the crime's aftermath to those acts the state has decided to prosecute. Indeed, from the victims' perspective it is hard to know how one could identify certain injuries as caused by specific conduct and delete other injuries caused by conduct for which the defendant was not charged. Crime does not arrive in such neat packages. From the defendant's perspective, however, it may be unjust to allow the victim to inflame the judge with descriptions of events that are not on the record. If the purpose of victim impact statements is to serve the state by introducing facts before the decision-maker, facts that would otherwise be obscured, then perhaps as one author suggested, if a victim chooses not to speak at sentencing or assist in a VIS, another party (a lawyer or family member) should be able to provide such information.[65]

The desire to curb prosecutorial discretion has prompted a more controversial suggestion for toughening victims' reforms. One legal commentator proposed a model statute that would allow a victim to challenge a prosecutor's decision not to prosecute. An *in camera* hearing would then be held, during which the judge would determine whether the prosecutor abused his or her discretion. If the judge so found an abuse, a declaratory judgment to that effect would be issued.[66]

Another proposal is to allow those victims who are especially vulnerable to revictimization (for example, spouse abuse victims) to:

> petition the court for a judicially initiated prosecution if the public prosecutor refused to file a charge. The petitioner must present evidence that the charge is justifiable and demonstrate that further injury is likely unless criminal prosecution is brought to deter the offender from continuing the illegal conduct. Upon this showing, a trial court would appoint a prosecuting attorney and initiate criminal proceedings.[67]

Many "victim supporters" part company with these approaches. Welling, for example, recommends against a course of action but suggests that victims could file grievances against a judge for violating the code of judicial conduct if the victim is not notified of her rights.[68] Others are concerned that too much victim participation will transform the criminal justice system into a forum for private prosecution, thereby jeopardizing the impartiality of public prosecutors.[69]

CONCLUSION

As the above summary has illustrated, legislative and judicial attention to victims' concerns has increased dramatically over the last fifteen years. Debates over the wisdom and necessity for these changes have often polarized people into warring camps, where victims' rights are seen as mutually exclusive with defendant's rights. Faced with this powerful distortion, many legislators have taken the easy way out and responded with superficial assistance to victims. Doing so placated those who press for improvement in how crime victims are treated, yet it does not challenge established patterns within criminal courts. The work group carries on as usual because, in practice, such reforms are often well-kept secrets that few victims know about or make use of to their advantage.

Such developments increase the need for researchers and policymakers to assess the true impact of victim reforms, evaluate what it would take to implement the reforms, and consider whether support for such reforms would evaporate if victims could invoke a legal remedy when deprived of their statutory rights. Perhaps, as two authors put it, "Victims' rights cannot be grafted onto the existing system without generally remaining simply cosmetic, nor can they be made potent without creating profound changes through the entire system."[70]

NOTES

1. Author Eleanor Chelimsky explains the police motivation for asking questions that appear to blame the victim for the crime: "Victims are, in fact, living reproaches to police claims of being competent ensurers of the public weal. In consequence, they often respond to victims aggressively, making them feel . . . responsible for the crime of which they are in fact victims." In "Serving Victims: Agency Incentives and Individual Needs." In Susan Salasin, ed., *Evaluating Victim Services* (Sage Publications, 1981) p. 86.

2. Bureau of Justice Statistics. U. S. Dept. of Justice, *Report to the Nation on Crime and Justice* (October 1983).

3. Kidd & Cajet, "Why Victims Fail to Report? The Psychology of Criminal Victimization," 40 *Journal of Social Issues* 34-50 (1984).

4. Dean Kilpatrick, Lois Veronen et al., *The Psychological Impact of Crime: A Study of Randomly Surveyed Crime Victims* (National Institute of Justice, 1983).

5. Frank Cannavele, *Witness Cooperation*, Institute for Law and Social Research, (New York: Lexington Books, 1975).

6. James Eisenstein & Herbert Jacob, *Felony Justice: An Organizational Analysis of Criminal Courts* 67-171 (1977).

7. Davis, Kunreuther & Connick, "Expanding the Victim's Role in the Criminal Court Dispositional Process: The Results of an Experiment," 75 *Journal of Criminal Law and Criminology* 491, 504-505 (1984).

8. Public Law # 97-291, 96 Stat 1248 (1982) 18 U.S.C. #1501.

9. National Judicial College, Conference on Victims, Statement of Recommended Judicial Practices II (1983).

10. Office of Justice Programs, U.S. Dept. of Justice, President's Task Force on Victims of Crime, *Final Report* (1982).

11. Barbara Smith, *Non-Stranger Violence: The Criminal Court's Responses* (National Institute of Justice, 1981).

12. Similarly, in a survey of 450 crime victims, 48% stated that they would have been more satisfied if they were better informed about the status of their case; 21% wanted more opportunity to let prosecutors or judges know their opinions about the case. J. Hernon and Brian Forst, *The Criminal Justice Response to Victim Harm* (1984) National Institute of Justice, Research Report at 45, 50.

13. Deborah P. Kelly, "Delivering Legal Services to Victims: An Evaluation and Prescription," 9 *Justice System Journal* 62 (1984).

14. One author has suggested that perhaps victim participation benefits the work group precisely *because* victims are outsiders and consequently their "presence would encourage the participants to fulfill their obligations in a responsible manner." Donald Gifford, "Meaningful Reform of Plea Bargaining: The Control of Prosecutorial Discretion," 1983 *U. of Illinois Law Review* 37, 89.

15. Dean G. Kilpatrick & Randy K. Otto, "Constitutionally Guaranteed Participation in Criminal Proceeding for Victims: Potential Effects on Psychological Functioning," 34 *The Wayne Law Review* 17 (1987) referring to Wortman, "Coping with Victimization: Conclusions and Implications for Future Research," 39 *Journal of Social Issues* (1983) 195-221.

16. *Id.* at 19.

17. *See.* Hernon and Forst, *supra* note 12: Gifford, *supra* note 14 at 90; Davis et al. *supra note 7.*

18. Abraham S. Goldstein, "Defining the Role of the Victim in Criminal Prosecutions." 52 *Mississippi Law Journal* 515, 536 (1982). Hernon and Forst's research supported this sentiment and indicated that judges usually do not appreciate the effect a crime has on victims, *supra* note 12 at 43. In a survey of judges, however, two-thirds believed that victim allocution was unnecessary because presentence reports included all the information they needed. Edwin Villmoore and Virginia V. Neto, "Victim Appearances at Sentencing Under California's Victims' Bill of Rights," (National Institute of Justice: August 1987).

19. See, for example, Kathleen B. Brosi, "A Cross-City Comparison of Felony Case Processing," Institute for Law and Social Research, 1979. 35-44.

20. A. Alschuler, "The Prosecutor's Role in Plea Bargaining," 39 *University of Chicago Law Review* 50, 53 (1968).

21. American Bar Association, Criminal Justice Section, Victims Committee. *Guidelines for Fair Treatment of Victim and Witnesses, Guidelines 6 and 10* (1983).

22. Std. 143.1(d) and Std 14.3.3(b)(1).

23. Pt. II, C(3)&(5), 48 Fed. Reg. No. 143, p. 33776 (July 25, 1983), reprinted in 33 *Criminal Law Rep* (BNA) 3329 (Aug. 3, 1983).

24. For a detailed description of victim participation in plea bargaining, see Sarah Welling. "Victim Participation in Plea Bargains," 65 *Washington University Law Quarterly* 301 (1987).

25. *See* Office of Justice Programs, Office for Victims of Crimes. U.S. Dept. of justice, *Victims' Rights and Services: A Legislative Directory 1988* (prepared by the National Organization for Victim Assistance), "NOVA Directory", at 11.

26. These states are Nebraska, West Virginia, South Carolina, Minnesota, Rhode island, Florida, and Indiana. *See* Welling, *supra* note 24 at 340-3.

27. Eduard Zeigenhagen, *Victims, Crime, and Social Control* (Praeger 1977) p. 100.

28. Anne Heinz and Wayne Kerstetter, "Pretrial Settlement Conference: Evaluation of a Reform in Plea Bargaining," 13 *Law and Society Review* 349 (1979). For the full report, *See Pretrial Settlement Conference: An Evaluation* (National Institute of Justice 1979).

29. Hernon and Forst, *supra* note 12 at 33-38.

30. Welling, *supra* note 24 at 355.

31. Guideline 11, *supra* note x at 17-22.

32. Rec. II A-6, B-2 at 21.

33. *Final Report, supra* note 10. Recommendations for the Judiciary at 76-78.

34. J. Hagan, "Victims Before the Law: A Study of Victim Involvement in the Criminal Justice Process." 73 *Journal of Criminal Law and Criminology* 317 (1982).

35. Maureen McLeod, "An Examination of the Victim's Role at Sentencing: Results of a Survey of Probation Administrators," 71 *Judicature* 162, 168 (1987).

36. VWPA amended the Federal Rules of Criminal Procedure to mandate that all presentence reports include a victim-impact statement. P.L. 97-292 Oct. 12, 1982.

37. NOVA Legislative Directory, *supra* note 25 at 9.

38. Although in some jurisdictions, this task is performed by the victim-witness office.

39. NOVA Directory, *supra* note 26 at 10.

40. Keisel, "Crime and Punishment—Victims' Rights Movement Presses Courts, Legislatures," 70 *American Bar Association Journal* 25, 26 (Jan. 1984).

41. Abraham Abramovsky, "Crime Victims Rights," *New York Law Journal* (February 3, 1986).

42. Lynne N. Henderson, "The Wrongs of Victims Rights," 37 *Stanford Law Review* 937, 951 (1985).

43. Indeed, a 1983 study of jurisdictions with victim-impact laws found that with the exception of Ohio, sentences did not increase when the statements were introduced. New York State Crime Victims Board, "A Quick Assessment and Evaluation of Victim Impact Statement Law," (unpublished study, May 1983). Presently, Rob Davis and Barbara Smith are engaged in a field experiment for the National Institute of Justice that will produce further data on this issue.

44. ___U.S.___, 107 S.Ct. 2529 (1987).

45. *Id.* at 2533 (quoting *Enmund v. Florida*, 458 U.S. 782, 801, 1982).

46. *Id.* at 2536.

47. Other commentators have noted the irony of this decision when compared to the Court's rulings concerning the felony-murder doctrine in *Tison v. Arizona* ___U.S.___, 107 S.Ct. 1676 (1987). "The effect of *Tison* is to make a defendant eligible for the death sentence even if he did not kill or intend to kill, whereas the effect of *Booth* may be to render a defendant ineligible for death, even though he intended to kill and killed in the course of commission of a felony." Jackson Sharmon, "Victim-Impact Statements and the 8th Amendment," 11 *Harvard Journal of Law and Public Policy* 583, 592 (1988).

48. *Booth v. Md.*, at 2542 (Scalia, J., Dissenting). emphasis in original.

49. *Id.* at 2536 (White, J., dissenting). The majority's ruling on victim-impact statements has thus far been confined to capital hearings. However, many defense attorneys believe the same arguments pertain to victim-impact statements an therefore all such statutes should be overturned. For a further discussion of *Booth, see* "Should Victim Rights Statements Be Used in Capital Cases?" 20 *Maryland Bar Journal* 2 (1987).

50. Bruce J. Schulte, "Victim Sentences Her Attacker," *The ABA Journal*, April 9, 1989, p. 28.

51. Deborah P. Kelly, *Rape Victims Perceptions of Criminal Justice* (Johns Hopkins University, 1982 unpublished dissertation), p. 209.

52. Final Report, *supra* note 10 at 114. In addition, a law review recently devoted its entire journal to this issue. *See* "Symposium: Perspectives on Proposals for a Constitutional Amendment Providing Victim Participation in the Criminal Justice System," 34 *Wayne Law Review* (Fall 1987).

53. Ala. Code ##15-14-5- to 47 (Supp. 1987).

54. NOVA directory, *supra* note 26 at 18.

55. Hagan, *supra* note 34 at 323-37. Others, however, have found that victims are more interested in information about their cases than the right to participate. *See* Villmoare and Neto, *supra* note 18.

56. Penal Code Section 1191.1.

57. Villmoare & Neto, *supra* note 19.

58. In a parallel survey, prosecutors' estimates of victim involvement were slightly higher than probation estimates. Prosecutors estimated that 26% of victims attended sentencing: 13% exercised their right to allocute, and 15% submitted written statements. Maureen McLeod, "An Examination of the Victim's Role at Sentencing: Results of a Survey of Probation Administrators." 71 *Judicature* 162, 164-165 (1987).

59. HR 235, 69th Leg. 1983.

60. Texas Crime Victims Clearinghouse. *Crime Victim Impact: A Report to the 70th Legislature* (1987) as reported in Kilpatrick, *supra* note 15 at 9.

61. Kilpatrick, *supra* note 15 at 27.

62. See Marlene Young. "A Constitutional Amendment for Victims of Crime: The Victims' Perspective," 34 *The Wayne Law Review* 51, 64 (1987).

63. In a survey reported by McCleod, 58% of probation officers said the victim-impact statement should relate to all crimes charged, McCleod, supra note 35.

64. *See* Abraham Goldstein, "Defining the Role of the Victim in Criminal Prosecution," 52 *Mississippi Law Journal* 515, 536 (1982).

65. McLeod, *supra* note 58 at 167.

66. Stuart P. Green, "Private Challenges to Prosecutorial Inaction: A Model Declaratory Judgment Statute," 97 *Yale Law Review* 488 (1988).

67. Note: Judicially Initiated Prosecution: A Means of Preventing Continuing Victimization in the Event of Prosecutorial Inaction," 76 *California Law Review* 727, 731 (1988).

68. Welling, *supra* note 24 at 353.

69. Juan Cardenas, "The Crime Victim in the Prosecutorial Process," 9 *Harvard Journal of Law and Public Policy* 357 (1986).

70. Villmoare and Neto, *supra* note 18 at 5.

Chapter 11

RESTITUTION AND VICTIM RIGHTS IN THE 1980s

SUSAN HILLENBRAND

From the crime victim's perspective, little is more axiomatic than the criminal justice system's ordering the offender to make restitution for the losses he has caused. It is not surprising, therefore, that restitution as a matter of justice to crime victims has been a persistent theme of the 1980s victim rights movement, if perhaps a relatively low-key one. The discussion that follows looks at how that movement has—and has not—affected crime victim restitution.

Following a brief history of restitution in the United States, this chapter turns to the continuing importance of restitution to crime victims and the new prestige it has been accorded by various national groups during the eighties. Subsequent sections address recent laws and state constitutional amendments that increase the opportunity for victims to participate directly or indirectly in the restitution process. Since programs that help set and enforce restitution orders may have a direct impact on the restitution victims receive, this chapter takes a look at how various types of restitution programs view their responsibilities to victims. Sections on the trial court and appellate court examine the judicial response: Are sentencing courts paying more attention to victims in deciding whether to order restitution and how much to order? Are appellate courts considering the victim in deciding restitution issues? This chapter concludes on a cautionary note to victims and their advocates about the necessity to remain vigilant, not only about *what* is happening in the restitution arena, but also about *why* it is happening.

HISTORY

The history of restitution has been described elsewhere in considerable detail and need only be reviewed briefly here.[1] It is relevant to recall, for example, that in Colonial times, prosecution was generally the responsibility of private individuals rather than the state. Victims not only were responsible for investigating the crime and prosecuting the accused, but they were the beneficiaries of criminal sanctions. While harsher sanctions, such as the death penalty, corporal punishment, the pillory, and the gaol, were frequently sought for more serious personal injury crimes, it is not surprising that the objective of private prosecution was often restitution in theft and property crime cases. This was commonly awarded in the form of multiple damages to victims. The impact on offenders was rarely considered; in fact, victims were sometimes authorized to sell indigent offenders into service for a period corresponding to the amount of the multiple damages.[2]

The decline of restitution as a criminal sanction has been traced to several developments in the criminal justice system.[3] One was the assumption by the state of the role of prosecutor. Once the state began to be viewed as the injured party, rather than the individual victim, and public prosecutors became responsible for criminal prosecution, restitution to the individual victim became a less obvious sanction. While many offenders were still literally required to pay for their crimes, the "victim" they were increasingly required to pay was the public through fines, rather than the individual through restitution. Victims who wished offenders to make good the losses they caused were steered to the civil justice system.

Restitution from the offender to the victim was struck a further blow by the advent of the penitentiary. Viewed as a humanitarian alternative to corporal punishment, the penitentiary originally was used only when restitution was not feasible. Eventually, however, it came to replace restitution as a punishment. Even if restitution were ordered in addition to incarceration, imprisonment severely limited the offender's ability to pay it.

Though the original rationale for victim restitution (making good victims' losses by those responsible for them) diminished over the years, the potential for restitution itself never completely disappeared as a criminal sanction. In the late nineteenth and early twentieth centuries, when offender rehabilitation became a major goal of the criminal justice system, restitution was revived, this time as a vehicle for instilling offender responsibility.[4]

Public confidence in rehabilitation as a sentencing goal is low today. Now, retributive justice is in vogue, as evidenced by the considerable outcry for more and lengthier prison sentences. Where once there were no penitentiaries at all, today there is no space in the prisons and jails.[5] The pressure for alternative sanctions is great, even at times by those who endorse the "punitive" approach but recognize the realities of economics and court orders aimed at overcrowded facilities. To the extent citizens perceive restitution as requiring offenders to pay for their crimes (and alleviating the public at large of the financial burdens of compensating their victims), many find restitution at least a grudgingly acceptable sentencing alternative.[6]

Others, including many in the victim rights movement, view restitution primarily as a matter of justice to crime victims.

VICTIM RATIONALE FOR RESTITUTION

Theoretically, victims have at their disposal at least three means other than restitution to pursue reparations for losses attributable to their victimization: civil suits against the offender, state compensation awards, and private insurance. Unfortunately, all have serious drawbacks.

Civil remedies are often expensive and time consuming: their outcome is uncertain; and they require the victim, who may have already undergone the rigors of the criminal justice system, to initiate yet another unwelcome relationship with the offender and the justice system. While there are now compensation programs in 45 states, most apply only to victims of violent crime, reimburse only above a certain minimum loss and below a certain maximum loss, and exclude victims of certain offenses. Private insurance for medical bills and property loss, of course, benefits only those victims who have had the foresight and the means to purchase it in advance of the crime; even for these relatively few victims, high deductibles may exclude reimbursement for many losses.

While little suggests that restitution was a foremost concern of the early victim rights movement, by the time the movement became a political force in the 1970s, victim restitution emerged as a logical and seemingly straightforward goal to pursue. Not only might restitution help make the victim "whole," it would place the responsibility for doing so on the offender who had caused the loss.

In December, 1982, President Reagan's Task Force on Victims of Crime released its *Final Report*, which contained 68 recommendations for improving the plight of the crime victim,[7] two of which related to restitution. Under the general heading of "Recommendations for Federal and State Action," the report urged that "legislation should be proposed and enacted to . . . require restitution in all cases, unless the court provides specific reasons for failing to require it."[8] The Report's "Recommendations for the Judiciary" stated that "judges should order restitution to the victim in all cases in which the victim has suffered financial loss, unless they state compelling reasons for a contrary ruling on the record."[9]

The rationale for the restitution recommendations was reflected in the accompanying commentary:

> It is simply unfair that victims should have to liquidate their assets, mortgage their homes, or sacrifice their health or education or that of their children while the offender escapes responsibility for the financial hardship he has imposed. It is unjust that a victim should have to sell his car to pay bills while the offender drives to his probation appointments. The victim may be placed in a financial crisis that will last a lifetime. If one of the two must go into debt, the offender should do so.[10]

While at first somewhat more cautious, the legal community also began to endorse restitution as a matter of justice to crime victims. In August 1983, the American Bar Association adopted a set of "Guidelines for Fair Treatment of Crime Victims and Witnesses," which contained a recommendation that "victims of a crime involving economic loss, loss of earnings, or earning capacity should be able to expect the sentencing body to give priority consideration to restitution as a condition of probation."[11] A comprehensive set of "Guidelines Governing Restitution to Victims of Criminal Conduct" approved by that same body five years later cautioned that "it should be remembered that victim restitution is not the primary goal of the criminal process; it is only a desirable and proper component of that process."[12] Nevertheless, these recommendations were considerably more expansive than the previous guideline, providing that "if the sentencing court finds that a victim or victims have suffered damages as a result of the criminal conduct of the defendant, and finds that the amount of such damages has been established by reliable and probative evidence, the court should make a finding as to the amount of those damages in addition to or in lieu of any other sentence or as a condition of probation."[13]

A "Statement of Recommended Judicial Practices" adopted by the first National Conference of the Judiciary on the Rights of Victims of Crime in early 1983 included a recommendation that "judges should order restitution in all cases unless there is an articulated reason for not doing so, whether the offender is incarcerated or placed on probation."[14]

LEGISLATIVE RESPONSE

Judicial authority to order defendants to make restitution to their victims is long-standing in the common law and has been codified in the federal system and in many, if not most, states for some time. However, the 1970s and 1980s have seen a spate of legislation on the subject. Much of this is novel in that it recognizes restitution *as a matter of justice to crime victims*, rather than solely as a punitive or rehabilitative measure.

Congress enacted the Victim Witness Protection Act in October of 1982. Its stated purposes were: "(1) to enhance and protect the necessary role of crime victims and witnesses in the criminal justice process; (2) to ensure that the Federal Government does all that is possible within limits of available resources to assist victims and witnesses of crime without infringing on the constitutional rights of the defendant; and (3) to provide a model for legislation for State and local governments."

The Victim Witness Protection Act authorizes restitution "to any victim of the offense . . . in addition to or in lieu of any other penalty authorized by law." If restitution is not ordered or is only partially ordered, the statute requires the court to "state on the record the reasons therefore."

Prior to the act, restitution in federal cases could only be ordered as a condition of probation, under the Federal Probation Act. The new act therefore represented a major shift in restitution theory that has been continued in the Sentencing Reform Act of 1984.[15]

On the state level, virtually every state enacted or amended restitution statutes from 1977 through 1987. Activity in the state legislatures was particularly active in the four years following the President's Task Force recommendations and enactment of the federal Victim and

Witness Protection Act. No fewer than 17 states passed restitution legislation in each of these years.[16]

In 1980, the first "victims rights" bill was enacted.[17] Although this statute does not explicitly address restitution rights for victims, at least 20 statutes enacted by as many states in the succeeding 7 years did so.[18] Much of this legislation recognizes a victim's right to restitution (or consideration of restitution) but is not explicit as to when or under what conditions. Several of these statutes merely assign responsibility for informing victims about the right to request restitution or for assisting them in obtaining it.[19]

In recent years, restitution has also been addressed in a number of other statutes extending the use of restitution either as a sanction itself or as a condition of other sanctions. While several of these clearly state a restorative purpose,[20] most do not.

By the end of 1987, restitution was authorized or required in virtually every state as a condition of probation. In addition, at least 23 states authorized it as a condition of parole, 14 as a condition of suspended sentence, and 10 as a condition of work release. At least 26 states provided for restitution in addition to, or in lieu of, other sentences.[21]

In addition to promoting restitution as a victim right, the victim rights movement has successfully promoted legislation to facilitate court-ordered restitution reflecting victim losses.

The federal Victim Witness Protection Act includes a requirement that the presentence report contain "information concerning any harm, including financial, social, psychological, and physical harm, done to or loss suffered by any victim of the offense" and "any other information that may aid the court in sentencing, including the restitution needs of any victim of the offense."

Virtually every state now also provides for some sort of victim impact statement prior to sentencing. Most states require probation officers to include impact information in their presentence reports. Usually, this is prepared by probation officials after consulting victims; occasionally, it is prepared by prosecutors or by the victims themselves. A number of states specifically authorize victims to submit written statements in addition to those submitted by officials. Nearly half the states explicitly allow victims to make oral statements at sentencing hearings. Whether statutes call in general terms for information about "the impact which the defendant's criminal conduct has had upon the victim" or enumerate specific types of information to be included in victim impact statements,[22] all provide a way for information about financial losses associated with the crime to be brought to the attention of the sentencing court.

In addition to recognizing a victim's right to input at the sentencing stage, some states have recognized the victim's right to consult with prosecutors before cases are dismissed or before plea or sentencing negotiations are finalized.[23] Others have recognized the victim's right to address the court before plea agreements are accepted.[24] Such rights enable victims to ensure that decision-makers are aware of their financial losses prior to major decisions about how the case will be disposed.

CONSTITUTIONAL AMENDMENTS

While victim rights legislation has been hailed as a major advance for crime victims, the fact that the rights are statutory, rather than constitutional, leaves victims little recourse if their rights are ignored or violated by the criminal justice system.[25] To address this problem, some victim advocates are urging states to provide constitutional status to crime victims.[26] To date, four states have done so. A Florida amendment speaks in general terms of a victim's right to be present and heard in criminal proceedings, but does not expressly mention the victim's rights to restitution.[27] Michigan's amendment enumerates the right to restitution, along with a number of other rights.[28] The amendment in Rhode Island states that a victim "shall be entitled to receive from the perpetrator of the crime financial compensation for any injury or loss caused by the perpetrator of the crime.[29] California's amendment expressly states the "unequivocal intention that . . . all persons who suffer loss as a result of criminal activities shall have the right to restitution from the persons convicted of the crimes for losses they suffer."[30] It is still early to assess the impact of these constitutional amendments on restitution law and practice.

RESTITUTION PROGRAMS

Even if the increased legislative and constitutional emphasis on victim rights results in more and larger restitution orders, such orders will be of little practical significance to victims if there are not programs to enforce them. Prior to the 1970s few formal restitution programs existed in the United States.[31] However, the 1970s seemed ripe for the creation of such programs. While the imprisonment rates surged,[32] there was a good deal of dissatisfaction with prisons. Existing rehabilitation programs did not appear to be working.[33] Moreover, crime victims were beginning to make themselves heard. Special programs to enforce restitution orders held a promise to inject new life into the restitutive sanction, a promise that seemed to meet a wide range of concerns within and without the criminal justice system. By the end of the decade, at least 82 restitution programs were operating.[34]

While a number of programs begun in the 1970s with federal funding disappeared when that funding was discontinued in the 1980s,[35] four basic types of restitution programs exist today: restitution components of victim assistance programs, victim/offender reconciliation programs, restitution employment programs, and restitution as a function of routine probation supervision.[36]

If the philosophy of legislators is ambiguous with respect to restitution, so is the rationale for restitution programs. While, by definition, restitution programs imply a goal of recovering victims' monetary losses,[37] this is clearly an ancillary goal for most restitution programs.[38]

Although certainly victim-oriented, most victim assistance restitution programs concentrate on obtaining the initial restitution order and have little involvement in seeing that the offender pays the restitution.[39] Victim/offender reconciliation programs have a somewhat broad goal of "reconciling" victim and offender; since the economic loss may be only part of the breach between victim and offender (and not necessarily the most important part), reconciliation need not result in economic recovery for the victim.[40] Restitution employment programs, on the other hand, may result in considerable restitution for victims. However, the rationale behind such programs is generally offender-oriented: rehabilitation, alternatives to more restrictive sentences, work experience, and strengthening of community ties. Finally, since probation itself is offender-oriented, it is unlikely that victim recovery is a primary concern of probation restitution efforts.

On a purely practical, cost-benefit basis, restitution programs probably would find it hard to justify their existence if the intended "benefit" were solely for victims. As a consequence of the "funneling effect"—the volume of crimes committed compared to the number of police reports, criminal apprehensions, and convictions—even the most successful programs are able to recoup losses for relatively few victims.[41] Moreover, if the sole aim is to reimburse victims, the cost of staffing and running programs relative to the funds collected might suggest that public monies would better be provided directly to crime victims through crime victim compensation programs.

Not surprisingly, therefore, many (if not most) advocates of restitution programs believe that victim restitution should *not* be the primary goal of such programs. One commentator has noted that "as the interests of the victim are given priority in restitution programs, other program goals would become almost totally unattainable. Program emphasis would have to be put on squeezing every last penny out of the offender, regardless of the consequence to him and his dependents."[42]

A practical result stemming from the offender orientation of restitution programs is that program evaluators have largely assessed outcomes in terms of correctional objectives rather than in terms of benefits to victims.[43] Victims, of course, view restitution programs from a different prospective. A recent American Bar Association study found that victims often feel programs do not do everything they could to increase offender payments. Moreover, many are dissatisfied with program's failure to consult them about their losses prior to recommending an award amount and to keep them informed about the restitution process.[44]

Regardless of the findings of this study or other studies on victim satisfaction with restitution programs, it is unlikely that existing programs will soon reverse their current emphasis on correctional objectives. Indeed, an abrupt reversal could be detrimental to the victims now benefiting from their efforts. As discussed below, appellate courts rarely view victim losses in and of themselves sufficient grounds for restitution, and programs with the sole goal of restoring victims might lose the essential cooperation of the trial courts whose orders are subject to review.

However, restitution need not be viewed as an all or nothing proposition for either victims or defendants in order to benefit both. The fact that the criminal justice system has goals other than restoration of crime victims should not be of concern to victims *as long as* their own needs are included among the goals of the system. If, in fact, the justification for restitution programs rests on their success in rehabilitating offenders by making them acknowledge the losses they have caused, it stands to reason that compliance and victim satisfaction are important factors in that rehabilitation.

TRIAL COURTS

Several judicial surveys conducted in the 1970s before the victim movement gained momentum found judges strongly supportive of monetary restitution and confident about its rehabilitative effectiveness.[45] Today the long-standing professional wariness on the part of judges about the propriety of the criminal justice system's attention to victim restoration (as opposed to offender rehabilitation) seems to be waning somewhat. Trial court judges are increasingly exposed to victims at least indirectly (e.g., through victim impact statements) and sometimes directly (through victim allocution). Moreover, their colleagues have accorded a degree of legitimacy to victim concerns.[46] It is not surprising, therefore, that many trial court judges report not only considering information about victim financial losses in their sentencing decisions, but using it to fashion restitution orders.

In a 1987 nationwide survey of 77 state trial judges for a study on the implementation of victim rights legislation, nearly 70% said that information about the financial impact of the crime was "very useful" to their sentencing decisions, and almost another 20% said it was "useful." A considerable majority reported impact information had a substantial impact on both the number and size of restitution orders. Moreover, *all* said they order restitution whenever the victim has suffered financial loss and the defendant seems able to pay.[47]

APPELLATE COURTS

In recent years, both federal and state appellate courts have addressed a number of restitution issues. In many instances, victims have fared well. However, to the extent that courts provide philosophical rationale for their decisions, their willingness to uphold restitution awards often has little to do with victims' "rights" to restitution as recognized in victim rights statutes and, more recently, in state constitutions. Ironically, even some of the decisions upholding restitution orders explicitly disclaim a victim rationale for doing so.

For example, the U.S. Supreme Court has ruled that state restitution orders are not "debts," but rather are criminal penalties that cannot be discharged under Chapter 7 of the Federal Bankruptcy Act.[48] While the decision was heralded as a victory for victims, compensation for victims was hardly its primary consideration, as explained by Justice Powell:

> Although restitution does resemble a judgment "for the benefit of" the victim, the context in which it is imposed undermines that conclusion. The victim has no control over the amount of restitution awarded or over the decision to award restitution. Moreover, the decision to impose restitution generally does not turn on the victim's injury, but on the penal goals of the State and the situation of the defendant. . . . Because criminal proceedings focus on the State's interests in rehabilitation and punishment, rather than the victim's desire for compensation, we conclude that restitution orders . . . operate "for the benefit of" the State.[49]

Similar reasoning had been cited earlier by a circuit court, which found that restitution imposed under the Federal Probation Act could not be discharged in bankruptcy because the "crucial point is that the probation condition is aimed mainly at punishing and reforming the defendant, not at making the victim whole."[50]

Because the Victim Witness Protection Act (VWPA) was enacted as victim-oriented legislation, it might be expected that appellate decisions concerning the act not only would uphold restitution orders, but be based on a victim rationale. This is often the case. However, even under this legislation, there is a certain ambiguity about the purposes of restitution. In considering an order imposed under the act, one court observed that "(c)riminal restitution rests with one foot in the world of criminal procedure and the other in civil procedure and remedy," but concluded that "because it is part of the sentencing process it is fundamentally 'penal' in nature."[51] Other courts have shared this conclusion.

For example, in upholding the constitutionality of the act, the Supreme Court found that 7th Amendment jury trial requirements were not relevant in determining the amount of restitution awards since restitution is a criminal, rather than a civil, penalty.[52]

On the other hand, some decisions have emphasized the compensatory purpose of the act. Courts have, for example, cited this in declining to limit restitution to victims or amounts set forth in charging instruments or plea agreements[53] and in allowing defendants to be assessed more than they benefited from the crime.[54] One court said the compensatory purpose of the act would not be served if the restitution order did not survive the defendant's death,[55] and another, noting the importance of the support and comfort the family of a sexual assault victim can contribute to the treatment of her psychological trauma, upheld restitution for the cost of a plane ticket to visit her family.[56]

Most courts reviewing VWPA restitution orders have interpreted the term "victim" rather broadly. For example, insurance companies[57] and other third parties who have reimbursed the victim,[58] government entities,[59] and indirect victims[60] have all been found to be "victims" under the act. Several courts explicitly mentioned Congress' intent on a broad interpretation of the term.[61]

After nearly a decade of such generally favorable appellate court decisions, many victims and victim advocates were dismayed at a 1990 U.S. Supreme Court opinion which failed to recognize any Congressional intent that restitution ordered under the Act could exceed the amount attributable to the offense of conviction.[62]

Not surprisingly, federal courts considering restitution orders imposed under the Federal Probation Act do not cite victim interests as often as courts considering orders imposed under the Victim Witness Protection Act. While the latter act requires sentencing courts either to order restitution for victims or give reasons for not doing so, the former authorizes them to order restitution as a condition of probation "when satisfied that the ends of justice and the best interests of the public as well as the defendant will be served thereby."[63] Nevertheless, some of these recent decisions, too, have benefited victims.

For example, courts have allowed restitution ordered as a condition of probation under the Federal Probation Act to exceed the amounts in the counts charged if the defendant agrees to pay restitution that goes beyond the amount attributable to the particular counts to which he has pleaded;[64] if the defendant knows that the amount that may be required can go beyond that attributable to the counts to which he pleads;[64] if the defendant enters a plea agreement in which the amount to be ordered exceeds the amount attributable to the conviction;[66] and if the amount of damages is established with specificity, part of a fraud, and admitted by the defendant.[67] Even if a defendant is convicted in a jury trial, a restitution order imposed as a probation condition is not necessarily limited by the amount of losses specifically charged in the indictment.[68] While not all of these opinions mentioned a philosophical basis, those that did noted that the rehabilitative goal of probation requires the probationer's acceptance of responsibility for his acts.[69]

To date, state appellate courts reviewing restitution orders have rarely cited their states' new statutes recognizing restitution as a matter of victims' "rights." Most have continued to look to probation, parole, and other sentencing statutes. Thus, similar to federal appellate courts considering restitution orders under the Federal Probation Act, even when these courts find "in favor" of victims, they rarely base their decisions on a victim rationale. To the extent any philosophical rationale at all is mentioned, it is likely to be offender rehabilitation.[70]

CONCLUSION

Restitution is once again viewed as a viable sanction in the U.S. criminal justice system. The victims rights movement has provided the popular and political justification for it and has successfully promoted techniques to facilitate it. Legislators, trial courts, and at least some appellate courts have been listening. State constitutional amendments may prove even more influential. Nevertheless, concern for victims is not the sole reason for the criminal justice system's receptivity to restitution. Other reasons include the search for economic and humane alternatives to incarceration and a continuing desire for rehabilitation opportunities for offenders. Despite (and in some instances because of) these non-victim based reasons, victims have benefited from recent developments in restitution law and programs. It would be a mistake, however, for victim advocates to assume that the criminal justice system will automatically take care of victims' restitution needs. If restitution is found ineffective as a means of rehabilitation or uneconomical as a rehabilitative tool, courts may come to rely on it less. Thus, while the victims movement may find it advantageous to "ride the crest" of the system's current interest in restitution, victim advocates should be looking beyond that interest to a time when restitution *for victims* may have to stand on its own.

NOTES

1. J. Gittler, "Expanding the Role of the Victim in a Criminal Action: An Overview of Issues and Problems," *Pepperdine Law Review*, Vol. II (1984); W. McDonald, "Toward a Bicentennial Revolution in Criminal Justice: The Return of the Victim, *American Criminal Law Review*, Vol. 13, (1976), p. 649.

2. McDonald, *supra* note 1 at 653.

3. Gittler and McDonald, *supra* note 1.

4. Gittler, *supra* note 1 at 137.

5. At the end of 1987 a record 581,609 prisoners were under the jurisdiction of federal and state correctional authorities, an increase of 76.3% since 1980. Most jurisdictions were operating above reported capacity. Bureau of Justice Statistics Bulletin, "Prisoners in 1987," April 1988.

6. *See* R. Immarigeon, "Surveys Reveal Broad Support for Alternative Sentencing," *The National Prison Project Journal*, No. 9, Fall 1986. Also see Research and Forecasts, Inc., *The Figgie Report Part V: Parole—A Search for Justice and Safety* (Richmond, VA: Figgie International Inc., 1985), reporting 67% of survey respondents agreeing with alternative programs as a solution to overcrowding.

7. *The President's Task Force on Victims of Crime: Final Report* (1982).

8. *Supra* at 18.

9. *Supra* at 72.

10. *Supra* at 79.

11. American Bar Association, *Guidelines for Fair Treatment of Crime Victims and Witnesses* (1983), at 22.

12. American Bar Association, "Guidelines Governing Restitution to Victims of Criminal Conduct," *ABA Reports with Recommendations*, Report IIIB (1988), Guideline 1.4.

13. *Supra* at Guideline 1.5.

14. National Institute of Justice, *Statement of Recommended Judicial Practices*, from the National Conference of the Judiciary on the Rights of Victims of Crime sponsored by the National Conference of Special Court Judges, National Institute of Justice and National Judicial College, (1983).

15. 18 U.S.C. 3556.

16. Compiled from information in the *1987 Legislative Directory*, National Organization for Victims Assistance, and primary sources.

17. WISC. STAT. § 950.01-07.

18. See, e.g., UTAH CODE ANN. § 77-3(1)(e), "Victims are entitled to restitution or reparations," and W. VA. CODE § 61-11A-4, "The Court when sentencing a defendant convicted of a felony or misdemeanor causing physical, psychological and economic injury or loss to a victim, shall order, in addition to or in lieu of any other penalty authorized by law, that the defendant make restitution to any victim of the offense, unless the Court finds restitution to be wholly or partially impractical."

19. See, e.g., MO. REV. STAT. § 595.209, which provides victims the right "to be informed by the prosecuting attorney of the right to request that restitution be an element of the final disposition of a case and to obtain assistance in the documentation of the victim's losses."

20. See, e.g., N.M. STAT. ANN. § 31-17-1(a), "It is the policy of this state that restitution be made by each violator of the Criminal Code of New Mexico to the victims of his criminal activities to the extent the defendant is reasonably able to do so," and ALA. CODE § 15-18-65, "The legislature hereby finds, declares and determines that it is essential to be fair and impartial in the administration of justice, that all perpetrators of criminal activity or conduct be required to fully compensate all victims of such conduct or activity for any pecuniary loss, damage or injury as a direct or indirect result thereof."

21. Compiled from information in the *1987 Legislative Directory*, *supra* note 16, and primary sources.

22. Statutes explicitly calling for financial information in written or oral impact statements include: ALA. CODE § 15-18-67; ALASKA STAT. § 12.55.022; ARIZ. REV. STAT. ANN. § 12-253 and § 13-702; CAL. PENAL CODE § 1191.1; COL. REV. STAT. § 16-11-102 and § 16-11-601; CONN. GEN. STAT. § 54-91a and c; DEL. CODE ANN. tit. 11 § 4331; FLA. STAT. § 921-143; GA. CODE ANN. § 17-10-1.1 and § 1.2; KY. REV. STAT. 421.520; LA REV. STAT. ANN. 46: 1841; MD. ANN. CODE of 1957, Art. 41 § 4-609; MASS. GEN. LAWS ANN. ch. 279 § 4A; MICH. COMP. LAWS § 28.1287 (763);

MINN. STAT. § 609.115; MO. REV. STAT. § 557.041; MONT. CODE ANN. § 46-18—242; NEV. REV. STAT. § 176.145; N.H. REV. STAT. ANN.§ 651:4-a; N.J. REV. STAT. § 2C:44-6; NY CRIM. PROC. LAW § 390.30: N.D. CENT. CODE § 12.1-32-08; OHIO REV. CODE ANN. § 2947.051; OKLA. STAT. ANN. tit. § 982; OR. REV. STAT. § 137-10; PA. STAT. ANN. § 180-9.3; S.C. CODE ANN. § 16-3-1550; S.D. CODIFIED LAWS ANN. § 23A-27-1.1; TENN. CODE ANN. § 40-35-207; TEX. CODE CRIM. PROC. ANN. Art. 56.01 (Vernon); UTAH CODE ANN. § 64-13-20; VT. STAT. ANN. tit. 13 § 7006; VA. CODE ANN. § 19.2-299.1; WASH REV CODE § 7.69.020; W. VA. CODE § 61-11A-2 and 3; WISC. STAT. § 590.04 and § 972.15.

23. See, e.g., KY. REV. STAT. ANN § 421.500, "The victim should be consulted by the attorney for the Commonwealth or the disposition of the case including dismissal, release of the defendant pending judicial proceedings, a negotiated plea, and entry into a pretrial diversion program." See also ABA *Guidelines for Fair Treatment of Crime Victims and Witnesses, Guideline 1, supra* note 13 at 16, and American Bar Association, *Standards for Criminal Justice* (Second Edition, 1980), Prosecution Function, Standard 3-14.31(d).

24. See., e.g., MINN. STAT. ANN. § 611A.03, providing for victims to be informed by the prosecutor of "the right to be present at the sentencing hearing and to express in writing any objection to the agreement or to the proposed disposition."

25. For an argument that existing federal constitutional protections extend to victims, see R. Aynes, "The Right Not to be a Victim," *Pepperdine Law Review*, Vol II (1984).

26. A national movement, "Victims CAN" (Constitutional Amendment Network), was established in 1986 to promote constitutional rights for crime victims in state constitutions. It is based in Fort Worth, Texas.

27. Florida Constitution, Art. 1, Sec. 16(b).

28. Michigan Constitution, Art. 1, Sec. 24.

29. Rhode Island Constitution, Art. 1, Sec. 23.

30. California Constitution, Art. 1, Sec. 28(b).

31. J. Hudson, B. Galaway (eds.), "Introduction," *Victims, Offenders, and Alternate Sanctions* (1980), p. vii.

32. A July, 1985 Bureau of Justice Statistics "Special Bulletin" on "The Prevalence of Imprisonment" reported that imprisonment rates increased 39% from 1970 to 1979.

33. J. Hudson, B. Galaway (eds.), *Restitution in Criminal Justice: A Critical Assessment of Sanctions* (1975), p. 5.

34. J. Hudson, B. Galaway (eds.), *supra* note 31.

35. A. Harland, "One Hundred Years of Restitution: An International Review," *Victimology* 8:1-2 (1983), 190-203.

36. D. McGillis, *Crime Victim Restitution: An Analysis of Approaches* (1986), p. 3.

37. *Supra*, p. 5.

38. H. Edelhertz, "Legal and Operational Issues in the Implementation of Restitution Within the Criminal Justice System," in *Restitution in Criminal Justice: A Critical Assessment of Sanctions, supra* note 33, p. 63.

39. McGillis, *supra* note 36.

40. Economic recovery may not be the primary concern of all victims. A recent study found that victims of burglary committed by juveniles were more concerned with offender rehabilitation than restitution. "Victim Understanding of Fairness: Burglary Victims in Victim Offender Mediation," (Research Report of Minnesota Citizens Council on Crime and Justice), 1988.

41. J. Stookey, "The Victim's Perspective on American Criminal Justice," in *Restitution in Criminal Justice: A Critical Assessment of Sanctions*, supra note 33, p. 23-24.

42. H. Edelhertz, *supra* note 38, p. 63-64.

43. *Supra*.

44. B. Smith, R. Davis, S. Hillenbrand, "Improving Enforcement of Court-Ordered Restitution to Victims: Executive Summary" (1989), p. 27-28, a study funded by State Justice Institute Grant No. 87-12I-E-.41.

45. S. Chesny, J. Hudson, J. McLargen, "A New Look at Restitution: Recent Legislation, Programs and Research," *Judicature*, Vol. 61, No. 8, p. 356 (March 1978).

46. *Statement of Recommended Judicial Practices, supra* note 14.

47. "Victims Rights Legislation: An Assessment of its Impact on the Criminal Justice System," a study of the American Bar Association's Victim Witness Project, funded under National Institute of Justice Grant No. 86-IJ-CX-0049 (S-1) (not yet published).

48. *Kelly v. Robinson*, 107 S. Ct. 353 (1986). But see *Pennsylvania Department of Public Welfare vs. Davenport* 495 US___(1990); 109 L.Ed.2d 588 (1990), holding that restitution obligations are "debts" subject to discharge under Chapter 13 of the Bankruptcy Code.

49. *Supra*, at 362-363.

50. *U.S. v. Carson*, CA5 (former) 2/17/82. Also see *U.S. v. Keith*, 754 F.2d 1388 (1985).

51. *U.S. v. Bruchey*, 810 F.2d 456 (4th Cir. 1987), p. 441.

52. *U.S. v. Satterfield*, 743 F.2d 827 (11th Cir. 1984), "In drafting the restitution provisions of the VWPA, Congress made clear in both the language of the statute and its accompanying legislative history that victim restitution would be imposed as a criminal, rather than civil, penalty," p. 836.

53. *U.S. v. Pomazi*, 851 F.2d 244 (9th Cir. 1988), "Given the VWPA's objective of providing full compensation to victims, and the language of the Act which expressly authorizes the sentencing court to order a defendant to 'make restitution to any victim of the offense' . . . we do not believe Congress intended to limit the amount of restitution to amounts set forth in an indictment or information," 248; *U.S. v. Hill*, 798 F.2d 402 (10th Cir. 1986), ". . . we believe limiting a victim's recovery to the amount charged in the indictment or the particular counts of the offense is unwarranted given the compensatory objectives of the VWPA. The decision of a prosecutor to indict a defendant and the manner in which a defendant is indicted have little, if anything, to do with the objectives of the VWPA," p. 405.

54. *U.S. v. Anglian*, 784 F.2d 765 (6th Cir. 1986), "It is true that, in the civil context, especially under the doctrine of unjust enrichment, restitution is sometimes measured by the benefit received. . . . We think it is unmistakable from the tenor of these statutes and from the legislative history, however, that Congress did not intend the term 'restitution' as used in the VWPA to be so construed," p. 767.

55. *U.S. v. Dudley*, 739 F.2d 175 (4th Cir. 1984). "(Under the VWPA,) an order of restitution, even if in some respects penal, also, has the predominantly compensatory purpose of reducing the adverse impact on the victim," p. 177.

56. *U.S. v. Keith*, 754 F.2d 1388 (9th Cir. 1985) *cert. denied* 106 S. Ct. 93.

57. *U.S. v. Durham*, 755 F.2d 511 (5th Cir. 1985); *U.S. v. Youpee*, 836 F.2d 1181 (9th Cir. 1986).

58. *U.S. v. Atkinson*, 788 F.2d 900 (2nd Cir. 1986).

59. *U.S. v. Ruffen*, 780 F.2d 1493 (9th Cir. 1986).

60. *U.S. v. Allison*, 599 F.Supp. 958 (1985).

61. *U.S. v. Youpee*, *U.S. v. Durham*, and *U.S. v. Allison* all noted that Congress intended the term "victim" to be interpreted broadly.

62. Hughey v. U.S., 495 US___(1990); 109 L.Ed.2d 408(1990).

63. 18 U.S.C. 3651.

64. *U.S. v. Woods*, 775 F.2d 82 (3rd Cir. 1986).

65. *U.S. v. Hawthorne*, 806 F.2d 493 (3rd Cir. 1986).

66. *U.S. v. Orr*, 691 F.2d 431 (9th Cir. 1982).

67. *U.S. v. Davis*, 683 F.2d 1052 (7th Cir. 1982).

68. *U.S. v. Sleight*, 808 F.2d 1012 (3rd Cir. 1987).

69. *U.S. v. McLaughlin*, 512 F. Supp. 907 (D. Md. 1981), p. 912. "The primary purpose of restitution as a condition of probation is to foster, in a direct way, a defendant's acceptance of responsibility for his or her unlawful actions. To permit a defendant who freely admits his or her guilt, and the amount of loss caused thereby, to avoid making the aggrieved party at least economically whole is intolerable from a societal perspective."; *U.S. v. Davis*, *supra* note 63. "Restriction of restitution (to the counts to which the defendant pleads) . . . would not comport with the rehabilitative purpose of restitution as a condition of probation, which is to foster a defendant's acceptance of responsibility for unlawful acts."

70. See, e.g., *State v. Barr*, 99 Wash. 2d 95, 658 P.2d 1247 (1983), "(a)ppellant's arguments ignore (the rehabilitative aspects) of restitution in favor of the view that restitution compensates the victim. Though partial compensation may be a concomitant result of restitution, it is not the primary purpose of such an order," p. 1250; *In re Trantino*, 89 N.J. 347, 466 A. 2d 104 (1982), "(t)he purpose of restitution in the setting of parole is not to make the aggrieved person whole but to assure rehabilitation of the offender and to prevent the recurrence of future criminal conduct," p. 111; and *Commonwealth v. Kerr*, 298 Pa.Super. 257, 444 A.2d 758 (1982), quoting *Commonwealth v. Erb*, 428 A. 2d 574, 580-81 (1981), ". . . an order of restitution is not an award of damages. While the order aids the victim, its *true purpose* and the *reason* for its imposition, is the rehabilitative goal it serves by impressing upon the offender the loss he has caused and his responsibility to repay that loss as far as it is possible to do so" (emphasis added), p. 760.

Chapter 12

THE "VICTIMS MOVEMENT" IN EUROPE

MIKE MAGUIRE
JOANNA SHAPLAND

In a short chapter, it is a tall order indeed to cover the huge range of developments in rights and services for crime victims that have taken place in Europe in recent years. A few general statements may be made with a fair degree of confidence. For example, it would not be a gross exaggeration to speak of a sea change in attitudes toward victims in most European countries, whereby the rhetoric, at least of the major relevant agencies (police, prosecutors, courts, social services, and policy-makers in the criminal justice field) now regularly includes concern for the interests of victims. Yet at the same time, there are major differences between countries and between agencies in the levels of resources committed, in the relative priority attached to particular aspects of victimization, and in the extent to which genuine changes in practice have been effected. All we can hope to do here is to convey a broad outline of what has been occurring and to pick out for special attention a few of what seem to us to be particularly significant or interesting developments.

The shape of the chapter is as follows. After a few general remarks about the varying social and legal contexts in which concern about victims has grown, we move to a discussion of specific kinds of development. We begin with a brief overview of the progress made by voluntary organizations, particularly in the area of victim support, where they have played the leading role in several countries. We then consider developments in compensation by the state and by offender, moving to more general comments on victims' services and victims' rights within the criminal justice system. We end with an assessment of the role and importance of research in encouraging change, and with some predictions about the future. For the sake of brevity, we confine our attention here to Western Europe, although it should be noted in passing that some Eastern Europe countries have also undertaken significant initiatives.

SIMILARITIES AND DIFFERENCES

In Europe, as in the United States, the "victims movement" has been in serious motion for less than 15 years, although there were isolated earlier developments (such as the introduction of state compensation for victims of violent crime in Britain in 1964). Indeed, in most European countries, the real thrust has occurred only during the past five years. This thrust was encouraged by a number of international initiatives, such as a convention and two important recommendations by the Council of Europe, in 1983, 1985, and 1987 (on, respectively, state compensation, the position of the victim in the criminal justice system, and on assistance to victims). Before this, only the United Kingdom, the Federal Republic of Germany (West Germany), and the Netherlands had been involved in major new initiatives. The reasons for the recent, unprecedented growth of interest in crime victims rights across the world are not totally clear, but the primary causes are probably no different in Europe than anywhere else: most obviously, public reactions against increasing crime rates combined with increasingly impersonal, uncaring and ineffective criminal justice systems, and growing awareness of the serious impact of crime on individuals.

Despite very wide agreement about the basic nature of the problem, responses have varied considerably. Indeed, at a very broad level, it is possible to draw some fundamental distinctions between the "victims movement" in Europe and in the United States. For example, since the early 1970s, many pro-victim groups in the States have adopted an aggressive, overtly political and campaigning approach, emphasizing the *rights* of victims (if necessary, at the expense of offender' rights) and a commitment to promoting new legislation to secure them; some, indeed, have campaigned for tougher sentences, including capital punishment (Hudson, 1984; Davis, Kumeuther, & Connick, 1984; National Organization for Victim Assistance, or NOVA, 1985; Fattah, 1986; Lamborn, 1986). In Europe, by contrast, there are few major groups that have taken an analogous approach. There tends to be greater consensus within each country, the rhetoric of government departments, police forces, and the most influential voluntary organizations alike referring much more often to desirable improvements in services for victims than to victims' rights or radical legislation on their behalf (Mawby & Gill, 1987; Maguire & Corbett, 1987, van Dijk, 1988a).

Of course, there are exceptions to this pattern. Many American groups are completely service-oriented, and some in Europe (e.g., "Victims of Violence" in England, and, to a lesser extent, the "Weisser Ring" in West Germany—the main victim assistance society there, which is run as a private and largely volunteer force) project a strong, campaigning, "anti-offender" profile. Nevertheless, it is a fair generalization. Though the reasons behind the contrast are complex, they clearly include differences in legal and political tradition (the existence of the U.S. Constitution being of major significance) and in the overall volume and seriousness of crime. Another major difference is the much greater focus on the criminal justice system in North America, typified by the prominence of victim-witness assistance schemes. This difference can likewise be explained by the progressive disillusionment and lack of cooperation on the part of American victims with well-publicized defects in their court system (Elias, 1983), a problem perceived as far less serious in Europe.

While is may be useful to draw broad comparisons of this kind between the United States and Europe, it is also evident that there are differences between the social and legal traditions of individual European countries; the differences, as we shall illustrate, have helped to produce some very different perceptions of, and responses to, victims issues. In West Germany, for instance, it has long been the practice in certain categories of criminal trials to allow the presence of an extra lawyer (*Neberklager*) to argue the case for the victim, whereas in Britain a victim has traditionally been treated simply as another witness with no right to an audience. Again, each country has its own traditions of social and medical services, ranging from the highly developed welfare state in Sweden and the Netherlands, to the much lower level of public provision for social or medical needs that obtains in most Mediterranean countries. While the flow of information and discussion between European countries about victims issues has increased enormously, while international initiatives are underway, and while some restandardization of practice is already occurring, basic differences of the above kind will continue to work against the development of anything resembling a homogeneous victims movement across Europe.

THE VOLUNTARY MOVEMENT AND VICTIM SUPPORT

Voluntary groups set up expressly to assist victims of crime are now in existence in virtually every European country. "Generalist" support services provided by volunteers have reached a particularly high level of organization in Great Britain and West Germany where pioneering groups formed in the early 1970s paved the way for the growth of the National Association of Victims Support Schemes (NAVSS) and the Weisser Ring, respectively. Both are already major organizations that have increasing influence on government policy toward victims. NAVSS, in particular, has promoted a model for the support of victims that has influenced the development of schemes in several other countries, notably in the Netherlands, Ireland, France, and Sweden.

More specialized services are provided by other voluntary groups in many countries, notably the counseling and assistance offered by rape crisis centers to victims of sexual assault and the shelter offered to battered women by women's refuges. Another development, of which there are examples in France, Spain, and Italy, is the voluntary provision, by suitably qualified groups, of legal advice and assistance to victims, principally in the area of claims or actions for compensation.

In this section, we explore some ramifications of one of the major issues currently affecting and preoccupying voluntary groups. The main voluntary organizations in the UK, the Netherlands, and West Germany that pioneered generalist services to victims have all experienced such massive increases in demand for their services that they have been forced into major expansion and reorganization. This has created practical necessities (for much greater financial resources and for more efficient management) that have had important consequences for the whole character and ethos of the victim support movement. Moreover, countries that have come late into the provision of victim services by volunteers (notably, France and Switzerland have tended to begin operations at a much more sophisticated and more centralized level of organization and with more secure funding, conditions which have greatly influenced their basic philosophy and approach. The results have varied between countries, but there is no doubting the general trend.

One of the most significant consequences has been what van Dijk (1988a) has called the "institutionalization of victim support." This phrase can be applied both literally and metaphorically. In more and more European countries, funding for the management and administration of voluntary schemes has come from central government. While direct government interference in the way they operate is unusual, there is clearly a degree of informal control. Organizations dependent on the renewal of short-term grants are not only accountable for how they have spent public money, but they tend to listen carefully to the general policy wishes of their funders. Moreover, the need to keep their own house in order tends to hasten any trend toward centralization and bureaucratization.

Perhaps the most interesting situation is found in Great Britain, where victims support schemes, which had struggled financially for several years, were suddenly in 1986 presented with a government grant of 9 million pounds for the next three years. This event is already transforming the organization from top to bottom (Corbett & Maguire, 1988; NAVSS, 1988).

Victim support in Britain began very definitely as a community-based, grassroots movement. Between 1974 and 1979, it consisted of no more than 30 independent voluntary groups, mostly funded on a shoestring by charitable donations, and administered virtually single-handed from a "co-ordinator's" own home. The names and addresses of victims, mainly of burglary or other crimes of low to medium seriousness, were passed to the coordinator by the place a day or so after the event, and volunteers were dispatched to visit them with offers of emotional or practical support. Any problems the volunteers were unable to deal with were, in theory, referred to agencies better equipped to handle them, although, in practice, it was often difficult to arrange this (Maguire & Corbett, 1987). While most of the early schemes operated according to this basic model, there were wide variations in, for example, their commitment to training, the kinds of victim they took on, and their concepts of service delivery. Moreover, they were fiercely independent and proud of their own mode of operation.

Even after 1979, when NAVSS was formed by a group of these schemes, many remained reluctant to allow any common standards or conditions to be imposed upon them. NAVSS could suggest basic policies and minimum standards in such matters as training, referral policy, record-keeping or management structure, but it had few effective sanctions against those who ignored them. Yet, over the years, NAVSS gradually achieved a stronger influence over local schemes by giving standard advice and information to new groups as they were formed, through conferences, newsletters, and its own higher profile in the media. This influence was enhanced above all by the new government funding, which is being administered through a committee; although independent, it is briefed and serviced by NAVSS. Schemes receive grants (mainly to pay coordinators, whose tasks now border on the Herculean in high-crime areas) only if they meet certain centrally agreed standards and requirements.

At the same time, NAVSS itself has been drawn closer to government, and there are fairly frequent meetings and discussions between senior NAVSS staff and both Home Office officials and government ministers. While NAVSS has taken few public stances on controversial issues involving victims, there is no doubt that it is both increasingly influenced by, and influential upon, policy-making behind the scenes. As it is the largest victims-oriented organization in Europe, containing over 350-member schemes with a total of more than 6,000 volunteers (NAVSS, 1988), this is no small matter (for further discussion, see Corbett & Maguire, 1988).

What effect has this institutionalization been having upon schemes at a local level? First of all, committees are being pushed to improve their systems of management and record-keeping, and volunteer visitors are being asked to undergo more training and to meet higher standards generally. Second, schemes are being asked to handle much more serious crime than has been the general practice in the past. Whereas the bread-and-butter work of volunteers has traditionally been one-off visits to burglary victims, most schemes are now assisting victims of rape and other very serious assaults, as well as the families of murder victims. This work often involves long-term support, which requires a much more professional approach, some training in counseling techniques, and expert back-up for the volunteers. While these developments are obviously beneficial to visitors, there is some worry among local schemes that they are gradually becoming professionalized to the extent where they could lose the very aspect that contributed most to their rapid growth in earlier years—their voluntary spirit or community base.

These issues are most acute in Britain, partly because of the relatively early and independent development of victim services, and partly because of its distinctive voluntary tradition: Britain has aptly been described as a nation of volunteers. A similar debate has been taking place in the Netherlands, although the effects have been less dramatic since several schemes there have employed professionals for many years. In West Germany, the Weisser Ring, which maintains over 200 offices, has remained nominally independent of government funding. Its status as a grassroots organization is questionable, however, due to the fact that it has for many years been allocated large amounts of money from "fines" paid by offenders in lieu of imprisonment and a large proportion of its membership is made up of ex-police officers and other criminal justice professionals. Although it, too, has expanded significantly, it has always had a firm organizational base. Moreover, since a much smaller proportion of its work is concerned with the emotional support of victims (unlike in Britain, where personal visits to homes and the provision of a "listening ear" form the keystones of victim support work) and its main services lie in the fields of legal advice and compensation, it has not been undergoing anything like the same traumatic process of "professionalization."

Perhaps the most fortunate country in regard to professionalization is France, which has achieved a good balance of professional and voluntary input without any major dissent. This is largely due to the fact that France was late to the field and was thus able to learn from the experience of others. France had little tradition of victim support before 1983, when a central organization was set up under generous funding from the Ministry of Justice, with the express purpose of developing (and hence directing) victim support across the country. There are now more than 150 local schemes in existence, with a ratio of 10:1 of volunteers to professionals.

Finally, on the subject of generalist victim assistance, it should be mentioned that while one may speak of Britain, the Netherlands, and West Germany as pioneers in victim services in Europe, with France and some Scandinavian countries as the "second wave" that benefit from lessons learned by the pioneers, there are still several countries—notably those around the Mediterranean—in which there are few groups in existence, if any, that have the specific objective of assisting crime victims. On the other hand, as we discuss below, some of these countries are more geared in other ways towards victims' interests (for example, in legal provisions facilitating the recovery of damages from offenders).

We end this section with a few comments about organizations that have seen less of the limelight recently, but which have been very influential in bringing the needs of particular categories of victims to public attention. Rape crisis centers and battered women's refuges, which have in most countries been run mainly by feminist groups, provide an important alternative model of victim assistance to that of the increasingly institutionalized, generalist organizations. They are usually fully independent of, and sometimes antagonistic toward, the police, encouraging victims to telephone them directly, even if they have not officially reported an offense. (By contrast, victim support schemes in Britain, for example, rely almost exclusively upon the police for the names and addresses of victims, whom they then contact with an offer of assistance).

Rape crisis centers often attempt to "radicalize" victims (or "survivors," as they prefer to call sexually assaulted women in Britain) while assisting them. They do not normally form national associations, and few receive government funding of any consequence; therefore, their voice is heard less often now that of their wealthier counterparts. Nevertheless, they have achieved a great deal in changing attitudes among police officers, judges, and the general public (for instance, in reducing the amount of victim-blaming by judges in rape cases and in securing better treatment for women who report sexual assaults to the police). On the other hand, it seems that in European countries, they have been less in the vanguard of the victims movement as a whole than has been the case in the United States (where some would argue that they began the whole thing).

STATE COMPENSATION FOR VIOLENT CRIME

As the impetus to improve services for victims has been picked up by governments, so ministers have looked around for measures they can introduce to show their government's willingness to support victims. One of the most obvious measures is state compensation for victims of violent crime. It is attractive because it is normally nationally introduced, administered, and controlled, and because it seems to given clear benefit to some of the most stereotypically deserving victims: victims of violent crime. In most countries, legislation has been required for its introduction. This is also an attractive option for states since legislation is something they can themselves control (as opposed to the amorphous diffusing of support networks throughout the voluntary sector) and, once passed, can thereafter be cited as a positive action by government. Given the striking popularity of victim issues throughout the political spectrum (Phipps, 1988; van Dijk, 1984a), passing the legislation rarely poses many problems. The main disadvantages of state compensation schemes, as far as governments are concerned, are their high initial cost and the relative inability of government to control cost and take-up thereafter. The first has deterred some countries from starting such programs and has led to restrictions in others. The second is only now becoming apparent in the older schemes.

The first state compensation scheme in Europe was the Criminal Injuries Compensation Board (CICB) set up in England, Wales, and Scotland in 1964. In a peculiarly British way, this was created not by legislation, but by administrative fiat, and run by a board of senior advocates under the supervision of the Home Office and Scottish Office. It was originally created as a very wide-ranging scheme, providing compensation to any victim of violent crime of any nationality who was victimized or injured in the course of preventing crime in Britain. It remains one of the most generous in Europe, paying out over 48 million pounds in compensation to nearly 22,000 victims in final awards and nearly 3,600 victims in interim awards in 1986-1987 (CICB, 1987). In the recent wave of concern about victims, it was seen as important to put the scheme on a proper legislative basis, and this is now being implemented under the provisions of the Criminal Justice Act of 1988. The new statutory scheme, however, is of almost identical composition to the old one.

State compensation schemes are now operative in the Netherlands, West Germany (through state-based schemes), Sweden, France, and Italy, among other countries, though the system in Italy is restricted to victims of terrorism. In Eastern Europe (for example, Poland and Czechoslovakia) and Scandinavia, the role of state compensation in aiding victims with their medical costs and recovery expenses is taken by standard social provisions and is not restricted to incidents of crime.

The Convention of the Council of Europe on state compensation for victims of violent crime (Council of Europe, 1983) sets out minimum provisions that it considers member states should provide. It seeks to ensure that victims residing or working in a state should be compensated by that state (thereby getting over the problem of migrant workers). It has currently been ratified by four member states (Denmark, Luxembourg, the Netherlands, and Sweden) and signed by many more. The convention was agreed with little dispute after having been produced by a committee in record time (Tsitsoura, 1988), and delays in ratification seem largely to be for budgetary reasons.

A comprehensive scheme is costly, as is shown by the example of the CICB. Even the CICB has tried to limit costs, by setting a minimum limit for claims to succeed; by restricting payment for clothing, spectacles, or other personal property damaged in the course of violent crime; and by ensuring that any payments of compensation by offenders are deducted. However, the relatively small numbers of offenders who are prosecuted and convicted, combined with their impecunious state, sets an intrinsic limit as to the amount that can be raised from offenders to offset costs (probably less than 10% overall). In Britain, amounts of compensation payable are tied to the level of awards made in the civil courts in personal injury cases. The cost of the schemes is therefore not under the control of the government. Increasing awareness of the scheme through the work of victim support agencies and media publicity has increased take-up rates to some extent, and there is now real worry about spiraling costs.

Miers (1983) has argued that state compensation is essentially a symbolic act by governments to show their concern for victims, but there is little real intention to follow through with hard cash. Though this seems to be true in some parts of the world, it is less applicable to Europe. The convention may be said to fall into this category (rapid passage, little implementation), but the fact remains that, where European countries have set up schemes, they have attracted applications and made awards.

What is pertinent, however, is Miers' other assessment of the implications of the symbolic nature of state compensation: that awards define the kinds of victims seen as being deserving by states. The convention and most states allow for awards to be reduced or refused if victims are not truly "innocent" victims—i.e., if they have contributed to the crime through provocation or have not helped the police quickly and without protest. This is a very unpopular part of the British scheme as far as victims are concerned (Shapland, Willmore, & Duff, 1985) and illustrates the difference between governmental and victim perceptions of such compensation. Victims see it (quite correctly) as a judgment by the state on the worth of their claims and their status as victims. However, the state's and the law's view of incidents and violence as being black and white, with a clear offender and a clear victim, does not match up with reality or the victims' perceptions of situations. Real incidents are usually muddy shades of gray, with no "ideal victim" (Christie, 1986) to be found. Disillusionment is to be found in the mismatch.

Though there are good commentaries on the setting up and procedures of the different state compensation schemes (see Joutsen, 1987; HEUNI, 1988; Miers, 1978), research into the operation of the schemes and the reactions of victims is more rare. There have been studies in

Britain (Shapland et al., 1985) and the Netherlands (Cozijn, 1984), the results of which parallel those of Elias on the New York and New Jersey boards (Elias, 1983). In Britain, in the early 1980s, awards were given to most victims who applied, and delays were running at less than one year. In general, victims were satisfied with the operation of the board, but their experiences did not affect their attitudes of other parts of the criminal justice system (Shapland et al., 1985). More recently, delays have increased, and there are signs of increasing dissatisfaction with the paper-based, centralized system. In the Netherlands, the procedures are very bureaucratic, requiring the participation of lawyers and ensuring delays of over two years before awards are made. There is great dissatisfaction with the operation of the scheme, such that victim support associations are not recommending it to victims (van Dijk, 1988b). Victims who have been through the scheme have been found to be more dissatisfied with the criminal justice system than those who never applied (Cozijn, 1984). Most important of all, in both countries, it seems that victims would prefer compensation from offenders to state compensation, even if this meant that they did not receive full compensation due to the limited means of offenders (Shapland et al., 1985; Maher & Docherty, 1988; Newburn & De Peyrecave, 1988; van Dijk, 1984b).

COMPENSATION FROM OFFENDERS

In Europe, compensation from offenders can occur by means of three different models: the *partie civile* procedure, the award of a compensation order as part of a sentence against the offender, and restitution made informally or as part of a diversion arrangement by the prosecution. The first two models have tended to be seen as mutually exclusive in jurisprudential terms, so that one country has favored one method while another country chooses the other, though the Netherlands is currently considering introducing compensation orders while retaining the possibility of using *partie civile*.

The *Partie Civile* Model

The *partie civile* model involves having the victim pursue a civil claim against the offender at the same time and in the same proceedings as the criminal trial. This process is active in countries with continental law jurisprudence (France and West Germany in particular and the Netherlands to a lesser extent). The advantages for the victim include the fact that he or she is an officially recognized participant in the trial; therefore, information regarding charges, court dates, and other considerations must be sent to the victim. In most countries, questioning by the victim or the victim's advocate is restricted to matters affecting damages. However, the West German Nebenklage procedure, available over a range of relatively minor offenses, allows for the victim to become, in effect, an ancillary prosecutor with wide-ranging powers of questioning and commentary on the trial and sentence.

There are several disadvantages to the *partie civile* method. In some countries, there are very low limits on the amounts of damages that can be awarded under this procedure (though there are moves, for example, in the Netherlands, to raise these). Typically, no mechanism is provided for enforcement so the victim is therefore forced to fall back on civil distraint procedures, which are slow and relatively ineffective. In some countries, in order to be a *partie civile*, the victim must attend all the relevant sessions, which imposes an impossible burden for victims who are in work or have small children. Finally, as with all compensation mechanisms, there is a problem of victims knowing about the procedures, so that they have low take-up rates. In France, leaflets explaining all the procedures are available at police stations, and victim support associations will give aid and advice. The first victim support scheme in Spain (at Valencia) has also adopted this as its chief role. Nonetheless, use of the *partie civile* is low in all countries in which research has been undertaken, namely in France, West Germany, and the Netherlands (HEUNI, 1988). It is now thought unlikely that the mechanism can be reformed to provide an adequate avenue for compensation from offenders (due to the intrinsic problems of using civil procedures that are most suitable for wealthy or institutional victims, for victims of crime who are relatively poor, and those who are legally ill-informed). Countries are increasingly looking with interest at the compensation order model.

Compensation Orders

Compensation orders were first introduced in England and Wales with the 1972 Criminal Justice Act. They permitted the sentencer to award compensation for any loss, damage, or injury suffered by an identifiable victim of crime as part of the sentence, though such compensation, like all financial penalties, had to take into account the means of the offender. The compensation orders were extended in the 1982 Criminal Justice Act such that, in the case of impoverished offenders, they could form the sole sentence and that, if both a fine and compensation were to be ordered, the compensation would take priority. Similar provisions were enacted in Scotland in 1980. Following the 1988 Criminal Justice Act in England and Wales, sentences will have to give reasons as to why they do not order compensation in a case with an identifiable victim. Compensations may be ordered for immaterial damages (pain and suffering, solatium) as well as for material loss.

The idea of compensation found immediate favor with magistrates in England and Wales, and the latest figures show awards in over 70% of criminal damage cases. There have always been more problems with injury cases because sentencers are unclear as to how to quantify awards (Shapland et al., 1985; Newburn, 1987; 1988) and do not always think to award compensation. In fact, in both studies, one of the principal factors differentiating cases in which an award was made from those in which no order occurred was whether the prosecution mentioned the word "compensation" in any context. Equally, sentencers are not being provided with sufficient information to enable them to quantify compensation. The amount of information on losses, and injuries that is suitable to prove the elements of the offense for conviction is much less than that needed for sentencing. The move toward codification of the law to make convictions technically easier to obtain has put a greater burden upon sentencers (Thomas, 1978), and the information mechanisms have not responded (Shapland, 1987).

In the Crown Court in England and Wales, and in the sheriffs' courts in Scotland, judges have clearly felt greater unease about mixing what they see as an essentially civil matter with criminal sentencing. Orders have been correspondingly less frequent (Shapland et al., 1985; Maher et al., 1988). This essential ambiguity about the role of compensation in sentencing has dogged both practice and academic debate. Should it be seen as a civil matter? Has it then a place in a procedure that is designed solely to marry the punishment demanded by the state with the resources of the offender, or should a criminal trial also address the wrong done to the victim? If so, should these needs be subordinated to the state's overall right to decide upon sentence according to its perceptions of what is important? How can it do so? Is there in actuality no problem because, in fact, punishment should include compensation, and compensation, no less than the fine, should be regarded as punishment? Is the real difficulty the fact that we have not yet sorted out a criminal scale for compensation and that merely translating across a civil scale produced in personal accident cases is insufficient? In different countries, the extent of the jurisprudential and practical division between civil and criminal law varies. Accordingly, so do their answers to the above questions. These are questions currently under active consideration in West Germany (Jung, 1988) and in the Netherlands, as both these countries debate whether to introduce compensation orders.

Victims have fewer worries. In England, Wales, and Scotland, victims approve of compensation orders made by offenders, even if the orders do not cover all their losses and if the payments come in the halting and uneven dribs and drabs of installments (Shapland et al., 1985; Newburn & De Peyrecave, 1988; Maher et al., 1988). The national victimization survey conducted in 1984 reflected these feelings (Hough & Mayhew, 1985). Dissatisfaction arises largely if awards are derisory (because of the reasons cited above) and if courts do not inform victims about the amount of the award or the reasons for nonpayment and the means being taken for enforcement.

Restitution and Diversion

Payment of money from offender to victim, whether it be restitution or compensation, can also occur earlier in the criminal justice process. In a few mediation schemes, still largely at the experimental stage (HEUNI, 1988), restitution may either be arranged informally and the crime not be referred to the police, or the police, alone or in combination with other social agencies, may supervise payment in return for dropping proceedings. Similar processes can occur with prosecutors. In all countries, it is likely that informal arrangements of this kind operate in a small minority of cases, even where a strict principle of legality applies. The disadvantages of this method are its relative invisibility and the lack of arrangements if something goes wrong, such as enforcing payment by offenders and uncovering corruption among criminal justice personnel. There is very little research in this area, and almost no estimates of its extent. However, the few published reports of mediation and diversion schemes suggest that restitution figures in only a small proportion of their cases, the majority ending with an apology or in some contract concerning the offender's behavior.

More formal arrangements have tended to start with juveniles. In Britain, juvenile liaison bureau diversion strategies can include the payment of restitution to a victim, but this is rarely achieved. In the

Netherlands, prosecutors can take into account compensation paid by the offender and require fines for certain offenses. Compulsory compensation may be introduced by this method, as opposed to at the time of sentencing. In West Germany, prosecutors can drop cases if compensation is paid, fines are paid to the state, or donations are made to certain charities. However, the form of the question posed to defendants and the attitudes of prosecutors render it currently inevitable that over 90% of this money is paid to the state or charity and only 10% to victims (HEUNI, 1988).

In general, there are two sets of issues to be addressed. One relates to the difficulty of changing the attitudes of prosecutors and ensuring greater uniformity in practice throughout the country. Diversionary compensation is discretionary and subject to all the problems of such a mechanism. Training guidelines, and pronouncements by senior functionaries are all helpful (and are being increasingly tried, for example, in the Netherlands). But disparities will still remain. The second issue is the inevitable lack of openness of such a system, and related problems of enforcement and corruption. The only way around this is formal mechanisms of rules, review, and appeal. However, in doing this, we may be in danger of re-inventing all the mechanisms already set up for sentencing—of re-creating a sentencing system lower down the process, with police or prosecutor as judge. Would it not be better to sort out compensation at the sentencing stage?

HELPING VICTIMS PARTICIPATE

There are three ways in which a victim's participation in the criminal justice system can be made smoother and more satisfactory for both the victim and the system. One is to reform criminal procedures by instructing professionals (police, prosecutors, court staff), through guidelines and orders, to be more sympathetic to the needs of victims. A second is to create a climate for changes of attitudes among those who operate the system. Here, research, victim support agencies, media publicity, and official pronouncements can all play a part. The final way is to change procedures through legislation or administrative ordinances so that victims themselves have usable rights in the process. All three of these means have been used in Europe, but the balance to date has lain with the first two. Victims' rights have only occasionally been changed or been important in effecting change. Indeed, the whole idea of bestowing greater justiciable rights on victims has been regarded with some suspicion and occasionally horror.

The pattern of change has varied in different countries more strongly in this respect than with compensation or victim support. Partly, this reflects different legal systems. In the common law tradition, which reaches its apogee in England and Wales, the accusatorial mode of discovering evidence has placed victims more firmly under the command of the prosecution and has made it more difficult to change procedures without affecting the experiences and rights of defendants and others. In inquisitorial jurisdictions (France, Spain, West Germany, Finland, and Poland), the use of examining magistrates to take evidence and prepare a case for trial has enabled victims to be allowed to tell their story without interruption as a matter of course, though the Dutch Ministry of Justice is now trying to change the practice whereby the police read out their statements first, in order to allow the victim instead to have the first word (HEUNI, 1988).

There are also cultural differences concerning the victim's wish to participate. In the Netherlands, research has shown that few victims wish to attend the main trial (they will already have given their story to the prosecutor). In West Germany, on the other hand, victims want to appear at the trial and have the opportunity to challenge the defense. They wish to give evidence in court. Note that this is congruent with the fact that the greatest opportunity for victims to have rights to appear and speak is also to be found in West Germany, under the Nebenklage procedure. In Finland, Aromaa has found that victims vary considerably in their desire to participate. A few want to participate in every way; while a few definitely do not want to take part. Most would like to avoid court procedures but, in order to make sure that their cases are dealt with properly, do attend (because of their distrust of criminal justice personnel). In France, the victim assistance movement helps victims go through the court process. They have found that victims are now more ready and more eager to play an active role, so that more now wish to speak out in court about their experiences. This may reflect the likelihood of increased support, greater acceptance of victim issues by the system, and/or media publicity (all references in HEUNI, 1988).

Schadler (in HEUNI, 1988) has queried whether, in fact, there can be a statement of what victims might like, were professionals' attitudes and practices sympathetic to victims, or whether victims' views merely reflect the cultural position of legal and court thinking in a given country. However, it seems that countries are beginning to move toward an acceptance of the diversity of victim views on participation (as set out in the Recommendation of the Council of Europe, 1985) and to set up ways in which these views can be taken into account. However, in all countries, it seems easier to influence police and prosecution thinking and procedures than those of court staff (see Shapland & Cohen, 1987, for the results of an English national survey; HEUNI, 1988, for the views of researchers in several European countries). Governments have agreed that police and prosecutors have duties toward victims. Acceptance of the idea that the courts have duties toward victims and that judges and court administrative personnel should ensure that victim requirements are met has not yet resulted.

As a result, though different methods have been adopted in different countries, all have been biased toward police and prosecution practices. It is rare to find provision of separate waiting rooms at court (Shapland & Cohen, 1987; HEUNI, 1988). Changing court procedures produces considerable controversy. However, guidelines have been issued for prosecutors in the Netherlands and backed up both by training and by the institution of an ombudsman to whom victims may appeal. The ombudsman is able to award damages against the Ministry of Justice if procedures have not been correctly followed (HEUNI, 1988). Guidance for police in the form of several Home Office circulars has been set out for England and Wales (Shapland, 1988a), with corresponding advise in Scotland. Sweden has training for prosecutors (HEUNI, 1988). Similar measures are being considered or introduced in most countries.

In contrast, relying on victim rights to speed change is considered impractical, unlikely, and even scandalous, a considerably different viewpoint than that found in the United States. There are several reasons for the difference. One is the lack of similar reliance on a written constitution. Another is the difficulty individuals have in taking test cases, without, in most states, provision for legal aid (though this is changing in several continental jurisdictions) or a contingency fee basis for actions. Yet another is the relative lack of pressure groups for victims in Europe.

Perhaps most important is the seemingly greater paternalism in the operation of the criminal justice systems in Europe and in the ways legislation is introduced. Tradition has it that once a need for change has been accepted by a profession or influential group within the legislature, that group considers how best to bring the change about itself within the administrative or legislative structures of the professions. A successful test case by an individual would be seen as a failure to anticipate the change. The difficulty is, of course, that this method of creating change is rather conservative (see Rock, 1988). Changes that fit the profession's self-image have a high chance of happening eventually. Changes that are inimical to professional self-images or which require fundamental, structural alterations can be stalled (Shapland, 1988b). Yet, change produced through the evolution of service delivery, as opposed to individual rights, does at least mean change that may be delivered effectively and relatively evenly across the country. Change based on individual cases where rights have been exercised can lead to patchy, limited effects.

PATTERNS OF CHANGE FOR VICTIMS

What of the future? It is very difficult to produce predictions when the history of concern over victim issues is so recent in many countries. Nonetheless, there are a few pointers.

One is the increasing institutionalization of victim issues. In Britain and France, for example, the idea of considering victim needs has now become embedded into the political way of life. Victims are not just the latest fashion—they are here to stay. In Britain, for example, ministers' speeches on most criminal justice problems are likely to contain a reference to victims, a fact that would have been unheard of only five years ago. In France, the recent change in government did not lead to the abolition of the previous government's initiatives on victim assistance and support, but, if anything, to their strengthening.

With permanence has come consolidation and broadening of the issues that are tackled. This is most clearly seen in victim assistance. In Britain, largely volunteer-motivated and run schemes of a few years ago are taking on a more professional ethos as their sources of funding become slightly more secure and the number of paid co-ordinators rises. It is not clear whether these changes will lead to an ossification of the type of service provided or greater selection of the clientele, but the firmer base has permitted schemes to expand into helping new types of victims (rape victims and relatives of murder victims) within the same model. Professionalization tends to imply a more conscious questioning of standards and philosophy, as well as a cementing of links with other agencies. Are we seeing the incorporation of victim support into the mainstream criminal justice response, with the victim support scheme taking its place alongside the probation service, forensic psychiatry, and police? An equivalent move from scattered volunteer initiatives to a country-wide centrally-funded agency occurred to the probation service in the first few years of this century. But with status come duties. Victim services have always been dogged by the question of whether they are operating for the benefit of victims (as defined by victims) or for the benefit of other groups (such as promoting the rehabilitation of offenders or making court officials' lives easier). In Europe, victims themselves have no organized voice. Unless there continues to be research on victims' own beliefs and needs, there is the danger that agencies set up for their benefit will come to serve only organizational goals.

We would argue that research results have been crucial in the spread of consideration of victim issues and of possible remedies in Europe. Research to date has been concentrated in a few countries, notably Britain and the Netherlands, with recent surges in West Germany and France. Though those studies may be ignored on occasions in their own land because they are seen as inappropriate to present political views, they have informed debate in other countries, both directly through publications and conferences, and more indirectly through their influence on the debates of the Council of Europe and the United Nations. It is now characteristic of countries that are thinking of expanding their repertoire of victim services to find out about research and practice in other countries with such a provision. Conferences may be held, individual academics or policy-makers may make visits to other countries, supra-national documents will be consulted. The effect has been a greater catholicism of provision. Countries within Europe are now prepared to consider provisions, such as compensation orders, which stem from an alien legal system. The influence of particular legal systems is waning, though services will still reflect national cultural and social differences.

This greater willingness to share and to learn from others is also sparking greater interest in forming pan-European links, urged on by the need to deal with the changes to be produced in 1992 within the European Economic Community. There is a European Association of Victim Support Organizations. There are greater links between European criminologists and legal researchers. This is not to deny the continuing relevance and influence of North American thought and practice. But there now seems to be an intermediate step between the importation of an idea and its implementation: the examination of its effects in another European country.

REFERENCES

Christie, N. (1986). The ideal victim. In E. A. Fattah (Ed.), *From crime policy to victim policy*. London: Macmillan.

Corbett, C., & Maguire, M. (1988). The value and limitations of victims support schemes. In M. Maguire J. Pointing (Eds.), *Victims of crime: A new deal?* Milton Keynes: Open University Press.

Council of Europe (1983). *European convention on the compensation of victims of violent crime*. Strasbourg: Council of Europe.

Council of Europe (1985). Recommendation No. R(85)11 of the committee of ministers to member states on the position of the victim in the framework of criminal law and procedure. Strasbourg: Council of Europe.

Cozijn, C. (1984). *Schadefonds Geweldsmisdrijven*. The Hague: Ministerie van Justitie.

Criminal Injuries Compensation Board (1987). Annual Report 1986-1987. London: H.M.S.O.

Davis, R. C., Kumeuther, F., & Connick, E. (1984). Expanding the victim's role in the criminal court dispositional process. *Journal of Criminal Law and Criminology*, 2.

Elias, R. (1983). *Victims of the system*. New Brunswick: Transaction Books.

Fattah, E. A. (1986). Prologue: On some visible and hidden dangers of victims movements. In E. A. Fattah (Ed.), *From crime policy to victim policy*. London: Macmillan.

HEUNI (1988, November). Report of the ad-hoc working group on the implementation of the U.N. declaration, HEUNI, November 1988. Helsinki: HEUNI.

Hough, M., & Mayhew, P. (1985). *Taking account of crime: Key findings from the second British crime survey* (Home Office Research Study o. 85). London: H.M.S.O.

Hudson, P. S. (1984). The crime victim and the criminal justice system. *Pepperdine Law Review, 11*.

Joutsen, M. (1987). *The role of the victim of crime in European criminal justice systems* (HEUNI Series No. 11). Helsinki: HEUNI.

Jung, H. (1988). Compensation order—*Eim Modell der Schadenswiedergutmachung?*, *Zeitschrift fur die gesamte Strafechtswissenschaft, 99*, Heft 3.

Lamborn, L. (1986). The impact of victimology on the criminal law in the United States. *Canadian Community Law Journal, 8*, 23-44.

Maguire, M., & Corbett, C. (1987). *The effects of crime and the work of victims support schemes*. Aldershot: Gower.

Maguire, M. & Pointing, J. (1982). *Victims of crime: A new deal?* Milton Keynes: Open University Press.

Maher, G., & Docherty, C., with McLean, S., & Campbell, T. (1988). *Compensation orders in the Scottish criminal courts, Scottish office central research unit papers*. Edinburgh: Scottish Office.

Mawby, R. I., & Gill, M. L. (1987). *Crime victims: Needs, services and the voluntary sector*. London: Tavistock.

Miers, D. (1978). *Responses to victimization*. Abingdon: Professional Books.

Miers, D. (1983). Compensation to victims of crime. *Victimology, 8*, Nos. 1, 2: 204-212.

National Organization for Victim Assistance (1985). Victim rights and services: A legislative directory. Washington, DC: U.S. Department of Justice.

NAVSS (1988). *Victim support*, Annual Report 1987-88. London: National Association of Victims Support Schemes.

Newburn, T. (1987). Compensation for injury in the magistrates' courts. *Home Office Research Bulletin, 23,* 24-27.

Newburn, T. (1988). The use and enforcement of compensation orders in magistrates' courts. *Home Office Research Study,* 102, London: H.M.S.O.

Newburn, T., & De Peyrecave, H. (1988). Victims' attitudes to courts and compensation. *Home Office Research Bulletin, 25,* 18-21.

Phipps, A. (1988). In N. Maguire & J. Pointing (Eds.), *Victims of crime: A new deal?* Milton Keynes: Open University Press.

Rock, P. (1988). Governments, victims and policies in two countries. *British Journal of Criminology, 28,* 44-66.

Shapland, J. (1987). Who controls sentencing? Influences on the sentencer. In D. Pennington & S. Lloyd-Bostock (Eds.), *The psychology of sentencing: Approaches to consistency and disparity.* Oxford: Centre for Socio-Legal Studies.

Shapland, J. (1988a). Producing change for victims in the criminal justice system—the U.K. experience. Paper given to Working Group meeting on the Implementation of the U.N. Declaration, HEUNI, Helsinki, November 1988. Helsinki: HEUNI.

Shapland, J. (1988b). Fiefs and peasants: Accomplishing change for victims in the criminal justice system. In M. Maguire & J. Pointing (Eds.), *Victims of crime: A new deal?* Milton Keynes: Open University Press.

Shapland, J., & Cohen, D. (1987). Facilities for victims: The role of the police and the courts. *Criminal Law Review,* 28-38.

Shapland, J., Willmore, J., & Duff, P. (1985). *Victims in the criminal justice system.* Aldershot: Gower.

Thomas, D. (1978). Form and function in criminal law. In P. R. Glazebrook (Ed.), *Reshaping the criminal law.* London: Stevens.

Tsitsoura, A. (1988). Victims of crime—Council of Europe and United Nations instruments. Paper given to Working Group Meeting on the Implementation of the U.N. Declaration, HEUNI, Helsinki, November 1988. Helsinki: HEUNI.

van Dijk, J. J. M. (1984a). Public perceptions and concerns: On the pragmatic and ideological aspects of public attitudes toward crime control. Paper given to British Society of Criminology Day Conference, 6 October 1984, London.

van Dijk, J. J. M. (1984b). *Compensation by the state or by the offender: The victim's perspective.* The Hague: Ministry of Justice.

van Dijk, J. J. M. (1988a). Ideological trends within the victim movement: An international perspective. In M. Maguire & J. Pointing (Eds.), *Victims of crime: A new deal?* Milton Keynes: Open University Press.

van Dijk, J. J. M. (1988b). Recent developments in the criminal policies concerning victims in the Netherlands. Paper given to Working Group Meeting on the Implementation of the U.N. Declaration, HEUNI, Helsinki, November 1988. Helsinki: HEUNI.

Chapter 13

WHICH VICTIM MOVEMENT?
The Politics of Victim Policy

ROBERT ELIAS

> It is time to recognize the larger contours and consequences of develop-
> ments political scientists have long studied as fragments. . . . Laws and
> official actions that reassure or threaten without much warrant . . . are
> doubtless conceived . . . as discrete events; but when, taken together, they
> reach a critical mass of complementary programs, they become an essen-
> tial part of a new political pattern . . . that converts liberal and radical
> watchwords of the past into conservative bastions of the future.
>
> —Murray Edelman

What would we say about a movement that apparently forgot to invite
most of its professed beneficiaries? What if we discovered, for example,
in the victims "movement," that victims were, politically, all dressed
up, but had no place to go? What kind of movement would it be? Would
it really be any movement at all?

Reviewing recent victim policy makes these questions all too appropriate. The movement to redress the victim's plight has been much
bally-hooed, but we must consider more closely what the movement
and its resulting policies represent politically and what they actually
achieve. Other than discussing relatively trivial legislative "debates,"
the victim movement has been presented mostly as if it had no politics
at all. Instead, we should examine the movement's political evolution,
particularly in the "Age of Reagan," which has set the context for victim
policy. We'll emphasize "legislative" policy: What changes have occurred, what new directions have emerged, and what's been the effect
of the politics of the 1980s and of the victim movement in particular?

Indeed, *which* movement has been receiving such great attention, and what political pattern does it reflect?

RECENT LEGISLATIVE POLICY

If we take the justice out of the criminal justice system we leave behind a system that serves only the criminal

—President's Task Force on Victims of Crime (1982)

The victim movement as legislative policy emerged in 1965 in California with the nation's first victim-compensation program. In the next decade and a half, national and state legislation steadily increased. Yet, the legislative movement for victims was most successful in the 1980s, which saw a tremendous outpouring of initiatives. Mostly, we're concerned here with U.S. state and national laws, but international legislation has also emerged during this period, casting the movement in a different light.

State Legislation

Most legislative activity has occurred in the states, providing victim services, changing the criminal process, emphasizing special groups, establishing victim rights, and dealing more harshly with offenders.[1]

Victim Services. These programs emphasize financial aid, logistical support, and personal treatment. Every state has laws bolstering the judiciary's common-law power to order restitution, in money payments, transferred property, or work. Half the states mandate restitution for many crimes unless the judge explains in writing why it is not to be imposed. Most states have authorized witness fees, some have raised their fee levels, and one pays lost wages. Thirty-five states reimburse rape victims for medical exams.

All but six states have compensation programs. Most impose eligibility rules, and pay for such losses as medical costs, psychological counseling, lost wages/support, funeral costs, and emergency awards, due to violent crime. Some impose a hardship test, allow pain and suffering awards, and provide some property coverage. A few states support local, non-profit victims groups, compensate parents of missing children and dependents of firefighters and police officers, and pay child care or for lost homes.

All but two states have funded domestic violence services (for safe refuge, and educational, training, housing, and emergency medical, legal, and psychological support). Half the states fund sexual assault programs for psychological and medical needs. Most states stress the victim's role in court: Thirty-four have created local victim/witness services to help victims exercise their rights, get timely information, and participate. A few states have special advocates programs.

Criminal Process. All states have laws to help the criminal process better serve victim needs, if not rights. All but two states allow a victim impact statement, an "objective" account (for the presentence report) of the injuries the offender caused, prepared by a probation officer, a victim advocate, or victims themselves. Thirty-five states allow a victim statement of opinion (oral or written) about the appropriate sentence. Many states have extended victim participation into other stages of the process, such as plea bargaining and parole hearings, and in the discharge, dispositional, mitigation, supervised, or early release, hearings.

Most states require victims to receive certain kinds of information about services, their court case, and their apparent offenders. Laws require police officers, hospital, or compensation officials to inform them about compensation programs, and prosecutors to inform them about witness fees. Other statutes require that victims be given notice of scheduled court proceedings, usually upon request, canceled hearing dates, pre-trial release, bail, plea agreements, sentencing, final disposition, parole hearings, pardons, work release, prisoner release, and escapes.

Fifteen states allow victims in the courtroom (waiving sequestration rules) at the judge's discretion, and one state makes court attendance a victim right. Eighteen states mandate speedy trials, although with no set time limits. Some states ban excessive cross examination of victims and reduced plea bargaining (or increase victim influence over the outcome).

All but four states protect against intimidation and retaliation, by toughening criminal penalties, specifying kinds of proscribed harassment, and allowing "protective orders." Several states have legislated against the long-term confiscation of recovered property, requiring officials to promptly examine its usefulness as evidence, and allowing photographic substitutes. Other laws help victims by explaining to employers the importance of court appearances. Some states even make it a misdemeanor for an employer to discharge an employee who misses work to attend court.

Victims have been given privacy protections, such as for their psychological treatments after victimization. Twenty-two states protect victims' names and addresses, but only for sexual assault victims in some states. Twenty-three states protect child identities. Five have blanket protections for counselor-client confidentiality. Twenty provide it for sexual assault counseling, and twenty-four have it for domestic violence counseling. Yet some oppose privacy, claiming it impedes press freedom, public records access, maximum information, and victim assistance.

Some states have changed statutory wording (such as rape-law reforms that reduce victims' burden of proof), broaden the proscribed conduct, use non-gender specific language, and recognize degrees of force. Other laws define new crimes, purportedly to better protect victims, such as against disclosing domestic-violence shelter locations. Finally, 17 states require training on victim issues for judges, prosecutors, and police officers.

Special Victims. Most states have passed laws for special victim groups. Some emphasize child victims. All but 9 try to make child testimony less traumatic, permitting a videotaped statement either alone (unsworn interrogatory) or under oath and cross-examination (deposition), or live testimony through closed-circuit television. Forty states have legislation about missing children, often creating clearinghouses to help find them. Over half the states have amended child-competency or hearsay-admissibility rules, required child guardians, or extended the statute of limitations for child offenses. Somewhat fewer states require speedy trials or protect child privacy during prosecution.

Twenty-four states allow background checks of child workers, including access to criminal records. Nineteen states require everyone, and all states at least require professionals (such as licensed teachers, medical staff, and child-care workers), to report suspected child abuse, backed by civil damages, or even criminal penalties. Some states have extended their adult bill of rights to children; 12 have children's bill of rights, requiring a guardian to tell the court the child's capacities, the trial's likely impact, when to use videotapes, and to help with emotional problems and court proceedings. Children are sometimes given easier access to compensation, and are exempted from testimony corroboration or grand juries.

Similar protections, such as services and shelters, have emerged for battered women. Better record-keeping, like monthly police reports, are required to track abuse patterns. Other laws provide protective orders, assign possession of the residence, get the defendant to pay support, and set custody and visitation rights. Thirty states authorize warrantless arrests for misdemeanor assaults; ten require it upon probable cause.

Sexual assault victims also receive special attention, with laws for services, such as hotlines and counseling, crime prevention and prosecution, and medical attention. At least one state requires sexual assault victims be given information about AIDS. And, changes have been made to reduce the victimization caused by traditional rape legislation.

Elderly victims have elicited laws allowing the victim's age to be used in determining sentences, producing tougher penalties and probation denial. Some states criminalize the abuse or neglect of the elderly. Many states require elderly-abuse reporting, especially by professionals, with 25 states protecting all vulnerable adults and 22 protecting older adults over a certain age. Some states mandate ombudsmen, speedy trials, abuser registries, hotlines, food, clothing, shelter, medical care, and other social services.

Other special victim groups have been added. Over 400 new laws related to drunk driving victims have emerged in recent years. Thirty-five states cover these victims for compensation, and all but one state has raised its drinking age to 21. "Dram shop" liability (for those serving intoxicated drivers) has been imposed by statute or case law in 42 states. Also, hate-violence victims have received some attention. Eighteen states criminalize acts infringing civil rights based on race, color, creed, religion, national origin, or sex; only one protects sexual orientation. Thirty states criminalize the desecration of religious property, and 22 ban the disruption of religious gatherings, and inappropriate hoods or masks. Forty-three states ban violence due to racial or religious hatred.

Victim Rights. Victim legislation has been increasingly packaged as statutory or constitutional rights. Since 1980, when the first victim Bill of Rights passed, 44 states have added similar laws, including the right to information, protection, transportation, property return, waiting areas in courtrooms, input, notification, employer and creditor intercession, speedy disposition, and court attendance. Most have passed formal bills of rights, but 5 states have packaged existing legislation and 4 have passed legislative resolutions.

As statutory rights with no real remedies for non-enforcement, some wonder whether these bills really provide rights. Some states encourage enforcement through an ombudsman or grievance procedure, yet officials are immunized against monetary damages for non-implementation. A few states have adopted constitutional amendments to reinforce their bill of rights. They elevate statutory rights to constitutional rights; specify rights to dignity, respect, sensitivity, restitution, compensation and to influence sentencing and be informed and present in the criminal process.

Offender Rights. By implication, some victim protections affect offender rights. Some initiatives specify that victim rights shall not erode defendant's rights, yet lack specific provisions for doing so. Indirectly, offender rights may be affected by victim participation in plea bargaining, sentencing, and parole decisions.

Directly, offender rights are curbed by "notoriety for profits" laws, which confiscate profits generated when offenders sell their crime story, and domestic violence laws, which allow warrantless arrests. Restitution is now an enforceable civil judgment, and offenders are often banned from being considered crime victims themselves. Laws have weakened evidence rules for convicting defendants, eliminated the insanity plea (sometimes for "guilty but mentally ill" laws imposing prison preceded by a mental-institution), and toughened (through "sentencing enhancement") criminal penalties (such as by distinguishing felonies and "serious" felonies).

Courts have reduced the exclusionary rule's curb on illegally seized evidence, and legislation has done likewise. Many states have challenged the bail system by allowing preventive detention that jails suspects even if they meet normal bail-release standards. Only "tort reform," which limits corporate liability for victimization, provides laws helping offenders, although obviously not those stressed by standard law enforcement.

Funding. Victim programs have been funded less and less through general revenues: only 16 states now do so. Some alternative sources are earmarked to fund particular programs, such as marriage license fees for domestic violence shelters; other sources are distributed more evenly.

Some resources come from offenders as a fixed or variable assessment for each crime, a criminal fine surcharge, a driver's license reinstatement fee, literary profits from crime stories, forfeited crime assets, recovered racketeering damages, and wages earned in prison, on work release, or while on parole. Other funds come from bail forfeitures or bondsman taxes, and from levies such as marriage, divorce, birth and death surcharges, alcohol taxes, income-tax checkoffs, and court filing fees. Funding also comes from the national government in block grants and from the Victims of Crime Act.

Pending Proposals. Much more legislation awaits enactment, such as proposals to reduce victim cross-examination, eliminate plea bargaining and the exclusionary rule, substitute affidavits for victim testimony, tighten bail requirements, require "truth in sentencing" standards from judges, and to add constitutional amendments. In areas such as drunk-driving, there's a campaign for increasing compensation, revoking driver's licenses upon arrest, confiscating license plates, incarcerating repeat offenders, issuing color-coded driver's licenses, and passing "open container" laws. Legislation may also begin addressing some neglected groups, such as rural or arson victims, and victimized members of deviant groups.

National Legislation

National legislation reflects the same concerns found in the states; indeed, it stimulated many state laws. Yet Congress has also passed its own laws that affect victims both directly and indirectly.[2]

Direct Legislation. Although not actually law, the heyday of victim policy began in 1981 with the Reagan administration's declaration of the National Victim Rights Week. In 1982, it established the President's Task Force on Victims of Crime, which soon provided a long list of recommendations, many of which have now been enacted or are being actively pursued.

In 1982, Congress passed the Federal Victim & Witness Protection Act (VWPA) to promote victims in the criminal process, address their needs, and provide model legislation for the states. It required victim-impact statements, sanctioned (by criminal penalties and protection orders) victim and witness intimidation, mandated restitution (or written justification why not), and tightened bail standards. It required the attorney general to set national guidelines for treating victims fairly in the criminal process, including services, notification, scheduling, consultation, accommodations, property return, employer notification, law-enforcement training, victim assistance, and crime-story profits. The guidelines came out in 1983, but carefully noted that they were not enforceable as rights.

In 1984, Congress passed the Victims of Crime Act (VOCA) to provide direct national resources, through the Crime Victims Fund, to help finance state compensation programs, and public and private victim/witness assistance agencies. The Fund had a cap of $100 million each year, to be gotten entirely from criminal fines, penalty fees, forfeited bail bonds, and literary profits, and not from "innocent" taxpayers. The first VOCA funds were spent in 1986, with a fund-limit increase to $110 million. In 1988, a new VOCA made a few changes, such as directing states not to exclude drunk-driving or domestic-violence victims, increasing the fund limit to $125 and then to $150 million and raising minimum-assistance grants per state.

Indirect Legislation. Some statutes have affected victims indirectly in omnibus programs, providing additional funding and easier procedures, or imposing tougher offender treatment. Before the 1980s, some aid came indirectly from agencies like the Law Enforcement Assistance Administration (LEAA), the Department of Health, Education and Welfare (HEW), and the National Institute of Mental Health (NIMH), and from federal crime legislation. The first general, federal aid from indirect sources in the 1980s came in the Justice Assistance Act of 1984, which provided block grants to states for improvements such as victim/witness assistance plans. That same year, Congress passed Acts on Bail and Sentencing Reform, which tightened laws against defendants to help victims, and urged states to do the same. The bail law allowed preventive detention, stiffened standards, and pushed the victim's role in bail decisions. The sentencing law restricted parole, limited judicial discretion, and mandated "truth in sentencing."

In 1987, Congress passed the Criminal Fines Improvement Act, which was to track down past offenders and upgrade fines collection, partly to increase Crime Victim Fund resources. In 1988, the new Justice Assistance Act made programs aiding child, spouse, and elderly victims eligible for new block-grant funding, provided some anti-drug financing, and authorized funds to drug-crime victims to help law-enforcement.

Special Victims. Since the 1970s, special victim groups have also been stressed on the national level. Child abuse laws began in 1974 with the Child Abuse Prevention & Treatment Act (CAPTA), which created the National Center for Child Abuse & Neglect (NCCAN) and funded public child-protection agencies, private treatment centers, and inter-agency cooperation projects. NCCAN helped stimulate child legislation in almost every state; in 1978, it began its first purported prevention program. In 1982, Congress passed the Missing Children's Act to address an apparent wave of child abductions. In the early 1980s, NCCAN's funding was slashed, but it was renewed again by 1985. In 1984, the original law was revised, emphasizing state treatment, identification, and prevention programs. In 1985, Social Services Block Grant Act money went to training child-care service providers against child abuse, and for health and protection for the next two years. In 1986, CAPTA first received VOCA money under the Children's Justice & Assistance Act, but those funds were cut significantly a year later.

Sexual assault laws emerged indirectly in the 1970s. The NIMH created the National Center for the Prevention & Control of Rape (NCPCR) and the Rape Prevention & Control Advisory Committee in 1976 to provide services, information, training, conferences, and technical aid, but no money for direct services. The LEAA funded some services but with non-federal resources, and almost never any feminist programs. LEAA programs emphasized victim cooperation and crime control, and its Stop Rape Crisis Center focused more on offenders than victims. In 1980, some aid came from the Rape Services Support Bill of the Mental Health Systems Act, but by 1981 that funding was cut, NCPCR was gutted, LEAA was dismantled, and rape centers abandoned the feminist model and dwindled dramatically. From 1981 to 1987, rape-center funding came from the Preventive Health & Health Services Block Grant of the Public Services Health Act, but by 1985 NCPCR had died.

Spouse abuse initiatives began in 1977 with LEAA's Family Violence Program, which helped begin in 1978 the National Coalition Against Domestic Violence, although it was reluctant to accept LEAA money and its abuse model. In 1980, HEW began an Office on Domestic Violence, but it died in 1981, which was also the last year for funding from CETA, ACTION, and HUD programs for battered women's shelters, programs which the Reagan administration mostly abandoned. In 1984, the Attorney General's Task Force on Family Violence guidelines were released, and the Family Violence Prevention & Services Act funded prevention and other assistance, augmented later by VOCA funds.

Elderly victim protections began in the 1970s in LEAA and the Administration on Aging, focusing on security and education, not on direct aid. The Safe Streets Act of 1975 and the Community Crime Prevention Program of 1976 required states and then localities to propose new legislation for the elderly. In 1977, the National Elderly

Victimization Prevention & Assistance Program emerged. By the mid-1980s, programs for the elderly still qualified for some general funds, but most had been completely cut several years earlier.

Other special victims have taken their place. Drunk-driving victims have been championed in Washington and given prime attention in the 1988 VOCA. Terrorist and torture victims have received some consideration. The Iranian hostage episode produced the Hostage Relief Act of 1980 and tax exclusions for government hostage victims. In 1986, the Omnibus Security & Antiterrorism Act provided monetary and non-monetary aid for terrorist victims. In 1987, the Torture Victim Protection Act provided alien victims judicial relief in U.S. courts for past torture victimization.

Federalism. Federal districts and territories have passed some laws, but far fewer than most states. The Virgin Islands has victim compensation, and Puerto Rico has used some VOCA funding. The District of Columbia has laws for rape examinations, victim compensation, marital rape, hate violence, vulnerable adults, child-abuse reporting, protection orders, restitution, victim privacy, and sexual-assault finding, and has proposed a victim bill of rights.

Following the new federalism of the 1980s, national policy has emphasized decentralized victim programs at more local levels. Little has been carried out by national programs, which have instead provided guidelines, funding, and requirements for local practice, such as the priority for such groups as children, the elderly, and sexual-assault and domestic-violence victims. National laws purportedly let the states set their own standards, yet many programs impose federal requirements anyway. VOCA funding for compensation has forced states to expand their medical coverage, maximum awards, and non-resident eligibility and to reduce minimum awards or deductibles and limits on family violence and drunk-driving claimants.

Pending Proposals. National initiatives have been numerous. The President's Task Force on Victims of Crime made 69 recommendations alone; others appear in the Attorney General's reports on victim assistance and family violence, in funding legislation, in annual reports to Congress, and piecemeal through other means.

The national proposals now pending include victim access to parole hearings, family violence statutes, privacy provisions, "dram shop" laws, sentencing, and bail and hearsay evidence reform. Most controversial are calls for preventive detention, more prisons, and capital punishment; limiting judicial sentencing discretion; admitting juvenile records in adult trials: an amendment to the U.S. Constitution; and eliminating parole, plea bargaining, and the exclusionary rule.

International Legislation

National and state laws are not the only ones that may affect U.S. victims. International or regional initiatives have addressed criminal victimization. The United Nations has passed such legislation, partly resembling and partly diverging from U.S. laws. International bodies have legislated even longer for victims more broadly defined.

Crime Victim Declarations. International and regional laws and standards have emerged since the late 1970s. The 5th UN Congress on the Prevention of Crime & Treatment of Offenders (PCTO) stressed victimization's economic and social effects. In 1980, the 6th UN Congress on PCTO addressed crime victims more directly (Lopez-Ray, 1985). By 1983, the Council of Europe passed a Convention on the Compensation of Victims of Violent Crimes, a regional model (Willis, 1984). Crime victims were included in the model legislation of the UN Institute on the Prevention & Control of Crime, the International Law Association's Committee on International Criminal Law, and the International Association of Penal Law (Schaaf, 1986).

The UN's 6th Congress was just as concerned with victims of the abuse of power, attributing to it far greater physical, psychological, and financial harm than common crime, and calling for global action (United Nation's Secretariat, 1980). The 7th Session of the UN Committee on Crime Prevention & Control in 1982 repeated the call. In 1985, at the 7th UN Congress on PCTO, acting on the World Society of Victimology's draft, the Declaration of Basic Principles of Justice for Victims of Crime & Abuse of Power was formally adopted and then ratified by the UN General Assembly (Lamborn, 1987a).

While a few nations, like the United States tried to limit the declaration to only victims in existing national criminal laws, almost all nations wanted (and got) broader definitions, encompassing political victimization (such as apartheid and disappearances) and economic victimization (such as by multinational corporations and national policy). The declaration covered both victim groups, but provided more specific standards for crime victims, such as access to justice, fair treatment, restitution, compensation, and services. It invoked international law to reinforce its protections, urged strong legislation against abuses of power, and called for global cooperation to prevent both kinds of victimization (Lamborn, 1987a).

Human Rights Declarations. The declaration and the preceding deliberations did more than consider different groups of victims simultaneously. It acknowledged relationships not widely accepted in the U.S. victim movement, recognizing that far more victimization comes from governments and business institutions than from those defined as criminal under national laws, and that social victimization causes crime. The declaration was predicated on existing international criminal law and human rights covenants. The former includes at least 22 recognized crimes, incorporating international instruments condemning crimes against peace, war crimes, crimes against humanity, genocide, slavery, hijacking, hostage-taking, and torture. It encompasses the "collective victims" of crime and abuses of political and economic power, as reflected in the standards of the International Society of Criminology, the International Society of Social Defense, and the UN Economic & Social Council's International Penal & Penitentiary Foundation (Bassiouni, 1985; Cataldo, 1985).

International human rights, invoked in the declaration, encompass the UN Declaration on Human Rights, the International Covenants on Civil and Political Rights, and Economic, Social and Cultural Rights, and the many specialized UN rights covenants on women, workers, torture victims, and others (Danielus, 1986). It also incorporated the human rights protections of the UN's Draft Code on Transnational Corporations (Lamborn, 1987a). It quite likely encompasses regional human rights declarations, such as from Europe and the Americas, and even non-governmental declarations like the Algiers Universal Declaration of the Rights of Peoples (Falk, 1981) and the International Tribunal on Crimes Against Women (Russell, 1984).

Pending Proposals. Passing the 1985 UN Declaration has shifted the context of victimization, at least in international discussions, toward a broader victim definition, beyond criminal victimization; it has set a precedent for incorporating victims into international law and for an expanded concept of victimization, which will likely provoke more international and regional legislation (Geis, Chappell, and Agopian, 1985). It's already stimulated implementation proposals for a covenant to bind signatories (Lamborn, 1987a). The declaration may inspire national legislation, like the proposed Canadian & International Charter of Rights for Crime Victims, which calls for protection, reparation, information, and treatment, as well as alternatives to the criminal process and the social system producing most injustice, conflict, and victimization (Normandeau, 1983).

EVALUATING VICTIM POLICY

The system's failure is only in the eye of the victim; for those in control, it's a roaring success!

—Jeffrey Reiman

We can evaluate recent victim policy through research and political analysis. What does this legislation provide? How well has it been implemented? What have been its tangible and symbolic effects? Has it helped victims? Has it eroded offender rights? What does it reflect about the victim movement? What is its political or ideological direction?

Program Implementation and Impact

The legislation reviewed above shows impressive victim activity in the 1980s. No wonder the period is viewed as a boon for victims. Indeed, these laws translate into many programs and much new financing. For example; between 1984 and 1986, nationwide victim compensation increased from $67 to $115 million (NOVA, 1988). Each year, the National Office of Crime Victims publishes an impressive list of organizations funded by VOCA money (OVC, 1988). Even some programs cut nationally have been resumed by state and city governments (Smith & Freinkel, 1988). New funding mechanisms have emerged, and rights have expanded. Some states have been especially innovative: California and Wisconsin, for their victim bill of rights, and Michigan and Florida, for their constitutional amendments. Programs are providing help, personally and in court, that would not otherwise be there.

Problems. Nevertheless, victim policy also has problems, when we look at its implementation and impact. Some advocates acknowledge what's been achieved, but claim much more remains to be accomplished, and it's happening too slowly: There's not enough victim rights legislation and funding, compensation restrictions remain, and victim bill of rights need enforcement (NOVA, 1988). Others view laws as not the most effective victim policy (since the laws are often not actually implemented), claiming the courts should lead the way (Austern, 1987).

Some worry that government may have promised more than it can deliver, ignoring, for example, information costs (Krasno, 1983; Anderson & Woodard, 1985). Others lament the fragmentation promoted by the "new federalism" (Smith & Freinkel, 1988).

More seriously, some question officials' real concern for victims, wondering why services get such short commitments, why programs must be diluted to avoid administration vetoes, and why other programs are abandoned before solving the problem. One comprehensive study of federal victim policies found them highly selective, underfunded, precarious, symptomatic, contradictory, and manipulative (Smith & Freinkel).

The state and local level seems to fare no better. Consider the victim groups given priority in the 1980s: Some states have created trust funds, protective programs, and preventive services against child abuse, but they are poorly funded. Sexual assault programs have increased in major hospitals, but have declined in community health centers; independent centers have dropped drastically (Smith & Freinkel, 1988). Spouse abuse programs have survived (with diversified funding strategies) and even increased a little, yet very unevenly, with a few states supporting most programs while the remaining ones eliminate services (Smith & Freinkel).

Elderly programs, always limited anyway to crime avoidance, almost completely stopped when federal funding ended; far fewer local services exist than a decade ago, even though neither elderly needs nor crime have been resolved (Smith & Freinkel, 1988). Restitution programs have been undermined by increased imprisonment and mandatory sentencing. Compensation programs have made more payments, but serve only a tiny fraction of all victims. Crime-control programs, enforcement crackdowns, and imprisonment have increased, yet crime has not declined (Elias, 1983a, 1985b).

Administration. Problems with victim programs may stem from more than poor resources and meager commitments. Some obstacles may be organizational, caused by internal structural and ideological conflicts. The new federalism may be an impediment. Conflicts have arisen between traditional institutions and alternative centers, and between governmental and non-governmental agencies, as the most appropriate sites for victim assistance.

Sometimes this is a matter of control: other times, it's professional ideology. Clashes emerge over using volunteers versus professionals, over independence versus institutionalization, and over philosophies of paternalism versus self-reliance. Conflicts arise among the law enforcement, mental health, medical, social service, and other perspectives found in victim programs (Smith & Freinkel, 1988). The problems don't end here: Victims have some of their worst administrative problems in the courts.

Victims in the Criminal Process

The victim's role in court has been much emphasized, producing many initiatives to improve treatment and participation. To implement them and help victims generally, dozens of victim/witness programs have emerged with the services outlined above. In sheer numbers, the initiatives are a success. Victim/witness programs have been helped, especially, by a federal funding priority given them in recent years. Many more victims now have help negotiating the criminal process and victimization's aftermath.

Misconceptions and Official Needs. Nevertheless, problems remain. While new initiatives, such as sexual assault laws, have redefined rape and changed evidence rules, some wonder if they've really helped most female victims in court (Beinen, 1981). Like other services, victim/witness programs serve a relatively few victims, even though they are better funded. Even victims who have been assisted (by transportation, waiting areas, and notification), much less those who are not, often get victimized again in court due primarily to apparent misconceptions about what victims need and want, and about how the courts typically work.

Policies assume that victims want to participate, that participating will satisfy their needs; that they fail to do so due to high costs, intimidation, insufficient rights, and opportunities; that court personnel want this participation; and that it's necessary for effective criminal punishments. Yet these assumptions, made by victim advocates, policymakers, victimologists, and the influential President's Task Force, may be wrong. Many victims have no big desire to participate and therefore shun opportunities to do so (Forer, 1980). A victim's testifying may not be a useful, cathartic experience, as argued, since the courtroom doesn't provide an appropriate setting (Henderson, 1985). Victims do not fail to cooperate because of high costs and are not needed (or sought) in most prosecutions; indeed, they are largely shunned as outsiders. Victims may not participate partly due to unresponsive officials or because they realize it will not produce the outcomes or influence they want.

More important, victims are irrelevant as to how most cases are resolved: by plea bargaining in routinized, courtroom work groups, where victims jeopardize negotiations, slow proceedings, and threaten outcomes. Victim/witness programs may help promote dissatisfaction by treating victims as prosecution witnesses, thus building false hopes (Davis, 1983; Elias, 1986). Attempts have been made to curtail bargaining, but they will fail: Officials rely on it for workload efficiency and professional goals. And eliminating pleas to get harsher convictions will not likely help victims since it is not necessarily what they really want or need (Henderson, 1985).

Ignoring Victim Needs. Despite apparent victim concern, most officials still view crime as victimizing the state or society, not the victim. Some victim protections in court were devised for official needs and may not help victims, especially with their psychological needs. Indeed, they may be destructive and prevent victims from resolving their experience.[3] Victims can participate in sentencing, yet it may satisfy no penal rationale or victim needs.[4] Despite the many initiatives, victim frustration with the courts apparently continues (Note, 1987). Participation may not be what victims want or need; non-participation or even noncooperation might be better (Elias, 1985c).

Rights and Punishments

Victim policy often assumes defendants have too many rights, despite contrary evidence (Rudovsky, 1988). It emphasizes a contest between victim and offender rights; thus, most of the former have come at the expense of the latter (Karmen, 1984). Yet victims are poorly served by curbing defendant's rights; indeed, we're all losers by eroding even further our minimal procedural protections.

Some rights curbs are less important, such as banning literary profits from crime. Others are more serious: preventive detention, warrantless arrests, capital punishment, weakening evidence rules, and eliminating the exclusionary rule and the insanity defense. Other changes are also disturbing: mandatory and increased imprisonment, longer sentences, and eliminating parole. These reforms seem to be a new dose of historically unsuccessful, get-tough policies that probably don't satisfy victim needs, including not being victimized in the first place. Unleashing the state against criminals does not empower victims to pursue their interests (Karmen, 1984). Beyond offender rights, victim policy may also infringe on the rights of child workers, the media, and the public generally.

The courts have found some victim policies unacceptable, ruling victim-impact statements unconstitutional in capital cases (Sharman, 1988), and the Victim & Witness Protection Act as denying defendants 5th, 7th and 14th Amendment rights. Yet other courts have disagreed, letting victim policies stand (Kahn, 1982). Those policies have helped produce, and have also resulted from, a climate that has pushed courts further toward eroding offender rights, upholding capital punishment, preventive detention, and exclusionary rule limitations (Viano, 1987). The U.S. Supreme Court has led the way, adopting a criminal review model that equates rights only with those who are clearly law-abiding, almost presuming guilt and no rights for defendants (O'Neill, 1984).

Constitutional amendments may further affect defendant's rights, providing a presumption for victim rights. They also seem poorly defined and hastily designed, have enormous yet unexamined effects on the U.S. legal process, have uncertain means for enforcement, and create rights conflicts with no apparent resolution (Symposium, 1987; Lamborn, 1987b). They assume an adversarial process that rarely occurs and that may be ill-advised. They promote a "rights" approach to society, pitting groups against each other in a high-stakes, zero-sum game not likely to benefit victims, even if appropriate to favor them over defendants (Viano, 1987).

Politics of Victim Policy and the Victim Movement

What political pattern does this reveal? We're concerned here not with narrow issues of how victim programs could be better funded or managed, or how they affect particular rights for victims, offenders, and others, but rather what the victim movement and policy represent as a macro-political phenomenon. Why have victim initiatives emerged as they have, and whose interests do they serve?

Who Gets What? Presumably, victims should benefit most. Yet for all the new initiatives, victims have gotten far less than promised. Rights have often been unenforced or unenforceable, participation sporadic or ill-advised, services precarious and underfunded, victim needs unsatisfied if not further jeopardized, and victimization increased, if not in court, then certainly in the streets. Given the outpouring of victim attention in recent years, how could this happen, and who benefits instead?

Offenders have gained since victim policy has not reduced crime, but such is not the case when apprehended, since their rights have deteriorated and prison sentences increased. Victim advocates, including many devoted activitists, may have gained from the emerging "victims industry," yet overall they've lost almost as badly as victims. That leaves only those holding political power who have devised contemporary victim policy: They've gained plenty.

It's hard to believe the apparent concern shown by politicians, not just because victim policy has achieved so little, but because it probably could have been predicted to do so. So why pursue such policies? Perhaps because they provide other benefits, both political and ideological.

Ideological Gains. Victim initiatives seem to perpetuate biased crime definitions conveyed in legislation, enforcement patterns, or the media, which limit our concept of victimization to "street" crime, usually ignoring the much more harmful "suite" crime, be it corporate or governmental (Green & Berry, 1985). They further narrow those victims to whom we'll devote our attention: *not* to lower class minorities, who are among the most victimized, but rather to the elderly and victims of child, female, and sexual abuse, who are not.

These victims are often treated paternalistically as helpless and frail and thus robbed of any sense of power and self-reliance (Smith & Freinkel, 1988). They are designated, although not permanently, as the "innocent" victims we all want to protect; they may also be "safe" victims, who can help bound the movement: an apparent exercise in social control (Marx, 1983; Elias, 1986). With offenders, it's no different. The President's Task Force narrows itself to a small array of common criminals, not producing the most harm, portraying them and their supposed rights in mythical terms, creating a biased view of crime and its sources (President's Task Force, 1982; Henderson, 1985).

Similar biases emerge in victim programs. Consider federal victim services and the "issue definition" process therein. The extremes of victimization are emphasized, where the most horror can be raised but the least victimization occurs. Emphasis is put on protection, services, and education, but rarely on prevention; when emphasized, it's defined only in conservative terms, never examining crime's social sources and instead exhorting victims to change their behavior. Programs are treated as temporary, requiring annual lobbying for renewal, perhaps to avoid suspicions that the United States has fundamental social problems or needs any deep-seated "welfare" programs: indeed, much is made of how offenders pay entirely for VOCA, and not "innocent" taxpayers.

As for specific programs, spouse abuse is viewed as part of a "cycle of family violence" in "some" families and never as sexism in the broader society. Child "abuse" is regarded as the problem, even though child "neglect" is far more prevalent. Sexual abuse is viewed as a problem of lax enforcement and victim indiscretions, never as a problem of male society. The elderly are viewed as victimized mostly by crime, not by the persistent poverty they often live in. Victimization's causes, when considered at all, never include things like class inequality, American cultural violence, or the bankrupt family. High-profile victims are shown apparent concern, yet it emerges more rhetorically than substantively. Worse, the few resources made available for victim services come with "strings" that spread these ideologies far beyond Washington (Smith & Freinkel, 1988).

The elderly were star victims in the 1970s, as were their programs. Yet by the early 1980s, they were off the victim agenda, with their needs and victimization unabated. Like a passing fad, the victim torch seems to pass to new celebrities, likewise championed without much substance. Victims of drunk drivers and abducted children are the recent focus, even though research finds these victimizations exaggerated and politically exploited, more safe yet dramatic victims whose stars will also soon fade (Ellison, 1982; Walker, 1985; Eliasoph, 1986)?[5] Is this short-term attention simply innocent politics or the management of dissent with token programs, used manipulatively until the fervor subsides (Piven & Cloward, 1971; Smith & Freinkel, 1988)?

Coopting and Manipulating the Movement. No wonder some believe the victim movement has been coopted (Henderson, 1985; Viano, 1987; Smith & Freinkel, 1988). The victim movement may be conservative and manipulated, it may be no movement at all, and it may be many movements of unequal influence, but it's hardly the politically neutral phenomenon it's been portrayed. The movement we hear most about may not very well satisfy the definition of social movement. The label "movement," like "rights," is often misapplied and overused.[6] A movement is a social or political phenomenon seeking fundamental change through mostly unconventional means (Garner, 1980). Yet the victim movement we know hasn't fundamentally challenged U.S. society in the fields of crime control strategies, social policy, or otherwise.

Government has never been conceptualized as crime victims' main obstacle—offenders have; thus the frequent alliance between victim advocates and government policy-makers. If ever a movement, it ceased when it became partners with government. This would be all right if government was really committed to helping victims and willing to admit its own contribution to victimization. Since it is not, the movement may be coopted, an important revelation since the term "movement" has a powerful symbolic appeal, implying significant change; yet, this change may not be occurring.

Aside from labels, how did the victim "movement" arise? It's been associated in the 1970s with liberal politics whose crime-control policies failed, thus ceding the filed to conservatives who, in their law-and-order crusade, championed the victim's cause. Yet, the liberal policy of rehabilitation failed because it was never seriously pursued; anyway, it's actually a conservative policy, designed not to question the society's performance but rather to help offenders accept it. An exaggeration of liberal/conservative differences often passes as "politics" in American society, perhaps diverting us from real politics and power. In fact, mainstream victim activity seems to be associated with conservative crime policies, even when liberals have held office.

In the 1980s, a coalition of so-called "strange" bedfellows of liberals and conservatives has produced, with Reagan administration guidance, current victim policy. Yet this may not be strange, but rather conventional politics,[7] and no real compromise of political perspectives, but instead a reiteration of conservative policies (Henderson, 1985).[8] The "movement" may have been coopted by being diffused, but also by being "used" for reforms that may have little to do with victims. Yet it allows them to be manipulated to enhance political legitimacy, government police powers, and an apparent agenda of further eroding defendant's rights: a symbolic use of politics to convert liberal rhetoric into thin air or conservative ends (Friedrichs, 1983; Edelman, 1988; Smith & Freinkel, 1988).

But it's misleading to view victim concern as a single movement; important strands exist beyond the conservatives and liberals (Elias, 1989). Some of the most useful initiatives have come from the "feminist" victim movement, but have been undermined in the "official" victim movement. There's also an "international" victim movement, described above, pressing for global initiatives, and recognizing the relationships between criminal victimization and abuses of power. But Washington does not embrace that movement's broader definition of victimization[9] nor does it take seriously another victim movement: the "human rights" movement, which considers more than merely crime victims, and whose perspectives (except for those stressing Soviet abuses) the Reagan administration has roundly condemned in favor of its international terrorism policy.[10]

In 1981, the victim movement got a national spokesman in Ronald Reagan, apparently launching the heyday of victim concern. Yet, whether measured by the victims of political or economic abuses (of human rights) at home and abroad, or the victims of an administration itself committing more crimes than any other, or the victims of government crime policies counderproductive to ending victimization by others, the Reagan years seem highly victim-conducive, if not victim-producing (Dorsen, 1984; Frappier, 1984; Kinoy, 1988). These are the abuses of power (human rights violations) the international victim movement has linked to the neglect, if not to the source, of criminal victimization. Should we trust such a government to be pursuing the best interests of the victims it has defined, or acquiesce to those it has not?

The recent NOVA Newsletter may not have exaggerated when it said that Congress, in renewing VOCA, was deciding which sectors of the victim movement it would be recognizing (Stein, 1988). We can probably predict *which* victim movements will continue to be included and which will not. U.S. administrations, whether liberal or conservative, seem unwilling to examine crime's social sources (which a human rights analysis might reveal) and make fundamental changes to significantly reduce victimization in the first place. Doing so would be the product of a real victim movement.

An Alternative Politics

The manipulation of victims for political gain may not have resulted from purposeful intrigue; it may have been merely opportune to do so as the movement developed. Nor have victim advocates been ill-intentioned or powerless in helping shape victim policy. We're concerned here not with individual motives, but with institutional constraints. Yet, however, we explain it, the adverse results are real enough. Is this the kind of victim movement we want?

Accepting financial aid and philosophical guidance from governments and groups concerned most with conservative crime policies risks cooptation and manipulation. Instead, we could pursue an alternative politics, building an independent domestic movement that's allied with the international movement, and practice a new victimology of human rights (Elias, 1985a).

NOTES

1. The following review of state legislation relies on National Organization of Victim Assistance (NOVA) (1988); Victims of Crime Resource Center or VCRC (1988); Anderson and Woodard (1985); Henderson (1985).

2. The following review of national legislation relies on Smith and Freinkel (1988); Henderson (1985); Office of Victim Services, or OVC (1988); Stein (1988); Trotter (1987); Murray (1987).

3. Preventive detention has been justified to make victims feel safe, yet victim fear may come less from the offender and more from the shock of victimization. Incarcerating the accused has been advocated under the untested assumption that it will satisfy the victim's desire for justice. Speedy dispositions will resolve trials quickly, but may not resolve the victimization, probably making it worse (Henderson, 1985: p. 976).

4. Victim involvement will not apparently enhance *deterrence*, and *incapacitation* relies on offender traits, not those of the victim. Victims can't help *rehabilitate*, except perhaps when related to the offender, where maybe the victim should help implement, but not determine, the sentence. Victim participation for *retribution*, which relies on assessing blame, would raise as many questions about victim blameworthiness as of the offender. It also assumes that retaliation best satisfies victim anger, when forgiveness may better promote psychological healing. Plea bargaining and mandatory incarceration render victim preferences for *restitution* irrelevant or futile (Henderson, 1985: p. 1001-1010). No wonder almost no victims use the victim-impact statement right (Villmoare & Neto, 1987).

5. The apparent concern for the elderly, women, and children comes from an administration that has massively cut social spending that might have spared these people victimization, both criminal and otherwise. And government policy has turned on the elderly in other ways: To shield them from financial victimization in their waning years, it's pushed "protective" plans that seem to confiscate their resources and place them in custody (Gordon, 1986). Government has gone from viewing the elderly as victims to viewing them as a new criminal class, the same treatment earlier given women, despite contrary evidence (Cullen, Wozniak, & Frank, 1985). How easy it is to manipulate groups: the elderly's main advocates promote the government's conservative, law-and-order crime policies. The government has also used ideological screens in women's programs: Shelters and independent centers are totally out of favor, and have been defunded, at least if they promote feminist goals of self-reliance and social change (Smith & Freinkel, 1988).

6. Here, rights serve as a powerful rhetorical device to exploit public concerns about crime (Henderson, 1985: 952). See also Scheingold (1974).

7. Non-decisions, or what's kept off the agenda, are a major power source in the U.S. system, which may routinely exclude real alternatives from policy consideration (Smith & Freinkel, 1988: 173).

8. Consider that the victim movement relies on an administration that supports (with few liberal objections) those who would force poor women to have unwanted children,

to end fetus victimization, yet, once born, subject children to a lifetime of real victimization (Edelman, 1984; Kimmich, 1985); that labels as victims Nazi criminals, Salvadoran death squads, and Nicaraguan contra "freedom fighters;" and that professes a (yet another) "war on crime," yet dismantled enforcement mechanisms, such as the anti-trust laws, and countenanced (if not welcomed) extensive corporate victimization, both criminal and otherwise (Green & Berry, 1985; Nader, 1986).

9. The United States was almost alone among nations in rejecting at the UN the relation between criminal victimization and the victimization caused by abuses of power. Although it finally voted for a weaker version of the declaration, it's not likely to ratify it, any more than it has most UN covenants (Frappier, 1984).

10. Yet in pursuing torture and terrorism policy, it designates politically approved victims (convenient for foreign-policy goals), ignoring most of the rest (Chomsky, 1988).

REFERENCES

Anderson, J. R., & Woodward, P. L. (1985). Victim & witness assistance: New state laws & the system's response. *Judicature, 68*, 221-244.

Austern, D. (1987). *The crime victims book.* New York: Viking Penguin.

Bassiouni, M. C. (1985). The protection of "collective victims" in international law. *New York Law School Human Rights Annual 2*(Spring), 239-257.

Beinen, L. (1981). Rape III: National developments in rape reform legislation. *Women's Law Reporter, 6*, 170-189.

Chomsky, N. (1988). *The culture of terrorism.* Boston: South End Press.

Cullen, F. T., Wozniak, J. F., & Frank, J. (1985). The rise of the elderly offender. *Crime & Social Justice, 23*, 151-165.

Danielus, H. (1986). The United Nations fund for torture victims. *Human Rights Quarterly, 8*(May), 294-305.

Davis, R. C., (1983). Victim/witness noncooperation. *Journal of Criminal Justice, 11*, 287-299.

De Cataldo Neuberger, L. (1985). An appraisal of victimological perspectives in international law. *Victimology, 10*, 700-709.

Dorsen, N. (1984). *Our endangered rights.* New York: Pantheon.

Edelman, M. (1988). *Constructing the political spectacle.* Chicago: University of Chicago Press.

Edelman, M. R. (1984). *American children in poverty.* Washington, DC: Children's Defense Fund.

Elias, R. (1983a). *Victims of the system.* New Brunswick, NJ: Transaction.

Elias, R. (1983b). The symbolic politics of victim compensation. *Victimology, 8*, 103-112.

Elias, R. (1985a). Transcending our social reality of victimization: Toward a new victimology of human rights. *Victimology, 10*, 6-25.

Elias, R. (1985b). Community control, criminal justice & victim services. In E. Fattah. (Ed.), *From crime policy to victim policy* (pp. 290-316). London: Macmillan.

Elias, R. (1985c). Victims and crime prevention: A basis for social change? *Citizen Participation,* Summer, 22-28.

Elias, R. (1990). *The politics of victimization: Victims, victimology & human rights.* New York: Oxford University Press.

Elias, R. (1990). The competing politics of victim movements. In Emilio Viano (Ed.) *Victims and Human Rights* (pp. 37-59), London: Taylor & Francis.

Eliasoph, N. (1986). Drive-in mortality, child abuse, and the media. *Socialist Review, 16*, 7-31.

Ellison, K. (1982). On the victims' side: A "bill of rights" or political hype? *National Law Journal, 46*(April), 1.

Falk, K. (1981). *Human rights & state sovereignty.* New York: Holmes & Meier.

Forer, L. (1980). *Criminals and victims.* New York: Norton.

Frappier, J. (1984). Above the law: Violations of international law by the U.S. government. *Crime & Social Justice, 23*, 1-45.

Friedrichs, D. (1983). Victimology: A consideration of the radical critique. *Crime & Delinquency,* April, 283-294.

Garner, R. A. (1980). *Social movements in America.* Chicago: Rand McNally.

Geis, G., Chappell, D., & Agopian, M. W. (1985). Toward the alleviation of human suffering. Rapporteurs' Report, 5th International Symposium on Victimology.

Gordon, R. M. (1986). Financial abuse of the elderly and state "protective services." *Crime & Social Justice, 26*, 116-134.

Green, M., & Berry, J. (1985). *The challenge of hidden profits: White collar crime as big business.* New York: William Morrow.

Henderson, L. N. (1985). The wrongs of victim's rights. *Stanford Law Review, 37*(April), 937-1021.

Kahn, L. A. (1982). Constitutionality of the Victim & Witness Protection Act of 1982. *Federal Probation, 48*(December), 81-82.

Karmen, A. (1984). *Crime victims.* Belmont, CA: Brooks/Cole.

Kimmich, M. H. (1985). *America's children: Who cares? Growing needs & declining assistance in the Reagan era.* Washington, DC: Urban Institute Press.

Kinoy, A. (1988). The present constitutional crisis. In J. Lobel (Ed.), *A less than perfect union* (pp. 32-40). New York: Monthly Review Press.

Krasno, M. R. (1983). The victim & witness protection act of 1982; Does it promise more than the system can deliver? *Judicature, 66*(May), 469-471.

Lamborn, L. (1987a). The United Nations declaration on victims: Incorporating "abuse of power." *Rutgers Law Journal, 19*, 59-95.

Lamborn, L. (1987b). Victim participation in the criminal justice process: Proposals for a constitutional amendment. *Wayne Law Review, 34*(Fall), 125-220.

Lopez-Rey, M. (1985). *A guide to United Nations criminal policy.* New York: United Nations.

Marx, G. T. (1983). Social control and victimization. *Victimology, 8*, 54-79.

Murray, M. H. (1987). The torture victim protection act. *Columbia Journal of Transnational Law, 25*(Summer), 673-715.

Nader, R. (1986). The corporate drive to restrict their victims' rights. *Gonzaga Law Review, 22*(December), 15-28.

National Organization for Victim Assistance (1988). *Victim rights & services: A legislative directory.* Washington, DC: Author.

Normandeau, A. (1983). For a Canadian & international charter of rights for crime victims. *Canadian Journal of Criminology, 25*(October), 463-469.

Note (1987). Victim rights laws sometimes bring frustration, survey finds. *Criminal Justice Newsletter, 18*(December), 3-4.

Office for Victims of Crime (1988). *Report to Congress.* Washington, DC: U.S. Government Printing Office.

O'Neill, T. P. (1984). The good, the bad, and the Burger Court: Victim's rights and a new model of criminal review. *Journal of Criminal Law & Criminology, 75*(Summer), 363-387.

Piven, F. F., & Cloward, R., (1971). *Regulating the poor.* New York: Vintage.

President's Task Force on Victims of Crime (1982). *Final Report.* Washington, DC: U.S. Government Printing Office.

Reiman, J. (1984). *The rich get richer & the poor get prison.* New York: Wiley.

Rudovsky, D. (1988). Crime, law enforcement, and constitutional rights. In J. Lobel (Ed.), *A less than perfect union* (pp. 361-376). New York: Monthly Review Press.

Russell, D. E. H., & Van Den Ven, N. (1984). *Crimes against women.* East Palo Alto, CA: Frog in the Well Press.

Schaaf, R. W. (1986). New international instruments in crime prevention and criminal justice. *International Journal of Legal Information, 14*(June-August), 176-182.

Scheingold, S. (1974). *Politics of rights.* New Haven, CT: Yale University Press.

Sharman, J. R. (1988). Constitutional law: Victim impact statements and the 8th Amendment. *Harvard Journal of Law & Public Policy, 11*(Spring), 583-593.

Smith, S. R., & Freinkel, S. (1988). *Adjusting the balance: Federal policy & victim services.* Westport, CT: Greenwood.

Stein, J. (1988). VOCA revisited, reauthorized, and revitalized. *NOVA Newsletter, 12,* 1-5.

Symposium (1987). Perspectives on proposals for a constitutional amendment providing victim participation in the criminal justice system. *Wayne Law Review, 34*(Fall), 1-220.

Trotter, K. A. (1987). Compensating victims of terrorism. *Texas International Law Journal, 22*(Spring-Summer), 383-401.

United Nations Secretariat (1980). Crime & the abuse of power: Offenses & offenders beyond the reach of the law. *UN Doc.A/CONF/87/6.*

Viano, E. (1987). Victim's rights and the Constitution. *Crime & Delinquency, 33,* 438-451.

Victims of Crime Resource Center (1988). Statutes of 1988 pertaining to crime victims. Mimeo.

Villmoare, E., & Neto, V. V. (1987). Victim appearances at sentencing under California's victims' bill or rights. *Research in Brief* (August), 1-5.

Walker, S. (1985). *Sense & nonsense about crime.* Belmont, CA: Brooks/Cole.

Willis, B. L. (1984). State compensation of victims of violent crimes: The Council of Europe Convention of 1983. *Virginia Journal of International Law, 25*(Fall), 211-247.

Chapter 14

CRIME VICTIMS
Practices and Prospects

GILBERT GEIS

During the past two decades, there has been a rapidly growing move-ment, especially in Canada, the United States, and Europe, pressing for greater consideration of the situation of crime victims and for their deeper involvement in the processes of criminal justice. The present volume offers an array of substantive and critical commentaries from both the United States and abroad regarding diverse aspects of these developments, including their roots, importance, achievements, short-comings, and prospects.

There also has come into existence a cadre of research workers who study the phenomenon of crime victimization. Some of these research-ers remain generalists, while others splinter evermore, as the victim movement itself proliferates, and concentrate on one or another finite aspect of the larger subject. At the same time, a vast network of service deliverers, the voices of the victims, has combined political and advo-cacy roles with those of nurturance and amelioration. The distinction seems pronounced between these service personnel and more tradi-tional social welfare workers, who all too often distance themselves from and condescend toward their clients.

Simultaneously, state-run compensation programs increasingly tend to the financial wounds of crime victims. These compensation efforts were the harbinger of the more far-reaching development of organized concern for victims. By the very nature of some of their patent in-adequacies, the victim compensation programs made imperative the inauguration of efforts to provide other kinds of support to crime victims who had discovered painfully that the recovery of money from a grudging bureaucracy was not the cure-all for the difficulties they experienced after being victimized.

Finally, and much more controversial, advocates of the cause of crime victims have begun to demand a prominent place in the processes of criminal justice. They increasingly are shaking up a system that has cozily coasted along virtually unaltered in basic ways through the past century. Victims may or may not deserve a more significant role in any program of criminal adjudication that aspires to justice and equality, but the questions that victims now are raising have rarely been asked before and, it is hoped, the answers that emerge can push a creaky system a little closer to ideals routinely parroted but too rarely realized.

It may strike some of us (as it does me) as unacceptable that vengeance-ridden victims will be able to secure tougher sentences against the offenders in their cases than those accorded criminals who happen to victimize more tolerant or compassionate persons. An illustration of the potential ferocity of victims' attitudes arose in 1987 in Portugal, where I was doing research on victimization. A 17-year-old boy in the town of Agueda was given a 4-year prison sentence after being found guilty of setting a forest fire in which 10 persons were killed. Widows and relatives of the deceased reacted in what the newspapers called an hysterical manner, denouncing the leniency of the sentence. The president of the court, however, declared that the defendant could be sentenced only for arson, not homicide, because the deaths occurred more than 8 hours after the crime and 12 to 14 kilometers from its original site. The judge also noted that it was a first offense and that the defendant had been intoxicated. He insisted that "nobody may expect that the courts, even involuntarily, should serve as instruments of revenge." In jurisdictions where, unlike Portugal, the tenure of the judiciary is at the will of the electorate, independence such as that shown in the sentencing of the arsonist could carry high career risks.

Nonetheless, the issue of the proper role for victims in the criminal justice process should in time force review of cognate matters, such as why we allow quixotic considerations, such as the amount of money stolen, to dictate a sentence? After all, a $50 burglary loss is likely to be much more hurtful to a poor person than a $2,000 loss to a millionaire. Similarly, a small fine can cripple an impoverished minor offender, while a more affluent person, who committed the same offense, shrugs it off as the most trifling of inconveniences. These kinds of issues, and a myriad others, may be kindled by the intrusion of victim concerns into the process of criminal justice.

VICTIMS AND THE WOMEN'S MOVEMENT

The crusading force of the women's movement also has been crucially intertwined with the growth of a crime victim's constituency. Women's groups first took a particular interest in crime victims with their focus on rape (Brownmiller, 1975), the quintessential male criminal offense. Later, they would locate in child sexual abuse another offense that had two powerful appeals: first, it traditionally has been seriously overlooked and ineptly dealt with; and, second, it characteristically makes men look bad, while rarely tainting the image of women.

The thrust of the women's movement into the criminal justice process has had profound impacts on that process that are only beginning to be satisfactorily analyzed. In earlier decades, liberal women, the core of the women's movement today, traditionally joined, almost invariably in subordinate positions, with liberal men to achieve what they defined as mutually desirable ends. But when the women came to take an independent path, they often scorned the agenda that had previously guided them. This matter is particularly well illustrated by the ferocious campaign by many women's groups against pornography, a campaign based on the view that pornography significantly contributes to the degradation and victimization of women, and that male liberals proclaiming First Amendment rights merely camouflage campaigns to exploit and dominate women (see generally Hawkins & Zimring, 1989).

Most notably, the women's movement has incorporated a strong anti-criminal offender plank into its ideological platform, a position that often is generalized throughout the victim's movement. In alliance with liberal men, especially Marxists, politically active women in the past typically saw offenders as victims themselves, done in by an oppressive economic and social system that forced them to break the law to retain any semblance of human dignity. Their acts were defined as political protests. When the women's movement focus came to rest upon rape, however, this explanatory structure almost totally disintegrated. Marxists themselves, now usually very sympathetic to the ideology of the women's movement, were left stranded, holding onto a distasteful contradiction: While other offenders could be defined as political protesters, rapists had to be seen as evil, macho chauvinists. At best, they might be regarded as weak masculine human beings, products of a sexual ethos perverted by capitalist competition, but it became taboo to hint that some rapes, like other human interactions, involve both a victim and offender who inevitably are the products of

their biology and their experience, persons trying to achieve, in however inexpert and self-defeating and ugly a manner, what they have
come to believe they need or want.

Undoubtedly, a significant reason why the women's movement came
to differentiate between victims and offenders in so unconnoted a
manner is that their views represent a strong reaction against the even
more primitive way in which earlier commentators had carried on a
program of victim-blaming when analyzing offenses such as rape. Such
derogation of the legally innocent party and implicit exculpation of the
wrongdoer was found to produce significant psychic harm in many
victims of sexual assault, who, like so many other victims, tended to
look inward to try to locate an explanation for what had happened to
them (Gordon & Riger, 1989). The concept of victim-precipitation,
felicitously coined in a pioneering study of homicide to capture the
similarity between victim and offender (Wolfgang, 1954), aggravated
the feelings of anyone with some sensitivity when it was unfortunately
brought to bear upon attempts to understand rape.

The interests of the women's movement in victims of male brutality
ultimately coalesced with the more generic concerns of the treatment
component of the larger victim's movement. As governments began to
bail out chronically underfinanced, largely volunteer victim service
programs, members of the women's movement had to make the painful
decision whether to share in such largess, a decision that would typically demand a broadening of their focus, or whether to retain their
ideological purity. Most succumbed to the financial lures, a development that Paul Rock (1986) has traced in consummate detail for Canada
in one of the most important analytical monographs on the victim's
movement produced to date. In Britain, on the other hand, as Maguire
and Shapland point out in their chapter in this book, rape crisis centers
usually have kept their distance from the state-subsidized victim-aid
organizations, and sometimes have sought to indoctrinate their clients,
called survivors, into aggressive feminism.

ORIGINS OF THE VICTIM MOVEMENT

It is difficult to disentangle the diverse elements that energized the
move toward greater recognition of the role and the importance of the
victim in the criminal justice system. Looking backward to the origin
of a now-established social movement sometimes produces a feeling of

mystified disbelief that it took so long to happen. The feeling is like that of protagonists in detective fiction, persons such as Agatha Christie's Hercule Poirot, who suddenly will exclaim as the story reaches its end: "Mon Dieu, it is so obvious. How could I possibly not have recognized it right from the beginning!" So it is with crime victims: Their condition for centuries aroused little comment or interest. Suddenly, they were "discovered," and afterwards it was unclear how their obvious neglect could have so long gone without attention and remedy.

Until a few decades ago, the plight of large numbers of crime victims in virtually all parts of the world was abominable. They were mugged, raped, their homes invaded, their handbags or wallets stolen. If that were not both bad and sad enough, they were double-victimized, first by the criminal offenders and then by the authorities. Police officers and prosecutors all too often had been hardened into cynicism from having dealt with too many crimes for too long, and they had come to forget that for most of us, victimization is rare, often a unique and novel experience. Further frustrated by their inability to do much about such offenses as burglary and car theft—those in which nobody saw and could describe the perpetrator—the authorities often were abrupt and dismissive in the face of victim despair.

About all victims were likely to get from crimes such as burglary was a story to tell their relatives, friends, and neighbors—a moment in the limelight. Part of what they had to tell, unfortunately, often dealt with the insensitivity and incivility of the investigating and other criminal justice authorities. These were the ills; it became the aim of the victim's movement to rectify them.

VICTIMS AND POLITICS

National political developments were largely responsible for moving the subject of victims of crime onto the stage, center front, in the United States. In 1964, Barry Goldwater, the conservative Republican candidate for the president, thrust the issue of crime in the streets into his campaign, the first time this had been done in the country's history. It was a phony issue in the sense that the federal government does not possess jurisdiction over most of the kinds of criminal activity that concern the average citizen.

Goldwater, however, touched a sensitive public nerve-ending. Lyndon Johnson overwhelmed Goldwater in the election, but he had been beleaguered by the issue of crime during the campaign, and he vowed that he would not be caught unprepared the next time, failing to foresee, of course, that the dramatically deteriorating situation of U.S. involvement in Vietnam would force him to abandon his 1968 presidential aspirations. By appointing a commission, the President's Commission on Law Enforcement and Administration of Justice, to study crime, Johnson chose a time-tested political strategy to defuse the issue. Resources and imagination were the key elements in bringing about the victimization work produced by the commission.

The commission's 1967 reports can be regarded as signaling the move to significance of the two earliest elements of the concern with victims. The commission pioneered in launching probes of the nature and extent of victimization, seeking in this manner primarily to improve on the accuracy and sophistication of statistical reports of criminal activity. In the most ambitious of its triumvirate of studies, the commission contracted with the National Opinion Research Center to interview a probability sample of 9,644 adult members of U.S. households about crime victimization experiences (Ennis, 1967). At the same time, it highlighted the recent appearance in New Zealand, Britain, and a few American and Australian states of programs to compensate victims of crimes of violence by including a 23-page, double-columned report on these developments as an appendix to a Task Force volume (Geis, 1967) and recommending support for such programs in its main report (President's Commission, 1967: p. 41).

Review of the archival material from the President's Commission, now available at the Lyndon B. Johnson Library in Austin, indicates some of the paths by which the Assessment Task Force, directed by Lloyd Ohlin, came to fix on an inventory of victimization. In addition, the files show the stunning speed with which the work was accomplished.

President Johnson started matters moving with a March 8, 1965, message to the nation. "Crime has become a malignant enemy in America's midst," he stormed, and, with italicized emphasis, he proclaimed that "we must arrest and reverse the trend toward lawlessness." By the end of July, he had established the commission, and charged it with determining, among other things, the causes of crime and delinquency, their prevention, the adequacy of law enforcement and the administration of justice, and the degree of public respect for the law.

To address such issues, the commission was authorized to "make such studies . . . as it deems appropriate."

By the end of September 1985, only a few months later, Albert Biderman of the Bureau of Social Research in Washington, D.C., submitted to Ohlin a path-breaking memorandum that outlined Biderman's vision of what might be done by the commission. "It is unlikely that any studies undertaken . . . can make more than a small contribution to advancing the state of knowledge," Biderman wrote. "This would be the case even if its efforts were massive." Therefore, there must be "a careful selection of priorities," and "some highly innovative approach to one or more of the problems."

Biderman first suggested that the experience as crime victims of high school and university students offered an as-yet unexplored area that could expeditiously be examined. Then he turned to a more ambitious item:

> Consider, for example, the accepted proposition that "offenses known to the police" are the "best" measure of crime because these are the data "closest to the commission of the crime." Insofar as offenses of victimization are concerned, it would seem that data developed directly from questioning the public would be "closer" to the crime and, for at least many classes of offenses, would suffer less from errors of undermeasurement than data derived from reports to the police and crime known directly to the police.

Though its points are obvious now, such a statement then represented an entirely new vision of how crime might be better understood.

Biderman went on to note that victimization studies themselves would be subject to "various types of errors and inadequacies," most notably their inability to learn about self- and mutual-victimizations, or about cases in which the victim is an impersonal entity. He suggested that a survey be launched in Washington involving 2,000 cases. Forms would be distributed by bulk mail and inserted in clip-out form in newspapers; then potential respondents could be encouraged by television campaigns to complete and return the forms. The effort would not only acquire new information, it would also serve to disseminate knowledge about crime.

In addition, Biderman proposed a random or purposive sample of the population to tap victimization, and suggested that such an effort might be subsidized by a commercial or media group.

By the end of the year, these ideas had been incorporated into the Assessment Task Force's work plan, which noted that "a few limited pilot studies may be launched to test the feasibility and political [ed. note: practical?] return from investigations in areas where our knowledge is especially fragmentary and uncertain." From early on, the surveys were seen primarily as providing a better—if only more novel and fresher—source of data than that found in the Uniform Crime Reports, whose shortcomings had bedeviled commission staff members intent on providing a sophisticated portrait of criminal activity. There were other ideas as well, though they rarely went beyond the blueprint stage. The Bureau of the Budget, for instance, chipped in the view that "attention might be directed to the characteristics of crime victims . . . and any behavior on their part which may facilitate the commission of crime." At the same time, the coterminous President's Commission on Crime in the District of Columbia was particularly interested in learning about public attitudes toward the police "and the relationship, if any, between good police-community relations and the degree of police-citizen cooperation (including the reporting of crime)."

In late January 1966, it became apparent that the Bureau of Census would be unable to carry out the national victim survey the commission had anticipated from it: that work then fell to the National Opinion Research Center, whose March 8, 1966, proposal was built upon "very encouraging" results from some "hastily written questions" about crime victimization that had been thrust into a November 1965 survey. These questions showed (N = 1,520) that 53% of the respondents reported no crime victimization, while 11% reported their most recent victimization in 1965, 9% in 1964, and 27% before 1964. The NORC saw its work as the exploration of a technique, the supplying of information to the commission, and the transfer of research data to the public, the scholarly community, and the police.

By June 1966, the first rough results were available from Biderman's work in the District of Columbia. They indicated that "conservatively" there might be ten times as much crime out there as became known to the police, a startling conclusion at the time. This preliminary information elicited a note from Ohlin to the members of the commission: "It is already apparent," he wrote, "that the public interpretation of these results and their implications will require careful consideration by the staff and the Commission." Victimization surveys, it is obvious, had made some significant initial strides, both politically and scientifically.

WHY CRIME VICTIMS?

There are a number of reasons why the concern with victimization and victim compensation displayed by the president's commission grew steadily thereafter. Especially important is the fact that governments are not likely to have much of an impact on the crime rate. The growth of cities, the continuing depersonalization of human existence, demographic forces (most especially the proportion of the population made up of young persons), class structure, materialism, the competitive urge—and most fundamentally the ethos of a social system—these and cognate factors largely will determine the level of criminal activity. Matters such as better household security and tougher prison sentences may alter slightly the total of this or that kind of crime, but the impositions on citizens by law-breakers are likely to remain constant or to increase as secularizing trends advance.

Rhetoric and promises by office-holders regarding crime control are notably dangerous because they may be remembered, particularly if there is a good file of television clips that can be replayed when the next round of crime figures is released. Sometimes attempts to find some hopeful sign in crime statistics can take astonishing forms. Recall, for instance, the ludicrous effort by then Attorney General John Mitchell to find a ray of sunshine in the mounting U.S. crime rate by his announcement that the Nixon administration was making inroads against crime, demonstrated by the fact that the previous year's 10% escalation had now been reduced to only an 8% increase. The attorney general apparently failed to appreciate, or hoped others would not, a fact that any run-of-the-mill statistician would know: that crime inevitably will show lower percentage rises in time because as the figures get higher, it takes astronomic changes to produce equivalent percentage increases.

Inherently, of course, the fundamental basis of the power of the victim's movement lies in public and political acceptance of the view that its clients are good people, done in by those who are bad. This item alone has made its growth irresistible. That it took so long to gain a foothold has to testify to political inertia and, particularly to the understandable fear that once financial commitments are made by governments, they are very likely to be with us for a long time: they will be defended vehemently against cutbacks by those committed to and dependent upon them.

The service element of the victim's movement has been accompanied by a vigorous research probe that began to develop about the same time and sought to determine the extent and correlates of victimization, matters addressed in this volume by John Laub. The origins and development of the two components of the focus on victims (surveys and service) appear to have had little in common; only an awkward kind of critical mass convenience seems to have produced a blending of practitioners devoted to both kinds of endeavors in such organizations as the International Society of Victimology. Victimization studies could, of course, be used to seek to learn if services to victims or other innovative programs make a difference in crime rates, but this application has found only peripheral employment (Kelling, Pate, Dreckman, & Brown, 1974).

Focus on victims, however, provides an opportunity to conciliate those who have been injured or deprived, and therefore are likely to be among the most disenchanted. Such a focus truly offers a decent chance to do something constructive and helpful about the generally intractable crime problem. The movement to aid crime victims made both logical and emotional sense. Their case is compelling, and they traditionally have been ignored. Strong overt opposition to programs providing assistance to crime victims is not likely to surface. Who, after all, is willing to go on record as opposed to so preeminently worthy a cause? There will be, of course, some reluctance to appropriate funds for crime victims, given competing budgetary demands and limited monies. And some persons with a philosophical turn of mind will carp and ask: Why *crime* victims? Why not *all* victims—those not only of crime, but of discrimination, earthquakes, workplace disease, or any of life's raw deals? The answer here has to be found in pragmatics. The plight of crime victims is dramatic and determinable. Their relief is feasible. It has strong social, political, and personal appeal. Any of us, at any time, could become a crime victim. And so a movement was born—and grew.

CRIME VICTIM SURVEYS

Crime victim surveys can be regarded as the scientific, as opposed to the humanitarian, element of the victim movement. They may help victims in an oblique manner by providing information on the extent of criminal activity and on the consequences of such activity for those who are victimized by it. But, most fundamentally, they are information-gathering devices, useful for taking the temperature of the body politic, for developing behavioral science and criminological theory, and for purposes of planning.

There are intense disputes concerning the best method to acquire victimization information, and there now exists a very sizable body of international literature offering precepts for the conduct of such surveys. That consensus has not as yet come to prevail may be illustrated by an inquiry that I dispatched via the Portuguese Ministry of Justice, where I was working on the plans for a national victimization study. My letter asked advice on sample size and sampling procedures from six experts, located in four countries. Not one was in agreement with any of the others on basic matters that were perplexing us. Each offered highly persuasive support for his position; several gratuitously threw in further tidbits of advice that took issue with what we until then had accepted as received wisdom. We were told, among many other things, to conduct surveys three years apart, rather than annually as in the United States, to request a history of lifelong victimization rather than to bound the time focus of the interviews, to raise or to lower the 12-year-age limit for interviews that is used in the United States, and to interview every member of the household about offenses rather than to use one member as a proxy for others in regard to certain kinds of victimizations. The absence of scientific agreement on key matters, as well as the disparate ground rules under which surveys have been conducted throughout the world, indicates how reckless it can be to compare the results from different countries as if they were measures of the same thing. There is, however, a plan underway to have a number of European nations, under the direction of the research branch of the Ministry of Justice in the Netherlands, utilize a similar measuring instrument and similar procedures so that a comparable portrait of victimization among these nations can be compiled.

The utility of the surveys—their cost-benefit ratio—inevitably is an arguable proposition. The best argument, I suspect, is the most difficult to render in a demonstrable way: It would follow along the line that the lifeblood of a democracy is information; that the better informed we are, the more competing viewpoints can adequately struggle for supremacy. Those endorsing such a view can now find support from what was once an unlikely source: In 1989, for the first time in 56 years, the Soviet government released detailed statistical information on crime rates. The earlier Russian view, promulgated by Stalin, was that knowledge of the amount of crime would tarnish the country's image abroad and encourage further crime. Now the government spokesman proclaimed: "It's better to know the real situation, so that the problems of our safety and the problems of the militia [police] become clearer" (Fein, 1989).

Nay-sayers probably would object that victimization surveys are little more than another marking-time attempt to try to "learn" more about a problem about which enough is presently understood to inform remedial programs, such as those that attack poverty and prejudice. Information-gathering, they might argue, tends to be a sop to put off those who need help, not data. There is no determinative way to adjudicate such a dispute as there is ample evidence to support either view (see, for instance, Moynahan, 1969; Silberman, 1978).

There also are sufficient analogous examples from other fields of endeavor to support either position, that favoring more knowledge before acting, or that for acting now. In medicine, the case for research informing policy is notably strong, though far from foolproof. In social reform, the tendency to throw research at problems when unencumbered money is in short supply is a commonplace. We certainly have become healthier; whether the quality of that quantitatively improved existence has improved is arguable.

All told, it seems to me that victimization surveys have and will continue to contribute to a more decent solution to problems of crime, problems both of offenders and of victims. They have already called dramatic attention to the short-comings of the Uniform Crime Reports as an adequate measure of criminal behavior, and have produced far-reaching reformulation of that statistical series.

Not that the surveys are without their problems. Methodological difficulties have been thoroughly explored in various chapters of this book; I would only highlight two major considerations. First, the particular paradox of the finding, duplicated worldwide, that individuals with the most education report themselves to be victims of the largest number of assaults. This counterintuitive result probably arises from the fact that episodes that working class youth pass off as inconsequential and commonplace are defined by better-educated persons as criminal and are therefore memorable. It seems reasonable that when you live amidst crime, you are likely to come to regard it more casually; such perceptions will be reflected in and will distort victim surveys. I focus on this particular situation because it serves to emphasize with some force the warning signals that should be posted when attempting to interpret the relationship between victimization figures and what truly may go on in the world that the figures are trying to characterize.

Emphasis should also be placed upon the fact that the surveys inevitably carry an ideological load. By concentrating only on traditional crime, they reinforce the idea that this is the essence of the crime problem. Many persons insist that greater menace lies in such matters as air pollution, nuclear neglect, bribery, and other forms of abuse of power. But victim surveys cannot discover white-collar crime victimization, primarily because the effects usually are so diffuse and those who suffer are so often unaware of what has happened to them. All societies undoubtedly ought to devote greater resources to provide well-publicized statistical temperatures of white-collar crime.

VICTIM COMPENSATION

Compensation from public funds for victims of crime to a considerable extent owes its contemporary origin to the pioneering efforts of Margery Fry, an Englishwoman and a Quaker, who devoted her life to the cause of correctional reform. Ms. Fry ridiculed the patent inadequacy of restitution as a court-ordered method for allaying the deprivations suffered by crime victims. For one thing, she pointed out, in many instances the offender is not apprehended, or, if caught, not convicted, so that no restitutive possibility exists. Even if there is a conviction, most offenders are too impoverished to pay much toward the cost of the victim's crime-associated expenses. For those offenders who are able to contribute something, the funds they give often have to be diverted from the support of their families, who then have to be subsidized by welfare monies.

There also are moral issues that too often remain unaddressed in discussions of restitution. Is it fair to allow some people to draw upon their own fiscal resources to escape some of the unattractive consequences of law-breaking, while other persons, without such resources, therefore suffer more heavily? Financial well-being has always polluted some aspects of the idea of equality in the criminal justice system. Note, for instance, how many victims of torts divert the authorities from criminal actions because they are fundamentally much more interested in winning a civil suit if the wrongdoer has significant funds or good insurance.

Ms. Fry's disenchantment with restitution prompted the British government to address the plight of crime victims. From the start, the focus has been exclusively on victims of crimes of violence. The supposition has been that property loss from crime typically is covered by insurance. For those without such coverage, the official attitude seems to have been that their absence of foresight (or of sufficient funds to afford foresight) is their own misfortune. Also, loss of goods does not possess the strong emotional appeal associated with bodily injury. Besides, the authorities were wary of the much heavier costs of including property offenses because of possible fraud. Inflation of insurance claims for burglary and car accidents is commonplace in the United States; indeed, professional burglars often attribute an element of their cynicism about the honesty of the average citizen to their experience of counting the value of their haul from the night before and then comparing that total to the much higher figure that the newspapers report on the basis of what the victim told the police and the insurance company.

From the start, crime victim programs have been perplexed by an inability to settle upon a satisfactory rationale for their existence. In Britain, in particular, the government was edgy about any hint that victim compensation inferred official liability that might be based, for instance, on the failure of the police to protect a citizen from victimization, particularly since most people are unable to secure a firearm with which to protect themselves. Only very recently has the British compensation program moved from *ex gratia* status, a benefit from a beneficent state, to a statutory footing.

Unlike the British, U.S. and Australian compensation programs at first tended to restrict compensation to persons who could not pay the costs of victimization by crimes of violence out of their own pockets. But the tragedies visited upon so many crime victims tended to produce changes that mitigated the harshness of this position: Some compensation boards, for instance, decreed that victims could receive state funds if their costs would in time exhaust their personal resources. Ultimately, many of the state programs eliminated the "needs test," a welfare principle, but some remain tied to an ethos of truculent acquiescence to a victim's requirements—a defensive stance that tends to regard the victim with bureaucratic suspicion. Inadequate awards for limited periods of time are common. Any suggestion that the victim was involved in behavior not morally blameless might lead to rejection of the claim (Miers, 1978). Often, too, the programs have been marked by red tape, inordinate delays in providing funds, insufficient aid, cumbersome application procedures, and a reluctance to take adequate steps to notify victims of their right to secure compensation.

Undoubtedly, as Robert Elias suggests in this volume, there has been some cooptation and corruption of benign intents in compensation efforts and victim assistance programs, but in most regards the world seems to me to be a somewhat better place for these developments. Elias' observations, generally iconoclastic and often refreshing, reflect, I believe, a failure to differentiate between progress and utopianism; an unwillingness to celebrate what has been accomplished, without finding within such accomplishment the seeds of self-interested conspiracy because what has been done has failed to achieve things that, in the best of all possible worlds, ought to be done. Victims of horrors that violate human rights should be identified and aided, torture ought to stop, and hunger should be alleviated. To say that not enough victims of not enough forms of injustice have been helped is to point out the self-evident, something that probably needs to be done to keep us alert. Certainly, crime will not be notably reduced unless there are systemic changes in a social system. But the costs of such changes are a matter of extraordinary complexity, matters that no one has satisfactorily addressed in (or outside) the parochial realm of behavioral criminology.

GOOD SAMARITANS

Good samaritans constitute an interesting sidebar in any overview of crime victims. The term, of course, derives from the Biblical parable (Luke *10*:29-36) about a member of the outcaste Samaritan sect who selflessly helped a robbery victim who was lying comatose along the road from Jerusalem to Jericho.

In the United States, the infamous rape-murder of Kitty Genovese has been taken as a cautionary tale said to demonstrate that residents of large cities at critical moments can be cold-bloodedly indifferent to the sufferings and pleas of their fellow human beings. The crime took place in a New York City suburb at about 3 o'clock on a March morning in 1964. Ms. Genovese was knifed in the back as she tried to run from her automobile to the shelter of a nearby apartment building entryway. She screamed: "Help me! Help me! Oh, God, he's stabbed me!" A neighbor leaned from his window and yelled: "Let that girl alone!" The assailant turned and fled from the scene.

Kitty Genovese then staggered about thirty yards, seeking sanctuary inside one of the nearby doors. Ten minutes passed before her assailant returned and began to hunt down his victim. He tried several places without success. When he finally located Ms. Genovese, he slashed her brutally with his knife, then raped her.

The most stunning aspect of the case was that 38 persons were found who admitted to having heard Ms. Genovese's cries for help. No one offered aid; no one bothered to call the police. A male friend of the victim probably had stood at the top of the stairs and seen her killed. He thereafter telephoned friends, asking their advice, and finally walked across the building rooftop to use another person's phone to call the police because he wanted to avoid being identified and involved. The murderer, when later apprehended, was asked how he dared to return to the scene: "I knew they wouldn't do anything," he said. "People never do."

Paradoxically, despite their leadership in the crime victims' movement, the English and U.S. legal systems take the position that a person ought not to be burdened and bothered with the responsibility of aiding another. As Peter Glazebrook notes (1980: p. 386): ". . . an able-bodied Englishman may with impunity watch a young child whose care he has not undertaken drown at his feet in a foot of water." An exception exists if a bystander has made an initial effort to assist; then he or she must carry through. Bystanders must also help those with whom they have a preexisting relationship, such as a spouse or kin; and those to whom they owe a contractual duty. In addition, two states (Vermont and Minnesota) now require intervention, while two others (Rhode Island and Massachusetts) mandate it only for cases of sexual assault.

Recently, Leslie Binder (1988) has suggested that the Anglo-American laissez-faire rule results from a masculine-dominated law-making system; were women in charge, she maintains, there would be a law more responsive to the feminist ethic of responsibility, interconnectedness, and cooperation. This position, though plausible, is weakened by the fact of the common existence of laws throughout Europe that punish failure to intervene to aid victims.

Portugal enacted its duty-to-aid law in 1982. One of the early convictions illustrates the statute's operation: In the evening of February 17, 1984, in a hamlet near Alcobaca, a 65-year-old man asked a 21-year-old woman to come to his house. While there, she agreed to engage in sexual intercourse. His pants off, the man became ill and then fainted. The woman left, taking his wallet: on her way out of the house, she stole some food from the refrigerator. As she was walking back to her own house, she met a person who later would testify that she never mentioned the condition of the victim. The unconscious man died four days later in the hospital from the brain hemorrhage he had suffered. The court sentenced the offender to payment of 30,000 escodos (about $200) or 131 days in prison, payment of court costs, and restitution of 10,000 escodos to anyone entitled to make a claim.

Available evidence does not appear to indicate any overriding practical or ethical objections to enactment in Anglo-American jurisdictions of a failure-to-aid criminal provision. Care would have to be exercised to make certain that the laws allowed an individual to protect himself or herself from a criminal label when the omission occurred for decent reasons. Henry Foster's (1967: p. 589) rule-of-thumb seems an appropriate guideline: "only egregious examples of wanton indifference should be subject to the law's clumsy sanctions." But there seems little doubt that failure-to-aid laws make reasonable ethical demands upon what, in the evocative French phrase, constitutes "egoisme excessif." That they have not been incorporated into the agenda of the Anglo-American victims' agenda is one of the anomalies of that movement.

CONCLUSION

It is undoubtedly banal and perhaps morbid to point out that all human beings ultimately are victims; in the end, each of us will be done in by one or another of the tragedies of human existence. The movement to learn more about crime victims and how to aid them has singled out one group of persons that has suffered from what often are the slings and arrows of an indifferent fate. The consequences of victimization by crimes have a certain dramatic tone, and they are rare enough so that we ought to be able to attend to them with some degree of success with a reasonable expenditure of attention and resources. It is a modest enough agenda. The chapters in this volume testify in detail to the extent and the adequacy of the effort, and to matters that require further effort. To study and aid crime victims also has a human side, in addition to its academic standing. To help others in need—both victims and potential victims—to protect or to restore or to improve the quality of their life, matters highlighted in the chapters in this volume, has to be regarded as one of the more admirable human enterprises.

REFERENCES

Binder, L. (1988). A lawyer's primer on feminist theory and tort. *Journal of Legal Education, 38*. 3.

Brownmiller, S. (1975). *Against our will: Men, women and rape.* New York: Simon & Schuster.

Ennis, P. H. (1967). *Criminal victimization in the United States: A report on a national survey.* Washington, DC: U.S. Government Printing Office.

Fein, E. (1989, February 15). Ending long silence Soviets report big increase in crime. *New York Times,* national edition, p. 46.

Foster, H. H., Jr. (1967). [Book review of J. Ratcliffe (Ed.), *Good Samaritan and the Law*]. *Notre Dame Lawyer, 42,* 589.

Geis, G. (1967). State compensation to victims of violent crime. In *Crime and its impact—An assessment* (pp. 157-177). Washington, DC: President's Commission on Law Enforcement and Administration of Justice.

Glazebrook, P. R. (1980). Criminal omissions: The duty requirement in offenses against the person. *Law Quarterly Review, 76,* 386.

Gordon, M. T., & Riger, S. (1989). *The female fear.* New York: Free Press.

Hawkins, G., & Zimring, F. E. (1989). *Pornography in a free society.* New York: Cambridge University Press.

Kelling, G. L., Pate, T., Dieckman, D., & Brown, C. E. (1974). *The Kansas City preventive patrol experiment: A technical report.* Washington, DC: Police Foundation.

Miers, D. (1978). *Responses to victimization.* Abingdon, Oxon: Professional Books.

Moynihan, D. P. (1969). *Maximum feasible misunderstanding: Community action in the war on poverty.* New York: Free Press.

President's Commission on Law Enforcement and Administration of Justice (1967). *The challenge of crime in a free society.* Washington, DC: U.S. Government Printing Office.

Rock, P. (1986). *A view from the shadows: The ministry of the solicitor general of Canada and the making of the justice for victims of crime initiative.* Oxford: Clarendon Press.

Silberman, C. (1978). *Criminal violence, criminal justice.* New York: Random House.

Wolfgang, M. E. (1958). *Patterns in criminal homicide.* Philadelphia: University of Pennsylvania Press.

INDEX

ABOUT THE AUTHORS

ROBERT C. DAVIS conducts research on crime victims and other criminal justice issues for New York's Victim Services Agency and the American Bar Association.

ROBERT ELIAS is associate professor of Politics and Chair of Peace & Justice Studies at the University of San Francisco; adjunct professor at the University of California—Berkeley and New College of California; a past researcher at the Center for the Study of Law and Society and the Vera Institute of Justice; and author of *Victims of the System* (1983) and *The Politics of Victimization* (1988).

LUCY N. FRIEDMAN has been executive director since 1978 of New York City's Victim Services Agency, an agency that assists more than 15,000 battered women each year. She has a Ph.D. from Columbia University and was previously an associate director of the Vera Institute of Justice.

GILBERT GEIS is professor emeritus, Program in Social Ecology, University of California—Irvine. He is a former president of the American Society of Criminology, and recipient of that group's Edwin H. Sutherland Award for outstanding contributions to research. He also received the Stephen Schafer Award for research from the National Organization for Victim Assistance.

MADELINE HENLEY, a recent graduate of Haverford College, is a research associate with the Victim Services Agency in New York City.

SUSAN HILLENBRAND has directed the American Bar Association Criminal Justice Section's Victim Witness Project since 1980. She holds a BS degree in political science from Marymount College and a paralegal certificate from the New York Paralegal Institute.

DEBORAH PERSIS KELLY is vice-chair of the ABA's Victims Committee and an attorney with the Washington, DC, law firm of Dickstein, Shapiro, and Morin. She received her M.A. and Ph.D. from Johns Hopkins University and her J.D., summa cum laude, from American University, where she was also a government professor for five years. (She also gave birth to triplets Kendal, Molly, and Kyle between the first and second draft of this chapter.)

DEAN G. KILPATRICK is internationally recognized for his work examining the psychological impact of criminal victimization and as an advocate for victims rights. He is currently a professor of psychiatry and director of the Crime Victims Research and Treatment Center at the Medical University of South Carolina.

JOHN H. LAUB is associate professor in the College of Criminal Justice at Northeastern University. His research interests are in the areas of juvenile offending, victimization, and the history of criminology as a discipline. With Robert Sampson, he is currently conducting a reanalysis of the Sheldon and Eleanor Gluecks' longitudinal data on juvenile delinquency and adult crime.

ARTHUR J. LURIGIO is a social psychologist. He received his doctorate from Loyola University of Chicago. He was formerly a visiting professor of psychology and a research faculty member at the Center for Urban Affairs and Policy Research (CUAPR) at Northwestern University. He is currently an assistant professor of criminal justice at Loyola University and a research associate at CUAPR. His primary research interests include reactions to criminal victimization, victim services, intermediate sanctions, expertise and statistical reasoning, and AIDS and the courts.

MIKE MAGUIRE has recently moved from Oxford University to the University of Wales, Cardiff, where he will lecture in criminology and penology. He has published two books on the subject of victims: *The Effects of Crime and the Work of Victims Support Schemes* (Gower, 1987, with Claire Corbett) and *Victims of Crime: A New Deal?* (Open University Press, 1988, with John Pointing). He has published in the areas of burglary, policing, and prisons.

PATRICIA A. RESICK is a professor of psychology at the University of Missouri—St. Louis. She also holds a fellowship with the Center for Metropolitan Studies at the university and has held faculty positions at the University of South Dakota and the Medical University of South Carolina. Her research has focused on reactions and treatment of victims of violence, particularly victims of rape. Her current research efforts are concerned with the cognitive treatment of post-traumatic stress disorder in victims of crime.

DAVID S. RIGGS is completing his graduate training at the State University of New York at Stony Brook. He has conducted a number of studies examining interpartner aggression in married and dating couples. He is currently a predoctoral fellow at the Crime Victims Research and Treatment Center.

JOANNA SHAPLAND, Ph.D., is a senior research fellow at the Centre for Criminological and Socio-legal Studies of the University of Sheffield, U.K. She has published widely on victim issues, including *Victims in the Criminal Justice System* (with Jon Willmore and Peter Duff, Gower, 1985) and *Policing by the Public* (with Joh Vagg, Routledge, 1988). She was a consultant expert to the Council of Europe Committee on the Victim, the criminal and social policy that drafted the convention and recommendations on victim services and rights.

MINNA SHULMAN is administrative director of the Victim Services Agency's national law enforcement training project on domestic violence. She has been with the agency for almost ten years and has developed and managed most of the agency's projects for battered women and batterers. She has an MSW from Washington University.

WESLEY G. SKOGAN is professor of political science and urban affairs at Northwestern University. He is the author of *Disorder and Community Decline* (Free Press, 1990), *Coping With Crime* (Sage, 1981, with M. Maxfield), and other books and articles on crime, victims, policing, and survey research methodology.

BARBARA E. SMITH, Ph.D., is a private consultant with the American Bar Association, New York City Victim Services Agency, and National Sheriffs' Association. She has conducted numerous national research projects and published widely on victims of crime, including child victims, victim rights legislation, crime prevention for victims, victim impact statements, crisis intervention, and issues related to criminal court processes.

IRVIN WALLER, professor of criminology, University of Ottawa, is vice president of the World Society of Victimology. A pioneer of the UN Declaration on Victim Rights, he has received awards for his work on public policy for victims from the National Organization for Victim Assistance and the World Federation for Mental Health. He has numerous publications on comparative crime policy, prisons, and social justice. He is currently working with local government in Europe and North America to make cities safer from crime.

NOTES